REGULATION-MAKING IN THE UNITED KINGDOM AND AUSTRALIA

This book shines a spotlight on the way in which parliamentary scrutiny of regulations provides the primary support for democratic legitimacy for regulations in the UK and Australia.

This democratic safeguard is supplemented by public consultation processes. Despite commonly expressed concerns that regulation-making is secretive and undemocratic, it can be recognised to be a democratically sound and important feature of modern law. There are, however, modern practices that remove or limit these safeguards on regulation-making, raising concerns about executive aggrandisement.

This book has two aims. The first is to explain the systems of parliamentary scrutiny in the UK and Australia and their historical development. The development of parliamentary checks on regulation-making through the 20th century established the primary basis for the democratic legitimacy of regulations.

The second aim is to examine recent developments in regulation-making that avoid or minimise this safeguard. Constitutional changes in the UK, transnational regulation, and emergencies such as the COVID-19 pandemic have affected regulation-making in a manner that avoids or minimises the parliamentary checks that were carefully developed and implemented in the 20th century.

The book contributes to public law in the UK and Australia by analysing recent developments that involve executive over-reach, with reference to the historical development of parliamentary checks on regulation-making.

Regulation-Making in the United Kingdom and Australia

Democratic Legitimacy, Safeguards and Executive Aggrandisement

Andrew Edgar

•HART•

OXFORD • LONDON • NEW YORK • NEW DELHI • SYDNEY

HART PUBLISHING

Bloomsbury Publishing Plc

Kemp House, Chawley Park, Cumnor Hill, Oxford, OX2 9PH, UK

1385 Broadway, New York, NY 10018, USA

29 Earlsfort Terrace, Dublin 2, Ireland

First published in Great Britain 2023

A catalogue record for this book is available from the British Library.

A catalogue record for this book is available from the Library of Congress.

Library of Congress Control Number: 2023947485

ISBN: HB: 978-1-50997-224-1
ePDF: 978-1-50997-226-5
ePub: 978-1-50997-225-8

Typeset by Compuscript Ltd, Shannon

ACKNOWLEDGEMENTS

I have many people to thank. The best place to start is with the two US administrative law scholars who inspired the main ideas and methodology for the book. The initial idea developed from reading Susan Rose-Ackerman's comparative analysis of regulation-making and democratic legitimacy in many articles and books. My initial plans for the book changed on reading Blake Emerson's *The Public's Law: Origins and Architecture of Progressive Democracy* (2019) and his historical analysis of the US administrative state. While I retained my comparative analysis, his book inspired the development of the historical focus of the book. Thanks too, to Eloise Scotford for persuading me early in the project to limit my comparative analysis to two countries, to ensure that I could analyse them in depth.

Then there are colleagues at Sydney Law School. Particular thanks to Shae McCrystal for enabling me to take leave to complete the book and to Rayner Thwaites for regularly talking through aspects of it. Thanks to Helen Irving, Anne Twomey and the late Nicola Franklin for mentorship and encouragement over the years. Thanks to the public law staff in the School, in particular the administrative law teaching team: Mary Crock, Ron McCallum, Rosemary Lyster, Belinda Smith, Emily Hammond, Rayner Thwaites and Grant Hooper.

I must also thank the senators and secretariat of the Senate Committee for the Scrutiny of Delegated Legislation. Although the work on the book started prior to commencing with the Committee as its legal advisor in 2018, the research and analysis has been influenced in important ways by my work there. I have learnt a great deal working through the problems that the Committee addresses with senators and the secretariat. Special thanks to Anne Twomey and Leighton McDonald for encouraging me to take on this role in the first place and to Committee Secretaries Anita Coles, Glenn Ryall and Fattimah Imtoual for their support and guidance. I would also like to directly thank Senators Concetta Fierravanti-Wells, Kim Carr and Paul Scarr for including me in their spirited scrutiny of regulations in a period in which regulation-making came to the fore.

Thanks to Kate Whetter and Verity Stuart of Hart Publishing for friendly support and help through the stages of the project.

Finally, thanks to my family. My parents passed away during the research and writing of this book. I know they would be proud of it, just as they were in each of the earlier stages of my studies and academic career. And last, thanks so much to Justine, my wife, who has shared my life for many years. The book is dedicated to you.

Sydney
June 2023

TABLE OF CONTENTS

1

Introduction

Administrative lawyers may recognise, or simply assume, that the laws they study are linked to forms of democracy, but the connections are rarely directly examined. This book raises and seeks to answer questions regarding the connection between regulation-making processes and parliamentary democracy in the United Kingdom and Australia. The general question concerns how regulation-making processes are connected to these norms. This question is supplemented by two more specific questions. What are the limitations of regulation-making processes, and how have those limits been addressed? Are there regulation-making processes and practices that cannot be reconciled with the forms of parliamentary democracy applying in the UK and Australia?

I answer the general question by analysing legal mechanisms for escalating problems with regulations to parliaments and courts. The controls on regulation-making laws in the UK and Australia do not require direct interaction with members of the public whose activities will be controlled by the regulation or those who will benefit from the regulation. Laws that require such direct interaction are often referred to as being a form of deliberative democracy. Regulation-making laws in the UK and Australia tend not to have general, judicially enforceable laws requiring such interaction.

There are numerous reasons why the answers to these questions can contribute to public law scholarship in Anglo-Commonwealth countries. The first (a point that is commonly made by those who study regulation-making) is that regulations are arguably the predominant form of legislative law in modern democracies, and most certainly in the two jurisdictions that I examine in this book, the UK and Australia. The UK legislation website shows that in the eight years from 2015 to 2022 the UK Parliament enacted on average 34 general public Acts per year while in the same period on average 1,482 statutory instruments were made each year.[1] At the federal level in Australia in the same period an average of 133 Acts were enacted each year and 1,868.5 legislative instruments each year.[2] As regulations are the predominant form of legislative law, public lawyers should have a strong

[1] Figures taken from the Legislation.gov.uk website and averaged by the author: www.legislation.gov.uk/ukpga and www.legislation.gov.uk/uksi.

[2] Figures taken from the Office of Parliamentary Counsel Annual Reports and averaged by the author: www.opc.gov.au/corporate-information/annual-reports. The office is responsible for administering the Federal Register of Legislation.

understanding of the laws and norms that apply to making them and how the processes established by those laws and norms can be understood as connected to, or enhance, a particular conception of democracy.

Secondly, there are signs that regulation-making processes may not be well understood, or at least slip between the cracks of public law scholarship in the UK and Australia. Anglo-Commonwealth public law scholars tend not to address regulations as a discrete topic. Constitutional lawyers focus on bigger-picture issues regarding the primary institutions, legislatures, courts and the executive, while administrative lawyers tend to study the smaller picture of judicial review of administrative action, tribunals, and ombudsmen, etc. Regulation-making fits between the two main fields of public law as, unlike other kinds of administrative action, it raises constitutional questions about delegation of law-making authority, includes a direct role for parliaments, and has a particular, subtly different set of standards and methods compared to judicial review of other forms of administrative action. Additionally, and importantly for this book, regulation-making processes prompt a fundamental question about law-making in a democracy; a question that does not arise for administrative decision-making such as for licences and permits: what justifies laws being made by administrative officials rather than elected representatives through parliamentary procedures?

The third reason for a study of this kind is that some recent uses of regulations in the UK and Australia can be seen to push beyond the accepted norms for regulation-making in these countries. If this is the case – and I will argue that it is – it is important for the democratic norms underpinning regulation-making to be clearly understood so that criticisms of particular practices or exceptions can be developed. One of the purposes of this book is to develop an historically informed understanding of the laws, norms and practices that parliaments and courts have developed for regulation-making in the UK and Australia. This provides a clear basis for engaging with the exceptions to the norms and regulation-making practices that seem problematic.

I. Is Regulation-Making Democratically Flawed in the UK and Australia?

Regulation-making processes in the UK and Australia have been criticised in recent years. The criticisms can be understood as involving systemic and non-systemic, practice-focused critiques. There are two forms of systemic critique. The first, the one I primarily focus on, is that regulation-making in parliamentary democracies such as the UK and Australia is insufficiently democratic. This criticism has been developed in comparative administrative law scholarship. This scholarship initially sparked my interest in the relationship between regulation-making and democracy and inspired the research for this book. The second systemic criticism relates to Australian law. It is that there are constitutional difficulties with delegation of regulation-making powers that have not been adequately dealt with by the High Court. These two systemic critiques can be distinguished from non-systemic, practice-focused criticisms. These are that the democratic safeguards that have been established are ineffective.

I will explain the various critiques in this section of the chapter and then set out my responses to them in the next. Briefly, I do not agree with the systemic critiques and think that the non-systemic, practice-focused critiques are a more fruitful line of research.

Susan Rose-Ackerman has developed the most well-known comparative administrative law research in recent years. This research includes an important argument about the democratic legitimacy of regulation-making in presidential and parliamentary democracies. In her most recent work, Rose-Ackerman explains that it is necessary to ascertain the democratic legitimacy of regulation-making due to it not being subject to the processes of law-making by elected legislatures.[3] This raises the fundamental question for Rose-Ackerman and is also the primary question for this book: what processes provide democratic support for regulations? Rose-Ackerman argues that the strongest form of democratic legitimacy is provided by legally enforceable public consultation processes, such as the notice and comment provisions in the Administrative Procedure Act 1946.[4] Focusing on the UK and Germany, she argues that democratic legitimacy of regulation-making in parliamentary systems is relatively weak due to the lack of general, enforceable public consultation provisions.[5]

Rose-Ackerman has developed this analysis in a series of publications. In her earlier comparative administrative law work, Rose-Ackerman pointed out that governments in parliamentary democracies will have no incentive to establish such requirements in legal form. She argues that in parliamentary democracies governments have a great deal of control over the legislature and that governments are not likely to support legislation that will limit their discretion.[6] Public participation requirements are likely to be restricted to encouragement of these processes but without making them enforceable by courts.[7] Accordingly for Rose-Ackerman, there are incentives in parliamentary systems, and in particular the parliamentary system in the UK, that affect basic features of administrative institutions and

[3] S Rose-Ackerman, *Democracy and Executive Power: Policymaking Accountability in the US, the UK, Germany, and France* (Yale University Press, 2021) 2.

[4] 5 USC § 553 (1946). Rose-Ackerman (n 3) 41–42.

[5] Rose-Ackerman (n 3) 83–84. For Rose-Ackerman's analysis of the UK in this work, see 7, 36–37, 51–53.

[6] S Rose-Ackerman, 'Policy-Making Accountability: Parliamentary versus Presidential Systems' in David Levi-Faur (ed), *Handbook on the Politics of Regulation* (Edward Elgar, 2011) 176–77. See also Susan Rose-Ackerman, *Democracy and Executive Power: Policymaking Accountability in the US, the UK, Germany, and France* (Yale University Press, 2021) 35, 53.

[7] See also CB Jensen and RJ McGrath 'Making Rules about Rulemaking: A Comparison of Presidential and Parliamentary Systems' (2011) 64 *Political Research Quarterly* 656, 660; S Rose-Ackerman, S Egidy, and J Fowkes, *Due Process of Lawmaking: the United States, South Africa, Germany, and the European Union* (Cambridge University Press, 2015) 17–18, 266–67.

processes and operate to make the safeguards providing the democratic basis for regulation-making ineffective.

Rose-Ackerman's analysis is that the weakness of democratic legitimacy of regulation-making in parliamentary democracies is due to executive control of parliaments being a primary characteristic of these forms of constitutional system. Rose-Ackerman's systemic analysis is highly significant. If it is right, the shift to heavy reliance on regulations as the primary form of legislative law in the UK and Australia has come at a heavy cost to democracy in each country. The democratic controls, in particular public participation but also parliamentary scrutiny, are weak and the institutional structures in each country work against the democratic safeguards being established.

There is a second systemic critique of regulation-making that has developed in Australia that focuses on constitutional principles developed by the High Court. The critique is that the High Court's analysis in *Victorian Stevedoring and General Contracting Company Pty Ltd v Dignan*[8] in the 1930s, and accepted since then, is too tolerant of broad delegations on regulation-making powers. I will analyse the *Dignan* case in more detail in chapter two but for introductory purposes it is helpful to note critiques of it developed in recent years. Professor Denise Meyerson has argued that Australian separation of powers doctrine should limit the legislature's powers to delegate law-making powers to the executive.[9] Similarly, Professor Gabrielle Appleby has argued that the separation of powers has not sufficiently been factored into the High Court's case law on regulations,[10] and she proposes substantive and procedural limits to be prompted and enforced by the High Court.[11] These are different systemic concerns to those raised earlier as they focus exclusively on the Commonwealth Constitution. They also focus on the role of Parliament in Australia's democratic system rather than forms of direct democracy. However, they are also relevant to the questions to be addressed in this book; how can regulation-making in Australia be recognised to be democratically legitimate?

There are of course also non-systemic critiques of regulation-making in regard to the UK and Australia. These criticisms focus on particular democratic safeguards that apply in these countries, and in particular on parliamentary scrutiny of regulations. The criticisms of parliamentary scrutiny are far more common in the UK and Australian scholarship than criticism of consultation procedures.[12] I will argue that the criticisms of regulation-making practices have particular significance within the regulation-making systems that have developed in the UK and Australia.

[8] (1931) 46 CLR 73.

[9] D Meyerson, 'Rethinking the Constitutionality of Delegated Legislation' (2003) 11 *Australian Journal of Administrative Law* 45, 48–49, 53.

[10] G Appleby, 'Challenging the Orthodoxy: Giving the Court a Role in Scrutiny of Delegated Legislation' (2016) 69 *Parliamentary Affairs* 269, 279–80.

[11] ibid 280–83.

[12] For criticisms of consultation processes, see ibid 276–77; A Edgar, 'Deliberative Processes for Administrative Regulations: Unenforceable Public Consultation Provisions and the Courts' (2016) 27 *Public Law Review* 18.

The concerns in regard to parliamentary scrutiny of regulations has been developed by public law scholars in the UK, often drawing on research and criticisms made by the Hansard Society, an independent association for research and advice on the UK Parliament. Adam Tucker referred to the legitimacy of regulations being 'persistently precarious' from a constitutional perspective and that parliamentary scrutiny of regulations is inadequate and fails to achieve the requirements of constitutional principles.[13] Jeff King came to similar conclusions and emphasised that this is also the view of parliamentarians.[14] The influential research conducted by the Hansard Society refers to the scrutiny provided by the UK Parliament as being 'utterly inadequate and inappropriate' and not 'fit for purpose'.[15] Similar criticisms have been made in Australia in regard to parliamentary scrutiny of regulations. The main theme of the Australian scholarship is that the scrutiny conducted by parliamentary committees is too narrow and not sufficiently policy-focused. This is due to the narrow scrutiny criteria that these committees apply and the commitment of those committees to bipartisanship.[16]

Each of these concerns have been raised over the last 20 or so years; long after the democratic safeguards on regulation-making in the UK and Australia were established. The comparative administrative law scholarship that I have presented emphasises a systemic problem that, at least according to Rose-Ackerman, makes it insufficiently democratic. The main point to draw from this analysis is that executive control of parliament establishes incentives to minimise legislation that controls regulation-making and in particular creates a disincentive to establish direct, and enforceable, forms of public participation for regulation-making. Australian constitutional lawyers have also criticised the High Court's separation of powers doctrine and emphasised the democratic shortfall arising through delegation of law-making powers by parliament to the executive. We have also seen domestic public law scholarship that focuses on the more detailed aspects of regulation-making in the UK and Australia and raises problems particularly in regard to the weakness of parliamentary scrutiny.

II. Outline of Argument

I can understand the concerns expressed in these arguments, and largely agree with those that relate to the democratic safeguards in practice. However, I do not agree with the systemic concerns and I will focus on them in this book. I will argue

[13] A Tucker, 'Parliamentary Scrutiny of Delegated Legislation' in A Horne and G Drewry (eds) *Parliament and the Law* (Hart Publishing, 2018) 347, 370.

[14] J King, 'The Province of Delegated Legislation' in E Fisher, J King, AL Young, *The Foundations and Future of Public Law* (Oxford University Press, 2020) 161–63.

[15] R Fox and J Blackwell, *The Devil is in the Detail: Parliament and Delegated Legislation* (Hansard Society, 2014) 25, 244.

[16] See M Aronson, 'Subordinate Legislation: Lively Scrutiny or Politics in Seclusion' (2011) 26 *Australasian Parliamentary Review* 4, 11–15; Appleby (n 10) 277.

that the general, systemic safeguards in both the UK and Australia go a long way to providing democratic legitimacy for regulations. There are very good reasons for relying heavily on delegation, and I will argue that delegation of regulation-making power is legitimate so long as democratic safeguards are in place. I will argue that systemic safeguards appropriate for a parliamentary democracy are well established and that the arguments raising systemic problems are understandable but not persuasive.

On the other hand, there are problems with regulation-making systems in both countries. I see these problems falling into two categories. The first category is parliament providing for exceptions from the democratic safeguards and, in particular, exceptions that enable parliamentary scrutiny to be minimised or avoided. The second relates to practices that reduce the effectiveness of the regulation-making system and the role of parliament within it.

The primary argument I make is against Rose-Ackerman's general point about systemic difficulties in parliamentary systems such as the UK and Australia. My primary point against her analysis is that it does not take sufficient account of the history of the development of democratic safeguards that developed in the twentieth century in the UK. I will show that very similar developments occurred in Australia in the same period. These developments included democratic checks on regulation-making. They were influenced by inquiries into regulation-making in the 1930s following concerns being raised in the late 1920s about broad delegation of regulation-making powers and insufficient parliamentary scrutiny. The inquiry in the UK was conducted by the well-known Donoughmore Committee[17] and a similar, but less well-known, inquiry was conducted by a Senate Committee in Australia.[18] Both recognised that the safeguards that had been used up to then – public consultation and judicial review – needed to be supplemented by parliamentary scrutiny. Parliamentary scrutiny in numerous forms was then added in both countries during the twentieth century. I will argue the result of these developments is a system of safeguards, parliamentary scrutiny, public consultation and judicial review, that is well established in the UK and Australia. Each safeguard has a particular democratic function and collectively they add up to a system that provides for democratic legitimacy.

It has long been recognised that regulations dealing with technical details of welfare schemes are a core feature of modern legislative law and that it is inevitable that such powers are delegated to the executive branch by parliaments.[19] The point at which problems arise is when regulations are used to make laws with broad-ranging social and economic significance. This is the democratic problem – using the regulation-making system with reduced parliamentary scrutiny for laws that

[17] Committee on Ministers' Powers, Report (London, 1932).

[18] Senate, *Report from the Senate Select Committee Advising on Establishing Standing Committees*, Parliament of Australia (Report, April 1930).

[19] See C Carr, *Delegated Legislation: Three Lectures* (Cambridge University Press, 1921), 20–21. See also JS Mill, *Considerations on Representative Government* (Floating Press, 2009) 131–32 and W Selinger, *Parliamentarism: From Burke to Weber* (Cambridge University Press, 2019) 186–88.

have broad political significance. The primary question is whether the democratic safeguards protect against this problem: whether regulations dealing with broad-ranging policy can be escalated and exposed for consideration by parliaments (primarily) and courts (secondarily). I will argue that these safeguards are generally in place in both the UK and Australia.

The difficult area is not the general system of safeguards on regulation-making but with exceptions to the system and poor practices. The exceptions to the general system are examined in part two of the book. They involve the democratic safeguards, in particular parliamentary scrutiny, being minimised or circumvented. Some examples are regulations that are exempted from parliamentary scrutiny and the use of Henry VIII clauses to enable Acts to be amended by regulations. I will examine these exceptions in part two and will argue that there are signs of these kinds of exception becoming more common and prominent in recent years. I will argue that these can be regarded as a form of 'executive aggrandisement'. I follow Tarunabh Khaitan in using this term as he persuasively argues that it better conveys the purposeful nature of recent forms of executive action, than other terms such as 'democratic backsliding'.[20] Khaitan also highlights that modern forms of executive aggrandisement occur through incremental yet systemic means that involve either legislative or informal changes, rather than big-picture constitutional reform.[21] Khaitan's use of 'executive aggrandisement' and his analysis of it, fit well with the different ways in which parliamentary scrutiny of regulation-making is avoided and minimised, that I examine in part two. The important point I will argue is that a strong awareness of the general system and its rationale is necessary to recognise and push back against the attempts to expand the exceptions.

There are also concerns about parliamentary practices that weaken its scrutiny of regulations, as referred to above in section I of this introductory chapter. These concerns must be distinguished from the concerns expressed in the comparative administrative law scholarship that there are systemic problems regarding the democratic legitimacy of regulation-making in parliamentary systems. The concerns regarding the effectiveness of parliamentary scrutiny in practice recognise that there are systems in place to support democratic legitimacy but highlight that they are not working sufficiently well.

These issues regarding regulation-making practices in the UK and Australia are not the primary focus of this book. They are better suited to empirical research rather than the methodologies used for the research for this book. I do however have some comments for introductory purposes and I make some further comments in chapter three, 'Parliamentary Scrutiny of Regulations'. The first comment is that criticism and reform of current practices is likely to be supported by the analysis provided in this book regarding the development of democratic safeguards for regulation-making. It is, of course, crucial to the system of safeguards that has

[20] T Khaitan, 'Executive Aggrandizement in Established Democracies: A Crisis of Liberal Democratic Constitutionalism' (2019) 17 *I•CON* 342, 350–51.

[21] ibid 352.

developed over the last century for parliamentary scrutiny to not only be operative but also effective. However, this point should be tempered with some realism. Democratic safeguards for all forms of law-making are likely to be subject to criticism that they are too weak, ineffective, or poorly focused. It seems inherent to democratic institutions and practices that they struggle to achieve democratic ideals.

The struggle to achieve the democratic purposes of regulation-making safeguards is true of regulation-making not only in the UK and Australia, but also the United States' notice and comment process; the form of democracy that is Rose-Ackerman's model for democratic legitimacy of regulations. The notice and comment process has been subject to famous criticisms. It has been criticised for becoming 'ossified',[22] overly onerous and restrictive, which limits regulating industries whose manufacturing processes or products raise risks of widespread social harm. It has also been criticised for being tokenistic: a form of Kabuki theatre that is treated by administrators as a formality after the main decisions and drafting have been finalised.[23] Rose-Ackerman mentions these difficulties,[24] but it is important to highlight that even within her model country for democratic regulation-making there are difficulties in practice.

At a high level of generality, it is important when studying regulation-making systems to understand the particular characteristics of democracy in the country being analysed. This is because the democratic features of regulation-making systems are, over time, exposed to new developments or expanding exceptions. Deep understanding of the development of the system in a particular country, or lower-level jurisdiction, provides a strong basis for critique of exceptions and practices. Democracy is never finally settled. Practices and institutions change; at times in democracy-enhancing ways and other times in democracy-avoiding or minimising ways. I will argue that the regulation-making systems in the UK and Australia, have systemic features that enable them to be regarded as generally democratic. There are of course practices and exceptions that are problematic, but they are to be evaluated and potentially criticised by reference to the democratic characteristics of the laws, norms, institutions and processes that are already built into our regulation-making systems.

III. Methodology

As I have already indicated, I use two methodologies to answer the questions raised about the democratic basis for regulation-making in parliamentary democracies:

[22] TO McGarrity, 'Some Thoughts on 'Deossifying' the Rulemaking Process' (1992) 41 *Duke Law Journal* 1385. See also JL Mashaw and DL Harfst, *The Struggle for Auto Safety* (Harvard University Press, 1990).

[23] ED Elliott, 'Re-Inventing Rulemaking' (1992) 41 *Duke Law Journal* 1490, 1492.

[24] Rose-Ackerman (n 3) 44.

comparative and historical. The topic was initially inspired by comparative administrative law scholarship, in particular the work of Susan Rose-Ackerman, and the book seeks to contribute to this field of administrative law by examining regulation-making in parliamentary democracies. The research for the book is also comparative as it involves comparison of the similarities and differences of regulation-making in the UK and Australia.

I supplement the comparative methodology with historical research in order to substantiate my arguments responding to the questions raised by comparative administrative law scholarship. The historical methodology facilitates identifying the normative context for current debates. The history of regulation-making safeguards in the UK and Australia highlights that these debates are longstanding and ongoing. They can be understood as part of the context of regulation-making. The norms of regulation-making that are highlighted in this history are flexible and commonly debated. They are similar to norms and debates in regard to the scope of judicial review of administrative action: judicial review has expanded and contracted through doctrinal developments and changes in judicial personnel. Both judicial review and regulation-making safeguards invite concerns and debates about the appropriate role for institutions and the techniques and approaches of officials who administer them.

A. Comparative Methodology

There are numerous reasons for using comparative methodology for the research for this book. The first and most obvious is that the UK provides a model for parliamentary democracy. Research limited to my home jurisdiction, Australia, would have missed analysis that is crucial to my argument – that regulation-making in parliamentary democracies can include safeguards that provide for democratic legitimacy. The second reason is that there has been mutual influence between the UK and Australia in regard to regulation-making. For example, Australia's initial legislation controlling regulation-making was a transplant from the UK. This is explained in chapter three. Also, as explained in chapter two, Australia's approaches to scrutiny of bills for delegation of regulation-making powers influenced developments in the UK in the late 1980s and early 1990s. Accordingly, it is helpful to see mutual influences in the development of regulation-making laws and norms in different countries that are parliamentary democracies. The striking similarities I have found in the development of regulation-making processes in the UK and Australia suggest that there are fundamental features of regulation-making in parliamentary democracies based on the Westminster Parliament.

The comparative analysis is limited to two countries, the UK and Australia. This narrow comparison enables detailed analysis of the debates preceding the development of laws and institutions that control regulation-making in each country and the reasons expressed for them.[25] The UK is often used as the primary example of a parliamentary democracy and is commonly used as the model in comparative political studies.[26] Australia varies from the UK parliamentary system due to its federal constitution and its upper house, the Senate, being an elected, equal body. We will see in chapter three that the difference between the forms of bicameralism in each country raises important differences to parliamentary scrutiny of regulations.

However, my primary focus is on the similarities between the two countries rather than differences. I point out differences throughout the book, but they are more in the details of legal and institutional arrangements rather than for the significance of the democratic basis for regulation-making. For example, the process for parliamentary scrutiny of regulations in the UK is included in each Act that delegates regulation-making power rather than a generally applicable, trans-substantive Act, as is the case in Australia.[27] That difference is important as it means that in the UK parliamentary scrutiny processes are negotiated and debated for each Act that delegates regulation-making powers. That is not the case in Australia where the Legislation Act 2003 provides for a general parliamentary scrutiny procedure. In regard to consultation, there are differences because the UK has more developed and broad-ranging judicial review principles for consultation.[28] And for judicial review of regulations, it is necessary to recognise the difference that the Human Rights Act 1998 makes.[29] Australia does not have an equivalent to that Act at the Commonwealth level; the Commonwealth level being the focus of in this book.

Despite these differences, the similarities between the two countries are more informative for understanding the principles and norms of parliamentary democracy for regulation-making. This is especially the case in regard to the development of parliamentary scrutiny committees. One important insight uncovered in the research for the book is that the developments in regard to parliamentary scrutiny have at times occurred simultaneously without express or direct influence of the other country and at other times been inspired or influenced by developments in the other country. For example, in chapter two I explain how inquiries were held in each country in the early 1930s into regulation-making safeguards with little or no inter-country prompting or influence. In chapter four we will see that the history of mandatory public consultation legislation is very similar in each country. At the start of the twentieth century both

[25] See also E Scotford, *Environmental Principles and the Evolution of Environmental Law* (Hart Publishing, 2017) 11–13.

[26] eg A Lijphart, *Patterns of Democracy: Government Forms and Performance in Thirty-Six Countries*, 2nd edn (Yale University Press, 2012) 10; TM Moe and M Caldwell, 'The Institutional Foundations of Democratic Government: A Comparison of Presidential and Parliamentary Systems' (1994) 150 *Journal of Institutional and Theoretical Economics* 171, 183.

[27] ch 3.

[28] ch 4.

[29] ch 5.

countries had legislative provisions which were repealed in the first half of that century. Identifying similarities such as these can help us to confidently identify the general features of democratic safeguards in parliamentary systems historically influenced by the UK.

The important point to be drawn from the comparative analysis is that the development of regulation-making processes and safeguards in the UK and Australia does not match what is said by Rose-Ackerman. There are systemic laws and institutions in each country that provide democratic safeguards despite the general control that the executive has over parliaments in parliamentary systems. That is enough for my project as Rose-Ackerman includes the UK in her work. I present a different understanding of regulation-making in these two countries to demonstrate the ways in which the democratic legitimacy of regulations is understood. This helps to make a more general point about comparative administrative law. It is helpful to engage closely with historical developments in administrative law and procedures to appreciate the connections with more general features of democracy and relevant institutional arrangements. I will demonstrate how this is true for regulation-making, and it is also most likely true for other laws that have democratic significance, such as electoral laws and laws applying to political communications and protests.

My focus on the UK and Australia is designed to contribute to knowledge of parliamentary democracies in comparative administrative law scholarship. While the research for the book was inspired by US–UK comparative administrative law scholarship; that comparison does not feature in the book. There is a history of comparative administrative law examining the UK and the US beyond the works already referred to that readers may want to seek out;[30] however, it does not feature in this book.

B. Historical Methodology

I focus on the historical debates about regulation-making processes and safeguards in the UK and Australia to substantiate my argument that the comparative administrative law scholarship has missed the ways in which democratic legitimacy is recognised in these countries in relation to regulation-making. This history reveals ongoing debates into the democratic legitimacy of regulations in each country and the efforts to implement them in the face of the strong resistance of governments. The analysis focuses on three periods in the development of

[30] B Schwartz and HWR Wade, *Legal Control of Government: Administrative Law in Britain and the United States* (Clarendon Press, 1972); PP Craig, *Public Law and Democracy in the United Kingdom and the United States of America* (Clarendon Press, 1990); E Fisher, *Risk Regulation and Administrative Constitutionalism* (Hart Publishing, 2007); P Cane, *Administrative Tribunals and Adjudication* (Hart Publishing, 2009); P Daly, *A Theory of Deference in Administrative Law: Basis, Application and Scope* (Cambridge University Press, 2012); P Cane, *Controlling Administrative Power: An Historical Comparison* (Cambridge University Press, 2016).

regulation-making laws in the two countries. The first is the initial development of the primary safeguards for regulation-making that were developed in the first half of the twentieth century. The second is the incremental reforms that implemented these safeguards (and at times removed them) that occurred since that period. The third is the developments that are potentially inconsistent with the laws and normative framework that was initially developed in the early twentieth century.

The starting point is the debates starting in the 1920s that led to inquiries and reports in each country in the early 1930s. The primary features of this period in the UK were Lord Hewart's *The New Despotism*,[31] published in 1929, and the Donoughmore Committee's report published in 1932. These are well-known features of the development of regulation-making laws for the UK and have been influential elsewhere. It is less well-known that similar debates occurred at the same time in Australia and led to an inquiry that made very similar, but less wide-ranging, recommendations to the Donoughmore Committee.

My analysis of this period involves examining the debates about regulation-making that prompted the inquiries in order to reveal the problems that were identified, and examining the reports of the inquiries to reveal how those problems were understood and the solutions that were recommended. It is important to recognise that the recommendations of the UK and Australian Committees in the 1930s were generally implemented – not necessarily soon after the reports, but over the twentieth century. The fact that the recommendations were largely implemented, even if they took time, supports recognition of these reports providing a relevant analysis of regulation-making processes and institutions.

Examination of the debates and reports helps us to understand the norms on which the democratic safeguards in each country have been built. The debates and reports are crucial to understanding the primary concerns regarding delegation of regulation-making powers in each country and the significance of the safeguards on regulation-making. These inquiries led to the inclusion of parliamentary scrutiny committees as a necessary safeguard to provide for democratic legitimacy of regulations. It is also important to recognise that beyond the Committee reports, the contributors that I refer to in these debates are primarily judges and lawyers. The academic lawyers contributing to the debates were some of the initial administrative law scholars in the UK. There were broader debates, particularly within the UK Parliament,[32] that I have not addressed.

The next step in the historical analysis is the implementation of reforms recommended by the committees in the 1930s. This implementation helps us to see that the norms were not merely abstract. We can be more confident of the status of the norms and their ongoing effect and relevance as they at times

[31] (Ernest Benn Ltd, 1929).

[32] See, eg, CM Chen, *Parliamentary Opinion of Delegated Legislation* (Columbia University Press, 1933); WH Greenleaf, *The British Political Tradition: Volume Three: A Much Governed Nation* (Methuen, 1987) 540–48.

directly influenced the development of the safeguards on regulation-making in each country and at other times are clearly consistent with the earlier recommendations. The 1930s inquiries and subsequent reforms tell us a lot about the characteristics of regulation-making systems and in particular the safeguards that make regulation-making democratically legitimate.

The implementation of the democratic safeguards through the twentieth century is relevant for more than its primary significance, that the norms expressed in the 1930s debates were turned into concrete form in laws and particular institutions, such as parliamentary committees. The history of their implementation reveals important institutional dynamics that are fundamental to regulation-making in these countries. The debates in implementation of the safeguards reveals strong and regular resistance by executive governments to the safeguards. The resistance revealed in these implementation debates helps to present a different picture of executive-parliament relationships regarding regulation-making than is presented in the comparative administrative law scholarship referred to earlier. The executive is a strong branch of government in parliamentary democracies and has much influence over parliaments. However, in each country the executive has not succeeded in resisting the primary democratic safeguards being implemented: parliamentary scrutiny committees. These committees have very important systemic significance for the democratic legitimacy of regulation-making in each country.

The third aspect of the history focuses on recent developments in which regulation-making power is delegated to administrative officials in a manner that restricts or excludes the democratic safeguards implemented in the twentieth century. My analysis of these current developments treats them as exceptions to the system. It draws on the norms that underpin the general system to critique the developments and to offer considerations and suggestions for reforms.

The historical methodology employed for this book relies quite heavily on the debates and recommendations made by committees in the 1930s. A question may arise as to why these Committee reports remain relevant when the characteristics of the state may have changed. We will see that the historical development of the welfare state was recognised to be a major contributor to the increased reliance on regulations in the decades prior to the 1930s. This raises a question as to why norms developed in that period are relevant now, a period of globalisation and deregulation.

My answer is that it has two aspects. The first is that some characteristics of regulation-making are different to the past and that the differences can be understood as being due to globalisation and, most likely, deregulation. For example, in chapter seven I examine the incorporation of privately made standards into regulations in order to support the harmonisation of laws in different countries. This is an example of the kind of changes to the state that we expect in the current period. The second aspect of my answer is that I want to emphasise that the 1930s debates help us to understand the characteristics of the core features of current regulation-making processes. In order to understand the impact of current regulatory developments on regulation-making processes and safeguards, it helps to have a strong understanding of the normative basis for those processes and safeguards.

Accordingly, the development of regulation-making safeguards and processes in the twentieth century is important for my argument. My general argument is that when examined historically a different conception of democracy underpins the regulation-making processes and controls in parliamentary democracies, at least in the UK and Australia. The primary democratic measure in these countries is parliamentary scrutiny. The history indicates that democracy is best understood not as a simple abstract concept but as being substantiated in different ways in different constitutional systems.

IV. Structure

The book is divided into two parts. Part one of the book examines the safeguards that are implemented and administered by parliaments, administrative officials, and the courts. Part two examines current legislative techniques that circumvent and minimise the effectiveness of the safeguards.

Part one focuses on the development of the regulation-making systems in each country and their democratic significance. Chapter two sets up this part by focusing on delegation of regulation-making authority. This includes how it became controversial in the 1920s and 1930s and the safeguards that were recommended in the 1930s reports and then implemented over the twentieth century. Chapter two should be regarded as supplementing this introductory chapter. It introduces the starting point for analysis of regulation-making, the delegation of power to administrative officials to make laws. Chapters three to five then examine the safeguards on regulation-making in each country: parliamentary scrutiny of regulations, consultation and other administrative deliberative processes, and judicial review. These chapters seek to establish two general points. They demonstrate that the democratic legitimacy of regulation-making in the UK and Australia involves contributions made by three safeguards. The primary addition made in the twentieth century was the introduction of parliamentary scrutiny, but consultation and judicial review remain important. These chapters also demonstrate that executives' control of parliaments in relation to safeguards is limited. Parliament has added checks and safeguards in the face of resistance of governments. We will see that governments have conceded to reforms being made or lost the vote for some, but not all, of the safeguards.

Part two of the book changes the focus to examine exceptions to the regulation-making systems and practices that avoid and minimise parliamentary scrutiny. In this part, I focus on current legislative techniques that create difficulties for the democratic legitimacy of regulation-making in the UK and Australia. This part highlights that if there are problems for democratic legitimacy of regulation-making in the UK and Australia, it is due to the expansion of exceptions and techniques that minimise parliamentary scrutiny, rather than there being no general system for regulation-making that provides for democratic legitimacy.

Chapters six to nine of part two examine the exclusion by statute of parliamentary scrutiny, incorporating by reference documents and private standards into regulations, broadening of Henry VIII powers, and the reliance on regulations in times of emergency for broad-ranging and highly restrictive laws. These aspects of regulation-making are often technical and complex, yet they are important because they reveal the way governments have taken steps to minimise and avoid controls on regulation-making. We will see that while they often succeed and seem to be becoming more common, they are also often subject to heavy criticism. The analysis in part two further highlights that it is better to understand the relationship between executive and parliament in parliamentary democracies not as involving simple or complete control of parliament by the executive, but as a relationship with ongoing tensions and conflicts.

V. Terminology

I can now explain some terminological choices made for this book. There are numerous different terms for regulations in each country. Some are formal terminology used in legislation such as, 'statutory instruments' in the UK and 'legislative instruments' in Australia. Some are informal and used by practitioners and academics, such as 'secondary legislation' and 'delegated legislation'. There is no particular difference in meaning of these terms; all refer to laws made by executive officials according to powers delegated by statute. To prevent confusion and unnecessary terminological differences, I use the general term 'regulations' in nearly all cases.

The terms 'UK' and 'Australia' are used throughout the book to mean the national level of government. I do not examine regulations made by UK-level officials for Scotland, Wales or Northern Ireland or regulation-making by devolved governments. I also do not examine regulation-making at the state and territory level in Australia. The exclusive attention on the national levels of government enables focus on the historical developments in detail. In my experience it is a common practice in comparative administrative law to limit the comparison in this manner.

I use the term 'parliamentary democracy' at many points in my analysis. In the early stages of the research for this book, I used the term 'Westminster-model democracy'. The reason for that terminology was to follow Arend Lijphart's famous comparative politics work, *Patterns of Democracy: Government Forms and Performance in Thirty-six Countries*, and in particular the way he distinguishes parliamentary democracies into majoritarian and consensus models.[33] However,

[33] (2nd edn, Yale University Press, 2012).

more recent scholarship in the UK has highlighted that the term 'Westminster-model' has either no meaning[34] or a meaning that is a vague family resemblance.[35] There is no need to enter this debate and it is enough for me to avoid using the Westminster model terminology. Instead, I use 'parliamentary democracy' and examine the features of regulation-making in two parliamentary democracies – the UK and Australia – that provide for democratic legitimacy.

I have used the term 'executive–parliament' relations in the current chapter and refer to it throughout the book. Meg Russell and Philip Cowley have made clear that it is overly simplistic in political analysis to refer to 'executive–parliament relations' due to the complexity of the two institutions and it is better to focus on particular forms of the relationship between the executive and parliament.[36] I focus on two particular aspects of executive-parliament relations: one involving parliaments' ability to establish democratic controls on regulation-making and the other on parliamentary scrutiny of regulations in practice.

I use a particular shorthand to refer to one of the primary contributors to the safeguards on regulation-making in Australia. The contribution was made by a Senate Committee in 1930, the Select Committee on the Advisability or Otherwise of Establishing Standing Committees of the Senate,[37] which I will refer to as the '1930 Senate Committee'.

VI. Contributions

There are three contributions that I seek to make with this book. The first relates to highlighting the reasons for why regulation-making can be regarded as systemically sound in parliamentary democracies, and in particular the UK and Australia. My intention is to provide comparative administrative lawyers with a deeper understanding of regulation-making systems that operate in parliamentary democracies.

The second is to contribute to public law in the UK and Australia. Better understanding of the democratic features of regulation-making in each country will provide a reference point for evaluation and potentially critique of the development of systemic exceptions and anti-democratic practices for regulation-making in these countries.

[34] M Russell and R Serban, 'The Muddle of the 'Westminster Model': A Concept Stretched Beyond Repair' (2021) 56 *Government and Opposition* 744; M Russell and R Serban, 'Why it Is Indeed Time for the Westminster Model to Be Retired from Comparative Politics' (2022) 57 *Government and Opposition* 370.

[35] M Flinders, D Judge, RAW Rhodes and A Vatter, '"Stretched But Not Snapped": A Response to Russell and Serban on Retiring the "Westminster Model"' (2022) 57 *Government and Opposition* 353. See also, P Norton, 'Is the Westminster System of Government Alive and Well?' (2022) 9 *Journal of International and Comparative Law* 1.

[36] M Russell and P Cowley, 'Modes of UK Executive–Legislative Relations Revisited' (2018) 89 *The Political Quarterly* 18.

[37] (Parliament of Australia 1929–30).

The third contribution is to prompt administrative lawyers to focus more attention on executive-parliament relations. This is an area in which constitutional lawyers in Anglo-Commonwealth countries study, but I think it is relevant to administrative law as well, particularly in relation to drafting of provisions that delegate powers to administrative officials and parliamentary scrutiny of the exercise of statutory powers. Parliamentary scrutiny of executive action is a common feature of accountability mechanisms in modern democracies and is ripe for administrative law scholarship. Administrative lawyers have focused much attention on the accountability of executive action to the courts in judicial review proceedings, but far less attention on accountability to parliaments.

PART I

Delegation of Regulation-Making Authority and the Development of Safeguards

2

Delegating Regulation-Making Authority

The primary purpose of this book is to seek answers to the question of how the exercise of regulation-making authority is managed for democratic purposes by legal procedures. But there is a prior question: why is it legitimate within the UK and Australia's parliamentary democracies to delegate such power? This question was subject to debates in the 1920s and 1930s in both countries. The purpose of this chapter is to examine these debates for what they reveal about both the concerns and advantages of regulation-making.

The 1920s–1930s debates and their resolution are crucially important to understanding the democratic basis of regulation-making processes in the two parliamentary democracies examined in this book. The two sides of the debate clashed over whether or not regulation-making can be reconciled with parliamentary democracy. Both sides framed their arguments in coherent, but very different, accounts of the constitutional arrangements in each country. The Donoughmore Committee's inquiry into the issue in the UK provided the framework for how regulation-making can be reconciled with a parliamentary democracy. Most of the measures recommended by the Committee were adopted by parliaments either in that period or subsequently. The equivalent debate in Australia in the same period occurred in both the Senate and the courts, as may be expected in a jurisdiction with a written, codified constitution that is structured on the separation of powers. My purpose in this chapter is to examine the ideas about regulation-making in the two parliamentary democracies, the proposals argued for, and those that were implemented.[1]

As in the other chapters in part one, this chapter examines more recent changes to implement the recommendations made in the 1930s. The later developments that are relevant in this chapter relate to parliamentary committees designed to review bills for whether they delegate regulation-making powers inappropriately. The House of Lords committee was established in 1992 and the Australian Senate committee

[1] For broader explanations of the historical developments examined in this chapter, see M Taggart, 'From "Parliamentary Powers" To Privatization: The Chequered History of Delegated Legislation in the Twentieth Century' (2005) 55 *University of Toronto Law Journal* 575, 576–600 and E Fisher, 'The Open Road? Navigating Public Administration and the Failed Promise of Administrative Law' in E Fisher, J King and AL Young (eds), *The Foundations and Future of Public Law* (Oxford University Press, 2020).

was established in 1982; long after committees in the 1930s recommended that they should be established. The establishment of these committees indicates the acceptance of delegation of regulation-making authority but that it needs to be managed, and that broad delegations should be explained and justified by governments.

By the end of the chapter we will see the development of general features of regulation-making that are similar in the UK and Australia. While concerns may still be raised about broad delegation of regulation-making authority, measures have been taken to manage it in both jurisdictions. It is the safeguards recommended by the committees in the 1930s and largely implemented in the twentieth century that make broad delegations of regulation-making powers tolerable in the UK and Australia. While very broad regulation-making powers are still understood to be problematic, the common reason for accepting them is the establishment of safeguards, in particular the introduction in the twentieth century of parliamentary scrutiny.

There are two primary differences between the two jurisdictions. The first is that a primary forum for the constitutional debate about broad regulation-making powers occurred in Australia in the courts rather than a committee inquiry, as was the case in the UK. Secondly, there is still a slight possibility in Australia for judicial review of statutory provisions delegating regulation-making authority. We will see, however, that this possibility is more apparent than real. The relatively minor nature of these differences suggests that the similarities represent fundamental features of regulation-making in the two parliamentary democracies. That is, delegation of regulation-making powers is tolerated when safeguards are in place. Concerns may remain about broad delegations and the institutional solutions to managing such concerns are parliamentary committees rather than courts.

I. Constitutional Concerns United Kingdom: Lord Hewart, John Willis and the Donoughmore Committee

The criticisms that arose concerning the delegation of regulation-making powers in the 1920s, the debates that ensued, and the Donoughmore Committee's report have had great significance for the laws that control regulation-making in the UK.[2] My approach is to examine the debates about broad delegation of regulation-making authority for how they refer to different understandings of parliamentary democracy in the UK. The questions I seek to answer are:

- What did the different sides of the debate recognise as being acceptable or unacceptable regarding regulations?

[2] CK Allen, *Law and Orders: An Inquiry into the Nature and Scope of Delegated Legislation and Executive Powers in English Law*, 2nd edn (Stevens & Sons, 1965) 50.

- What understandings of parliamentary democracy can be understood to underpin the different sides and the Donoughmore Committee's analysis and recommendations?

A. Lord Hewart of Bury's Critique

The concern raised by Lord Hewart was the increased reliance on regulations in WWI which continued into the 1920s.[3] He recognised that by this stage regulations were more common than Acts, that regulations were being made under 'skeleton Acts' – Acts that enable officials to make the laws with policy significance – and that regulations were commonly the laws that control the conduct of citizens.[4] But it was not just that this form of law had become the primary form by the 1920s. Hewart's concern was that regulations were made without any particular structure, decision-making procedure, rules of evidence or requirement for reasons.[5] More generally, his argument raised concerns about arbitrary law-making.[6]

Hewart presented these concerns within an argument about administrative officials over-reaching their appropriate role in the UK's parliamentary democracy. It was that departmental officials were using their role in drafting legislation to include provisions that empower themselves to make regulations and to limit review of these regulations by the courts.[7] This was the 'new despotism' of the title of Hewart's book. The old despotism was the Tudor and Stuart Kings' direct challenge to the authority of Parliament.[8] The new despotism was that department officials use Parliament as a means to increase and consolidate their own authority. Hewart stated:[9]

> In these days the method is to cajole, to coerce, and to use Parliament – and it is strangely successful. The old despotism, which was defeated, offered Parliament a challenge. The new despotism, which is not yet defeated, gives Parliament an anaesthetic. The strategy is different, but the goal is the same. It is to subordinate Parliament.

Hewart's argument has rightly been referred to by commentators, both of the time and more recently, as a conspiracy theory.[10] As we have just seen, he saw it as a strategy. Hewart also referred to it as being 'systematic' and a 'well-thought-out plan' to expand administrative powers.[11]

[3] Lord Hewart of Bury, *The New Despotism* (Ernest Benn Ltd, 1929) 15, 43, 99–100. See also CK Allen, *Bureaucracy Triumphant* (Oxford University Press, 1931) 28.
[4] ibid 84, 100–01.
[5] ibid 43–44.
[6] ibid 20–21, 44.
[7] ibid 6, 11.
[8] ibid 11, 108.
[9] ibid 11.
[10] See Allen, *Law and Orders* (n 2) 294–95; Taggart (n 1) 576.
[11] Hewart (n 3) 159.

What then did Hewart seek as the solution to this? Along with others at the time who I will refer to further below, he referred to providing safeguards: parliamentary scrutiny of bills; judicial review; and public consultation.[12] However, his main focus was on provisions of Acts that delegate regulation-making authority. His preference was for such provisions to be repealed or amended.[13] He also wanted public awareness of the problem that would discourage such provisions being enacted into the future which could be supported by a parliamentary committee to review bills for their inclusion of such provisions.[14] The media could expose these provisions in order for opposition to be raised in particular cases and act as a deterrent more generally.[15]

Hewart's criticism of the broad delegation of regulation-making authority was that the expansion of administrative law-making power came at the expense of parliamentary and judicial authority. Parliament was retreating from its law-making role and was being subordinated to the executive.[16] He worried about whether political officials exercised any control of regulations that were made and the thoughtlessness of Parliament passing legislation that included provisions that exclude review of regulations by the courts.[17] The two key features of the UK's parliamentary democracy, the role of Parliament in law-making and the role of the courts in the rule of law, were being undermined by power-grabbing administrative officials. In his words, 'a despotic power which at one and the same time places Government Departments above the sovereignty of Parliament and beyond the jurisdiction of the Courts'.[18]

What form of parliamentary democracy does Hewart's analysis invoke? One point that he did not refer to was that broad delegation of regulation-making authority does not threaten parliamentary sovereignty, at least in form. Parliament can always repeal the statutory delegation of authority, as was made clear at the time.[19] However, delegation of broad regulation-making authority does threaten Dicey's understanding of parliamentary sovereignty; that the representative nature of the House of Commons establishes political limits on law-making in a parliamentary democracy.[20] This is consistent with understandings of parliamentary democracy developed prior to the twentieth century where laws are expected to be made according to public deliberation.[21] Laws made by parliaments according to

[12] ibid 86.
[13] ibid 153.
[14] ibid 153–54.
[15] ibid 153–55.
[16] ibid 11.
[17] ibid 73, 100.
[18] ibid 8.
[19] C Carr, *Delegated Legislation* (Cambridge University Press, 1921) 27; F Port, *Administrative Law* (Longmans, Green and Co, 1929) 145.
[20] AV Dicey, *Introduction to the Study of the Law of the Constitution*, 8th edn (Macmillan and Co, 1915) 78–81.
[21] W Selinger, *Parliamentarism: From Burke to Weber* (Cambridge University Press, 2019) 1–4.

deliberative processes cannot be regarded as arbitrary and are accordingly no real threat to liberty.[22]

Hewart's *The New Despotism* was influential when it was published. It was preceded to an extent by CK Allen, Oxford Professor of Jurisprudence, in a series of articles in the 1920s and 1930 that were later published as a collection entitled *Bureaucracy Triumphant*.[23] Many scholars have stated that Hewart's *New Despotism* raised the attention of the public to the issue and that, importantly, it prompted the Donoughmore Inquiry being established which I deal with in section II.C below.[24]

B. The Functionalist Response

There was an alternative to Hewart's view that was expressed in the developing administrative law literature of the 1920s and 1930s. The conceptual basis and methodology of the response, particularly that of John Willis, is sometimes referred to as 'functionalism'. Martin Loughlin explains the methodology of the 1920s and 1930s functionalist scholars as being focused on facts and practice, rather than generalisations, as well as on historical development.[25] This is clearly apparent in John Willis's *The Parliamentary Powers of English Government Departments*,[26] his response to Hewart's, *The New Despotism*. Willis's argument was based on the key features of functionalist legal analysis and legal realism:[27] the use of broad delegations of regulation-making authority in practice rather than their inclusion in legislation, which was the focus of Hewart's book.[28] Willis concluded that when regulations are studied in this way, Hewart's argument was 'out of all proportion'.[29] He also took a longer view of history than Hewart, placing the issues regarding delegation of regulation-making powers in the context of shifts in the form of legislation and changes in the purposes of government occurring in the mid nineteenth century.[30]

Although Willis's book is not the only work of the time that provides an alternative understanding of the significance of regulations in the UK's parliamentary democracy,[31] it was a direct response to Hewart. It is convenient to focus initially on Willis's reasoning and then come back to some of the other contributors of the time that broadly shared Willis's view.

[22] ibid 7–8, 23–24.
[23] Allen, *Bureaucracy Triumphant* (n 3) ch 4.
[24] J Willis, *The Parliamentary Powers of English Government Departments* (Harvard University Press, 1933) 38–39, 174; SA de Smith, 'Delegated Legislation in England' (1949) 2 *Western Political Quarterly* 514, 515; Allen, *Law and Orders* (n 2) 49–50; Taggart (n 1) 578–79.
[25] M Loughlin, *Public Law and Political Theory* (Clarendon Press, 1992) 168.
[26] (Harvard University Press, 1933).
[27] Most likely influenced by his time at Harvard writing the book: Taggart (n 1) 582–83.
[28] Willis (n 24) 4, 57.
[29] ibid 170.
[30] ibid 11–26.
[31] See also Carr (n 19); Port (n 19).

Rather than focus on Willis's main argument, that the application of broad delegations of regulation-making authority (law in action) was not as worrying as they seemed in the particular statutory provisions (law in the books), it is worthwhile highlighting Willis's criticism of Hewart in regard to the historical reliance on regulations in the UK. Willis agreed with Hewart that in the post-WWI period, Parliament was delegating broad regulation-making powers to administrative officials, and that administrative law-making had effectively replaced parliamentary law-making.[32] However, Willis characterised Hewart's concern as being part of a conservative legal theory that no longer matched the realities of institutional arrangements.[33] For Willis, it was necessary to go back to two particular developments in the nineteenth century.

The first related to changes starting in the industrial revolution; in particular, the introduction of worker's health and safety laws and the development of political parties competing on promises of social reform.[34] Willis expressed these changes as representing a shift from the state being 'soldier and policeman' to 'protector and nurse'.[35] The post-WWI period was particularly important as it included reconstruction of society and the economy.[36] Accordingly for Willis, and others who provided alternative accounts to Hewart,[37] the important starting point was not the emergency circumstances of WWI that had carried on after the war. It was inherent in the governmental arrangements developed with the welfare state in the nineteenth century.

The second was the shift to including the details of legislated laws in regulations rather than statutes. Willis recognised that this shift was incremental. In the second half of the nineteenth century some legislation included great detail, but Parliament was also starting to legislate in general forms, including provisions delegating regulation-making authority to administrative officials.[38] The important point for Willis was that social and political change during the nineteenth century came with changes in the forms of legislative law and administrative functions.[39] The different functions of Parliament and government had become clear by the 1920s. Willis understood legislative assemblies as being 'a battleground for conflicting ideals of society', but when Parliament has enacted laws then administration, and their functions of interpreting and implementing Parliaments' legislation, comes to the fore.[40] This is very different to Hewart's concern of Parliament being subordinated to the executive. Willis understood

[32] Willis (n 24) 4–5.
[33] Willis (n 24) 29–30.
[34] Willis (n 24) 12. See also FW Maitland, *The Constitutional History of England* (Cambridge University Press, 1913) 416–17.
[35] Willis (n 24) 13.
[36] ibid 31–33.
[37] Carr (n 19) 19–20; Port (n 19) 67–87, 125–27.
[38] Willis (n 24) 14.
[39] ibid 13–15.
[40] ibid 171.

that in the democratic era, Parliament and the executive had developed particular functions. Parliament to deal with macro-politics and broad directives on social policy and administration to deal with the micro-political details of implementation.

Willis also had a response to Hewart's concern about the arbitrariness of the increased reliance on regulation-making. It was that the shift to regulation-making included efforts to ensure that the regulations made by administrative officials were based on facts and evidence rather than conjecture.[41] He substantiated this by pointing to the establishment of special commissions dealing with matters such as the coal industry, the poor law and local government, and the inclusion of provisions in legislation establishing advisory committees to inform the exercise of regulation-making powers.[42] Willis understood the development of advisory committees as providing specialist knowledge and enhancing public confidence.[43]

Willis therefore highlighted ways in which Parliament was establishing forms of administrative governance. He recognised that administrative regulation-making has its own forms of deliberation, often established by legislation. This suggests that Willis did not see regulation-making as a threat to parliamentary democracy, but involved developments, demanded by an expanded electorate, for welfare-based reforms. The implementation of such reforms inevitably involved administrative techniques and the forms of deliberation associated with administrative governance.

Although Willis's book has become the most famous response to Hewart's *The New Despotism*,[44] other administrative law scholars of the period accepted the increased reliance on regulations in the post-WWI period. Two of these works were Cecil Carr's *Delegated Legislation* and Frederick Port's *Administrative Law*. These authors had numerous common reasons for the growth and legitimacy of regulation-making: parliamentary time is limited for the demands on political officials to make new laws;[45] administrative officials are likely to have more expertise than parliamentary officials on the matters that Parliament was by then seeking to regulate;[46] regulations were the most appropriate form of law for dealing with emergencies;[47] and regulation-making was helpful for making experimental laws.[48] While Willis's book addressed Hewart's argument directly, other administrative law scholars of the time published books that set out the benefits of regulation-making and indicated why such laws were inevitable in the era of the welfare state.

[41] ibid 35.
[42] ibid 35–8.
[43] ibid 37.
[44] See, eg, Loughlin (n 25) 168; Taggart (n 1) 580–90.
[45] Carr (n 19) 19–20; Port (n 19) 138.
[46] Carr (n 19) 20–21; Port (n 19) 139.
[47] Carr (n 19) 22–6; Port (n 19) 137.
[48] Port (n 19) 144.

These works are also important for adding a dimension that was not the focus of Willis's book. It was that while regulation-making is inevitable and potentially advantageous due to the development of the welfare state, its legitimacy is dependent on safeguards. Both Carr and Port spent many pages setting out the safeguards that should be established for regulation-making. The first, and most obvious, was an existing aspect of the broader constitutional arrangements, that Parliament always has power to repeal or amend provisions delegating power.[49] They added the following:

- Regulation-making authority should be granted to a trustworthy delegate;[50]
- The provisions that delegate regulation-making authority should include clearly stated limits in order to support parliamentary and judicial scrutiny;[51]
- Provisions should be included for tabling regulations in Parliament and for Parliament to have powers to annul regulations;[52]
- Regulations must be published;[53]
- Judicial review should be available;[54] and
- Consultation processes should be employed.[55]

The first four of these safeguards involve steps for Parliament. This is consistent with views expressed by Willis and Carr that political and parliamentary control as being the most appropriate safeguard on regulation-making.[56]

The point that may be drawn from this is that Hewart's opponents denied that the delegation of regulation-making authority is inconsistent with the UK's parliamentary democracy. The increased reliance on this form of law was an evolution responding to political demands rather than administrators' conspiracies. They included in their analyses the adaptations of parliamentary democracy in the form of safeguards that accommodated this evolution. For them, administrative law-making is inevitable in the shift to the welfare state but work should be done to improve Parliament's role in the process. If Hewart's argument can be understood as referencing a deliberative model of parliamentary democracy, with Parliament as the deliberative forum, Willis, Carr and Port can be regarded as referencing a new model of parliamentary democracy, one in which administration plays an important role.

[49] Carr (n 19) 27; Port (n 19) 145.
[50] Carr (n 19) 27–28.
[51] ibid 29.
[52] ibid 38; Port (n 19) 145–7.
[53] ibid 36.
[54] Port (n 19) 147–151.
[55] Carr (n 19) 31; Port (n 19) 152–54.
[56] Carr (n 19) 49; Willis (n 24) 113.

C. The Donoughmore Committee

As referred to earlier, the Donoughmore Committee was established as a response to Lord Hewart's book. Its terms of reference were clearly reacting to Hewart's argument, stating that the Committee was to be established to[57]

> consider the powers exercised by or under the direction of (or by persons or bodies appointed specially by) Ministers of the Crown by way of (a) delegated legislation and (b) judicial or quasi-judicial decision; and to report what safeguards are desirable or necessary to secure the constitutional principles of the sovereignty of Parliament and the supremacy of the Law.

The Committee concluded that there is no general problem with delegation of regulation-making powers so long as safeguards are in place. It therefore rejected Hewart's argument that delegations of regulation-making powers should be repealed or amended. The Donoughmore Committee's report received mixed reactions. Willis regarded it as an 'anti-climax'.[58] On the other hand, CK Allen, a supporter of Hewart, referred to it as a 'constitutional document of the highest value'.[59]

The Donoughmore Committee expressly dismissed Hewart's concern that delegation of regulation-making power is basically a conspiracy employed by administrative officials to use Parliament to empower themselves. Instead, the Report referred to delegated legislation as 'legitimate and constitutionally desirable' so long as safeguards were established.[60] The Committee elaborated this view as follows:[61]

> We do not agree with those critics who think that the practice is wholly bad. We see in it definite advantages, provided that the statutory powers are exercised and the statutory functions performed in the right way. But risks of abuse are incidental to it, and we believe that safeguards are required, if the country is to continue to enjoy the advantages of the practice without suffering from its inherent dangers.
>
> But in truth whether good or bad the development of the practice is inevitable. It is a natural reflection, in the sphere of constitutional law, of changes in our ideas of government which have resulted from changes in political, social and economic ideas, and of changes in the circumstances of our lives which have resulted from scientific discoveries.

While purportedly dismissing Hewart's primary argument, the Committee also acted consistently with one of Hewart's suggested solutions by recommending that a Parliamentary committee be established to report on bills for whether the

[57] Committee on Ministers' Powers, Report (London, 1932) ('Donoughmore Committee report') v.
[58] Willis (n 24) 175.
[59] Allen, *Law and Orders* (n 2) 50.
[60] Donoughmore Committee report (n 57) 51.
[61] ibid 4–5.

limits of regulation-making powers are clearly defined, impose taxes, or include Henry VIII powers, etc.[62] This recommendation was not implemented in the UK or Australia until much later (see section III below). Accordingly, while the Donoughmore Committee recommended a safeguard on the *inclusion* of delegation powers in Acts, it was only one of the two solutions that Hewart sought and was not implemented at the time. That means that in the first half of the twentieth century, the safeguards on the *exercise* of regulation-making powers became the focus of attention.[63] This can be regarded as the Donoughmore Committee's recommended solution to the problems raised by Hewart. It shifted the focus from the legitimacy of including delegation of regulation-making powers in Acts to acceptance of such powers so long as safeguards were in place. The questions then became a decision for Parliament and governments in regard to which of the range of safeguards should be implemented.

The Committee expanded on the safeguards they regarded as necessary. They will be dealt with in more detail in subsequent chapters. For now the important point is that they confirmed what we would now see as the basic safeguards: parliamentary scrutiny of bills and regulations;[64] the availability of judicial review;[65] and public consultation.[66]

The Donoughmore Committee's report can be regarded as supporting a particular form of parliamentary democracy. The view that Parliament must be the institution for debating policy choices underpinning all legislative laws was raised by Hewart and dismissed by the Donoughmore Committee. That outcome, and the reasoning in the Donoughmore Committee's report, suggests a different understanding of parliamentary democracy. That is that at least for Acts written in general terms and including broad delegation of regulation-making authority, Parliament's role has shifted from the forum for policy debates and deliberation to the forum for escalating problematic policy decisions that occur within administrative institutions.

II. Constitutional Concerns Australia: The *Dignan* Case

Parliamentary democracy has been adapted in Australia to accommodate its federal constitution. One of the early landmark cases regarding the nature and form of this accommodation was raised in a case, *Victorian Stevedoring and General Contracting Co Pty Ltd and Meakes v Dignan*,[67] decided five months prior to the Donoughmore Committee's report. The *Dignan* case plays a similar role for Australian constitutional principles as the Donoughmore Committee report plays

[62] ibid 62–63, 67–68.
[63] de Smith (n 24) 17.
[64] Donoughmore Committee report (n 57) 63, 68–69.
[65] ibid 61–62.
[66] ibid 44, 62, 66.
[67] (1931) 46 CLR 73.

in the UK. It is a key case in the High Court's ongoing management of the tension between the aspects of the Constitution dealing with the separation of powers and the aspects dealing with responsible government.

The mixing of these different constitutional systems in the Commonwealth Constitution has been referred to using the shorthand, 'Washminster' system, initially coined by Elain Thompson in her article 'The Washminster Mutation'.[68] In constitutional cases the Australian High Court has been required at times to consider a choice between US constitutional principles, in *Dignan* the non-delegation principle,[69] or the British principle of political rather than legal restrictions on delegation of regulation-making authority. The High Court in *Dignan* primarily chose the political model, with some minimal legal restrictions.

In this section, I analyse the *Dignan* case to highlight the similarities and differences between the Australian solution and the Donoughmore Committee's recommendations when concerns were raised about the broad delegation of regulation-making authority. As we will see, the similarity is that the judges' reasoning focused on delegation of regulation-making authority, and the breadth of such authority, primarily being a matter for political judgment. The differences are that the Commonwealth Constitution sets out the subject areas in which the Commonwealth Parliament can legislate that provides limits on the Parliament's powers that are enforced by the courts. There is also an important institutional difference that should be highlighted. The Commonwealth Constitution with its justiciable, enforceable provisions enables the question of broad delegation of statutory powers to be litigated. The consequence of that is that rather than the constitutional concerns regarding broad delegation of regulation powers being dealt with by a commission of inquiry (as occurred with the Donoughmore Committee), the matter was determined in Australia by a court. The High Court's reasoning is quite restricted and formal. It is largely limited to the question of authority to enact such provisions rather than the range of potential safeguards. The restrictions that were referred to were general and minimal.

A. The *Dignan* Case

The *Dignan* case involved a conflict between political parties over regulating workers on the wharves. The Labor Government made regulations, the Waterside Employment Regulations under the Transport Workers Act 1928, giving priority

[68] E Thompson, 'The Washminster Mutation' (1980) 15 *Politics* 32.

[69] The non-delegation principle requires statutory regulation-making powers to be limited by an 'intelligible principle' or general policy or standard that controls the scope of the official's authority: *Gundy v United States* 588 US_ (2019) 15–16. It is worthwhile noting that the US Supreme Court has not struck down any legislation on this basis since 1935 (*Panama Refining Co v Ryan*, 293 US 388 (1935); *ALA Schechter Poultry Corporation v United States*, 295 US 495 (1935)), which has led US public lawyers to acknowledge that the non-delegation principle provides little restrictiveness: see PL Strauss, *Administrative Justice in the United States*, 3rd edn (Carolina Academic Press, 2016) 46.

to union members who were available to work.[70] The important steps leading to the High Court's hearing occurred within a few dramatic months. The regulation was made on 26 June 1931. The company who brought the case in the High Court was charged on 17 July 1931 of an offence under the Regulations and was convicted on 24 July 1931. The Regulations were disallowed by the Senate on 29 July 1931; that is, after the appeal to the High Court was lodged and before the hearing on 11–13 August 1931.[71]

The case before the High Court raised the question of the constitutional authority to enact broad delegation of regulation-making powers. The provision of the Transport Workers Act 1928 delegating regulation-making authority was very broad. It provided a regulation-making power in the form of a Henry VIII clause stating:

> The Governor-General may make regulations, which, notwithstanding anything in any other Act but subject to the Acts Interpretation Act 1901–1918 and the Acts Interpretation Act 1904–1916, shall have the force of law, with respect to the employment of transport workers, and in particular for regulating the engagement, service, and discharge of transport workers, and the licensing of persons as transport workers, and for regulating or prohibiting the employment of unlicensed persons as transport workers, and for the protection of transport workers.

The applicant drew on the High Court's separation of powers principles for their argument. The particular point was that previous case law determining that judicial power could not be granted to another body,[72] also applied to legislative power so that legislative power could not be granted to the executive.[73] The argument was elaborated in this way:[74]

> On the proper construction of the Constitution, read as a whole, the threefold division of powers indicates the intention of the Imperial Parliament that the legislative power was to be exercised only by the body which was composed of representatives of the people.

The Commonwealth responded by arguing that the High Court had dealt with the general issue in previous cases without determining that regulation-making powers breached the separation of powers in the Constitution. They also argued that there was no express restriction on delegation of regulation-making authority

[70] For the political context of the *Dignan* case, see GS Reid, 'Parliament and Delegated Legislation' in JR Nethercote (ed), *Parliament and Bureaucracy: Parliamentary Scrutiny of Administration – Prospects and Problems in the 1980s* (Hale and Iremonger, 1982) 149, 154–55; J Stellios, *Zines's The High Court and the Constitution*, 6th edn (Federation Press, 2015) 203–04; G Williams, S Brennan and A Lynch, *Blackshield and Williams, Australian Constitutional Law and Theory*, 7th edn (Federation Press, 2018), 485–86; G Appleby, 'Challenging the Orthodoxy: Giving the Court a Role in Scrutiny of Delegated Legislation' (2016) 69 *Parliamentary Affairs* 269, 274.

[71] *Victorian Stevedoring and General Contracting Co Pty Ltd and Meakes v Dignan* (1931) 46 CLR 73, 74–77.

[72] Citing *Waterside Workers Federation of Australia v JW Alexander Ltd* (1918) 25 CLR 434.

[73] *Victorian Stevedoring and General Contracting Co Pty Ltd and Meakes v Dignan* (1931) 46 CLR 73, 79.

[74] ibid.

to the executive and that the issue involved policy matters unsuited to determination by the High Court.[75]

The High Court rejected the applicant's argument. The famous judgment was given by Dixon J, who presented the issue as a choice between US and British approaches to delegation of regulation-making powers. Dixon spent many pages examining the US case law only to conclude that it could not be adopted in Australia. His main point was that although the Commonwealth Constitution is structured on the executive, legislative and judicial powers as being apparently separate functions, there is no separation between the executive and legislative powers that meant law-making powers could not be delegated to administrative officials.[76] As the High Court had by then started its development of principles for separating the judicial power from the executive and legislative powers, Dixon referred to the outcome in *Dignan* as being asymmetrical.[77] He based his acceptance of it on Australia's British heritage; stating that the result was based, 'less on juristic analysis and perhaps more on the usages of British legislation and theories of English law'.[78]

The significance of resolving the constitutional problem in this way were that regulations gain their authority from the Act that authorises them and that Parliament has control over the regulation because it has control over the Act that provides the authority for it. That is, Parliament can always repeal or amend the Act.[79] A regulation relies on its empowering legislation for its efficacy not only when it is made but also in a continuing sense.[80] The only restrictions that Dixon J referred to were that the delegating provision must be within a head of power under section 51 of the Commonwealth Constitution and that Parliament cannot abdicate its law-making power by establishing an institution with general law-making power.[81]

Accordingly, the consequence of Dixon's decision to take the approach most consistent with British history was that the legal restrictions on regulation-making powers were minimal. The primary focus was on statutory authority and Parliament's ongoing ability to control delegated legislation. Whereas the Donoughmore Committee's report was able to address a much broader range of safeguards, Dixon's reasoning, as may be appropriate in a case raising a question as to whether statutory delegation of broad regulation-making authority is authorised by the Constitution, focused on legal authority and the constitutional provisions that control Commonwealth legislation.

Evatt J gave the other important judgment in the *Dignan* case. His reasoning was consistent with Dixon J in regard to reliance on ministers' responsibility to

[75] ibid 81.
[76] ibid 101–02.
[77] ibid 101.
[78] ibid 101–02.
[79] ibid 102.
[80] ibid.
[81] ibid 96.

Parliament and that Parliament ultimately has control which it can use to repeal or amend an empowering Act or a regulation.[82] He also referred to Parliament not being able to abdicate its power and that section 51 of the Constitution provides the primary limit on the exercise of regulation-making powers.[83] He elaborated with regard to how courts should determine whether Acts that include delegation of regulation-making powers are within the powers granted to the Commonwealth Parliament by section 51. He stated that very broad grants of regulation-making powers may not be regarded as within particular heads of power in section 51 and that courts are likely to employ a stricter view when Acts delegate to non-departmental agencies which are a step removed from responsible government controls.[84] These elaborations highlight how Evatt J accommodated his acceptance of broad delegations of regulation-making authority to the provisions of the Commonwealth Constitution.

These features of Dixon J's and Evatt J's judgments highlight the Washminster aspect of Australia's constitutional arrangements. The outcome has an important similarity to the UK position; that broad delegations of power are constitutionally permissible. However, there are important differences. The question was resolved by litigation and the limits set out in the case are not provided by safeguards but by constitutional means that are quite narrow and unlikely to be engaged. The safeguards that have been developed in Australia are due to developments prompted by Parliament, rather than being required, or prompted, by the courts in constitutional litigation. The High Court has not added to the criteria in *Dignan* for delegations of regulation-making powers. There have been recent cases in which plaintiffs have challenged broad regulation-making provisions of legislation, but the High Court has either determined that the delegation is acceptable notwithstanding the breadth[85] or avoided resolving the case on this basis.[86] The significance of these recent cases is that the parameters set out in the *Dignan* case have not been elaborated.

B. Significance of *Dignan* for Parliamentary Democracy

The *Dignan* case more generally tells us that the High Court will not insist on the Commonwealth Parliament being the primary institution for deliberation regarding policy issues. Framework Acts (or more pejoratively 'skeleton Acts') of which the Transport Workers Act 1928 that was challenged in *Dignan* was a classical example, do not raise constitutional concerns in Australia. This was confirmed by the High Court in the 1950s when it accepted that Acts that provide broad

[82] ibid 114, 118.
[83] ibid 119, 121.
[84] ibid 120.
[85] *New South Wales v Commonwealth (Workchoices case)* (2006) 229 CLR 1, 174–82 [395]–[418].
[86] *Williams v Commonwealth of Australia (No 2)* (2014) 252 CLR 416, 456–57 [32]–[36].

delegations of regulation-making authority and provide only 'outlines of policy' indicate 'an intention of leaving it to [administrative officials] to work out that policy by specific regulation'.[87]

The primary limits considered by the High Court in *Dignan* were the Commonwealth Parliament's ultimate authority to control regulations via its control of Acts and the High Court's judicial review of legislation for whether it fits within the heads of power in section 51 of the Constitution. Other potential safeguards that came to the fore in the Donoughmore Committee's report (parliamentary scrutiny, judicial review and consultation provisions) were not raised and, to be fair, were not at issue in the case. The contribution to the twentieth century norms of regulation-making in parliamentary democracies is that broad delegations do not, on their own, cause any constitutional difficulty. This is the formal version of Australia's parliamentary democracy. Parliament is the ultimate controller of delegated legislation but is not necessarily the forum for debate and deliberation in the making of laws.

A question then arises as to how these ideas of parliamentary democracy that underpin the reasoning in the *Dignan* case align with more recent case law in which the High Court has drawn on the democratic features of the Commonwealth Constitution (particularly that the houses of Parliament are to be directly chosen by the people': Constitution sections 7 and 24) to develop an implied right to vote and an implied freedom of political communication. In these cases the High Court has developed principles of representative and responsible government from the text and structure of the Commonwealth Constitution.[88] At some points in the case law, the judges have explained the freedom of political communication as being to ensure openness, participation and accountability of government to the people.[89] This is the terminology of deliberative forms of democracy developed within a parliamentary democracy.[90]

Do these principles of representative government in the constitutional case law contradict the High Court's approach in *Dignan*? The answer is no. Doctrinally there is no difficulty: the implied freedom is a limit on laws made by Australian parliaments and does not require parliaments to take particular actions.[91] More

[87] *Morton v Union Steamship Company of New Zealand Limited* (1951) 83 CLR 402, 410.

[88] *Australian Capital Television Pty Ltd v Commonwealth* (1992) 177 CLR 106, 137–38; *Nationwide News Pty Ltd v Wills* (1992) 177 CLR 1, 47–48; *Lange v Australian Broadcasting Corporation* (1997) 189 CLR 520, 557–62; *McCloy v New South Wales* (2015) 257 CLR 178, 222–30 [100]–[124] (Gageler J), 279 [301] (Gordon J).

[89] *Australian Capital Television Pty Ltd v Commonwealth* (1992) 177 CLR 106, 138–39; *Nationwide News Pty Ltd v Wills* (1992) 177 CLR 1, 47–48; *Lange v Australian Broadcasting Corporation* (1997) 189 CLR 520, 571; *Unions NSW v New South Wales* (2013) 252 CLR 530, 551 [28]–[29], 571 [104]; *McCloy v New South Wales* (2015) 257 CLR 178, 222–30 [45]. See also SA Mason, 'The Interpretation of a Constitution in a Modern Liberal Democracy' in C Sampford and K Preston (eds), *Interpreting Constitutions: Theories, Principles and Institutions* (Federation Press, 1996) 13, 21–22, 27.

[90] See also H Patapan, *Judging Democracy* (Cambridge University Press, 2000), 59–60; Stellios (n 70) 609.

[91] *Lange v Australian Broadcasting Corporation* (1997) 189 CLR 520, 560; *Unions NSW v New South Wales* (2013) 252 CLR 530, 554 [36], 571 [109]; *Brown v Tasmania* (2017) 261 CLR 328, 359 [88] (Kiefel CJ, Bell and Keane JJ), 407 [258] (Nettle J), 430 [313] (Gordon J).

generally, the focus on representative and responsible government principles in these cases are not focused on ensuring parliamentary deliberation of proposed laws. Representative government protects public debate about political matters, which is based on the accountability of political representatives to electors and restricting laws that infringe on public discussion and debate.[92] Responsible government ensures that ministers are accountable to Parliament: government functions are exercised by ministers and agencies who can be questioned in Parliament.[93] While these principles may suggest that they are designed to protect Australia's version of parliamentary democracy, they do not go so far to insist on Parliament, the primary deliberative forum of parliamentary systems, exercising all legislative powers. The important feature of the Australian High Court's analysis is that Parliament can exercise control of governmental functions, including the making of delegated legislation.

A recent case illustrates this point. In *Williams (No 1)* the High Court determined that an agreement between the Commonwealth Government and a religious group to fund school chaplains was invalid.[94] The Commonwealth had not relied on statutory authority to make the agreement and other potential sources of authority were not available. Parliament then enacted legislative provisions enabling the authorisation of Commonwealth funding agreements by delegated legislation.[95] The relevant provision is particularly broad. It authorises government funding where the Commonwealth otherwise does not have power to make such arrangements or grants.[96] When the same plaintiff challenged the same form of funding that was challenged in *Williams (No 1)*, one of the issues was whether the delegation by the statute of such broad authority to the executive to make delegated legislation was invalid. The High Court read the delegating provision down so as to avoid dealing with that question.[97] It instead determined that the particular regulations were invalid for not being within the subject matter that parliament can legislate in section 51 of the Constitution.

The significance of this approach is that it suggests that broad delegations of regulation-making authority are unlikely to be determined to be invalid. The courts have other options; in this case determining whether the regulations (rather than the Act) were authorised by the Constitution and, in other cases, reviewing regulations by reference to administrative law principles.

[92] *Australian Capital Television Pty Ltd v Commonwealth* (1992) 177 CLR 106, 138.

[93] *Lange v Australian Broadcasting Corporation* (1997) 189 CLR 520, 558–59; *Egan v Willis* (1998) 195 CLR 424, 451 [42]; *Comcare v Banerji* [2019] HCA 23, 267 CLR 373 [56]–[65].

[94] *Williams v Commonwealth* (2012) 248 CLR 156.

[95] Financial Management and Accountability Act 1997 (Cth), s 32B (now titled the Financial Framework (Supplementary Powers) Act 1997 (Cth)).

[96] ibid.

[97] *Williams v Commonwealth (No 2)* (2012) 252 CLR 416, 457 [36].

C. Senate Inquiry into Standing Committees

The catalyst for establishing the Australian parliamentary committee for review of regulations did not come from the judiciary, as in the case in the UK with the publication of Lord Hewart's *The New Despotism*, but from the Senate. In particular it arose from an important dynamic in Australia's parliamentary democracy, an upper house in which the Government usually does not have a majority but has power to veto Acts and regulations. The dispute underlying the *Dignan* case involved high-stakes politics that crystallised in a conflict over regulations made under the Transport Workers Act 1928 (Cth). The context for that conflict was the Labor Party being elected in October 1929 with a substantial majority in the House of Representatives but no majority in the Senate. It was a period in which the Senate asserted its position in legislation-making and in holding the Government accountable.[98]

The Senate's steps to assert its scrutiny role were apparent in its decision to establish a committee to inquire into standing committees. The Senate decided in December 1929 to appoint a select committee to inquire into establishing Senate standing committees in four different areas: regulations; international relations; finance and; private members bills.[99] Senator Elliott's speech proposing the inquiry started by arguing that the Senate needed to develop a stronger role. He stated that the 'Senate has not taken full advantage of its wonderful opportunities to render service to Australia' and that the proposed committees would 'enable honorable senators to take a keener interest in matters and to bring a considered opinion to bear on the measures that are presented to Parliament'.[100] Regarding regulations, Senator Elliott expressed two primary concerns: that very brief, framework, legislation was being passed authorising a large volume of regulations and that these regulations were not being read by senators even though both houses of Parliament had powers to disallow them.

The Senate established a committee to advise the Senate on the important aspects of regulations made by government.[101] This decision to establish a committee to inquire into the issue was prompted by proposals regarding the Senate's role in Parliament. Although this occurred in the same year that Lord Hewart's book was published it was not referred to at the time the decision to establish the Committee was made. However, Lord Hewart's book was subsequently referred to in the Senate Committee's report[102] and, in a supportive manner, in the Senate as a whole when the report was being considered.[103] So while Lord Hewart had

[98] Reid (n 70) 149, 153, 157.

[99] Commonwealth, *Parliamentary Debates*, Senate, 5 December 1929, 745 (Senator Elliott).

[100] ibid 745–46.

[101] ibid 747.

[102] Senate, *Report from the Senate Select Committee Advising on Establishing Standing Committees*, Parliament of Australia (Report April 1930) para 16.

[103] Commonwealth, *Parliamentary Debates*, Senate, 1 May 1930, 1313.

some influence in the process, the concerns regarding regulations initially arose independently.

The 1930 Senate Committee accepted the basic problem for regulation-making at the time: regulation-making powers were very commonly included in Acts[104] and that the regulations that were made according to such powers were not being reviewed by senators. The 1930 Senate Committee's recommendation to establish a committee to review regulations was accepted and implemented soon after the 1930 Senate Committee published its report.

The 1930 Senate Committee was less clear in relation to scrutiny of bills. It initially recommended that its proposed scrutiny committee should review the provisions of bills authorising regulations to be made for whether such powers should be exercised by Parliament.[105] However, after further debate in the Senate as a whole[106] its final recommendation was for a committee to review only regulations tabled in Parliament.[107] The final recommendation regarding bills was for a separate committee to review *particular* bills referred to it by the Senate.[108] This final recommendation meant that while the 1930 Senate Committee played an important role in the development of controls on the exercise of regulation-making powers, it had no effect on scrutiny of *all* bills for their inclusion of regulation-making powers.

III. Establishing Scrutiny of Bills Committees

The result of the Donoughmore Committee's report and the *Dignan* case was confirmation that broad delegations of regulation-making powers are accepted, maybe reluctantly, but nevertheless accepted in the UK and Australia. The forums in which the debates about this issue occurred varied (consistently with the different forms of parliamentary democracy in the UK and Australia) but the outcomes were fairly similar. That is, broad delegations of regulation-making authority were accepted in the primary controversies of the first half of the twentieth century.

However, the Donoughmore Committee's recommendation that bills be reviewed by a parliamentary committee for whether they include broad delegations of regulation power was not implemented at that time.[109] This was recommended as a solution to members of parliament being unaware that particular bills include such powers.[110] Although scrutiny of regulations committees were established before and after the Donoughmore Committee reported, it was not until the second

[104] Senate 1930 Committee (n 102) para 13.
[105] ibid para 23.
[106] Commonwealth, *Parliamentary Debates*, Senate, 8 May 1930, 1548–61; Commonwealth, *Parliamentary Debates*, Senate, 15 May 1930, 1802.
[107] Senate 1930 Committee (n 102) para 1.
[108] ibid para 2.
[109] Donoughmore Committee report (n 57) 67.
[110] ibid 63.

half of the twentieth century that scrutiny of bills committees were established in both the UK and Australia. The committees in both countries were established as part of renewed development of parliamentary committees from the late 1960s.[111]

As we will see, these committees in the UK (Delegated Powers and Regulatory Reform Committee) and Australia (Senate Standing Committee for the Scrutiny of Bills) are specifically designed for reviewing bills for delegation of regulation-making powers. There are other committees in both countries that scrutinise bills. For example, the House of Lords Constitutional Committee can consider delegation of regulation-making powers as part of its function of scrutinising bills for their 'constitutional implications'.[112] Of course, the constitutional implications of delegation of broad regulation-making authority were squarely raised by Lord Hewart. While it must be recognised that the House of Lords Constitution Committee plays a role in parliamentary scrutiny of bills, my focus will be on the committees in both countries that were specifically designed for this purpose.

A. United Kingdom

The Delegated Powers and Regulatory Reform Committee was initially established in 1992. Its general role is to scrutinise bills for whether they inappropriately delegate regulation-making powers or enable an inappropriate degree of parliamentary scrutiny.[113] The scrutiny of bills role implements the recommendations of the Donoughmore Committee that reported 60 years prior to the Committee being established.[114]

The starting point for establishing the Committee came from a speech by Lord Rippon in the House of Lords in 1990. Lord Rippon expressed his concern as follows:[115]

> Bill after Bill contains Henry VIII clauses; that is to say, clauses giving the Minister power to amend or even repeal primary legislation by order. Moreover, there is an increasing reliance on enabling powers of one kind or another. So I believe that we have to consider what checks Parliament itself can impose.

He turned to Australia for the institutional reform that he thought would provide the necessary check on the drafting of bills. As will be explained below, the

[111] See Select Committee on the Committee Work of the House (Earl Jellicoe) (HL 1991–92, 35-I) paras 13–18; M Russell, *The Contemporary House of Lords: Westminster Bicameralism Revived* (Oxford University Press, 2013) 209–11; House of Lords Library Note, *Select Committees in the House of Lords* (2017), 2; Harry Evans, *Odgers Australian Senate Practice*, 14th edn (Department of the Senate, 2016) 464.

[112] See, eg, House of Lords, Select Committee on the Constitution, *The Legislative Process: The Delegation of Powers* (HL 2017–19, 25) para 40.

[113] D Natzler and M Hutton (eds), *Erskine May's Treatise on The Law, Privileges, Proceedings and Usage of Parliament*, 25th edn (2019) para 40.48, available at erskinemay.parliament.uk.

[114] Donoughmore Committee report (n 57) 62–63, 67–68.

[115] HL Deb Vol 515, cols 1407–37 (14 February 1990).

Australian Senate initially established its Scrutiny of Bills Committee in 1981. Lord Rippon stated in his House of Lords speech that the Australian Committee should be studied to determine whether something similar could be adopted by the House of Lords.[116]

Two years later, the Jellicoe Committee included in its report a recommendation that the Delegated Powers and Regulatory Reform Committee be established. It expressed the concern as being that, 'in recent years there has been considerable disquiet over the problem of wide and sometimes ill-defined order-making powers which give Ministers unlimited discretion'.[117] Earl Jellicoe confirmed in the House of Lords that the Australian Scrutiny of Bills Committee was studied in its inquiry.[118]

There was much agreement with the proposal to establish such a committee in the speeches made in the House of Lords when Earl Jellicoe's report was tabled. However, Lord Wakeham, representing the Government, stated that the Government had reservations.[119] The reservations were expressed by the Lord Chancellor who stated that without such a committee the House of Lords had no difficulty raising concerns about broad delegations of regulation making power. He also stated that the Australian Scrutiny of Bills Committee was not a good precedent for the House of Lords as the report on it that was received by the Lords indicated that there was less opportunity for the Senate as a whole to debate such powers which meant that there was additional need in Australia for a committee to conduct scrutiny.[120] The general point was that the House of Lords already provides an effective check on broad delegations of regulation-making powers being included in bills. There was no need to establish a specialist committee for that purpose. However, in the end the government agreed to the Committee being established.[121]

The Delegated Powers and Regulatory Reform Committee has now operated for over 30 years; long enough for assessments of its effectiveness to be carried out. Meg Russell's research of Parliament identifies the Committee as being particularly effective at requiring changes to bills that have overly broad delegation of such powers or include Henry VIII clauses.[122] Fox and Blackwell in their study of delegated legislation in the UK, refer to the Delegated Powers and Regulatory Reform Committee as 'perhaps the biggest success story in the delegated legislation process in recent decades'.[123]

[116] ibid.

[117] Jellicoe Committee (n 111) paras 60, 133 and Annex 4.

[118] HL Deb Vol 537, col 899–937 (3 June 1992).

[119] ibid col 899–937.

[120] ibid col 946–1016.

[121] HL Deb Vol 540, col 96 (10 November 1992).

[122] Russell (n 111) 187–89, 219–20; M Russell and D Gover, *Legislation at Westminster: Parliamentary Actors and Influence in the Making of British Law* (Oxford University Press, 2017) 219–23, 227–28.

[123] R Fox and J Blackwell, *The Devil is in the Detail: Parliament and Delegated Legislation* (Hansard Society, 2014) 71.

B. Australia

We have just seen that the development of the House of Lords, Delegated Powers and Regulatory Reform Committee was influenced by the Australian Senate Scrutiny of Bills Committee. The Scrutiny of Bills Committee has a wider role than the House of Lords Committee. Its first three scrutiny criteria relate to impact on rights and liberties that are harsh, are based on insufficiently defined powers or are not reviewable. The two criteria relating to regulation-making powers are whether particular bills 'inappropriately delegate legislative powers' or 'insufficiently subject the exercise of legislative power to parliamentary scrutiny'.[124]

The Committee was established due to what will now be recognised as familiar problems. The reform process started with two reports of the Senate Standing Committee on Constitutional and Legal Affairs in 1978.[125] The Committee's first report set out the constitutional framework regarding delegation of regulation-making powers. It considered the *Dignan* case, along with two other High Court cases, and concluded that the limits established by the High Court (Parliament cannot abdicate its authority and always has overarching authority to amend or repeal the empowering Act) are not helpful in practice.[126] It concluded that 'This situation creates a responsibility in the Parliament to ensure that the delegations when first made are appropriate, carefully framed and subject to adequate supervision'. The remainder of the report went on to examine different forms of problematic delegations of power: referred to as inappropriate delegations, uncontrolled delegations, and insufficiently defined delegations.[127] In its second report tabled in the Senate on the same day, the Senate Standing Committee on Constitutional and Legal Affairs set out its analysis of and recommendations for a scrutiny of bills committee.[128]

Unlike in the UK, where the Government initially resisted establishing the Delegated Powers and Regulatory Reform Committee but then shifted to supporting it, the Australian Government rejected the recommendation to establish the committee throughout the process.[129] The reasons it gave for doing so were that the Government itself considers the same matters when drafting bills that the committee would consider and so do the two houses of Parliament. Additionally, the committee would be a new element for the Parliament that would distort

[124] Standing Order 24(1)(a)(iv), (v).

[125] Senate Standing Committee on Constitutional and Legal Affairs, *Report on Delegation of Parliamentary Authority* (Parliamentary Paper No 331/1978); Senate Standing Committee on Constitutional and Legal Affairs, *Report on Scrutiny of Bills* (Parliamentary Paper No 329/1978).

[126] Senate Committee, *Parliamentary Paper No. 331/1978* (n 125)) paras 2.8–2.13.

[127] ibid chs 4–6.

[128] Senate Committee, *Parliamentary Paper No 329/1978* (n 125).

[129] Commonwealth, *Parliamentary Debates*, Senate, 22 November 1979, 2795 (Ministerial statement). See also Commonwealth, *Parliamentary Debates*, Senate, 17 November 1981, 2418; A Missen, "Senate Committees and the Legislative Process" in JR Nethercote (ed), *Parliament and Bureaucracy: Parliamentary Scrutiny of Administration – Prospects and Problems in the 1980s* (Hale and Iremonger, 1982) 125, 131.

and frustrate the process of making legislation.[130] The committee was ultimately established, initially on a temporary basis, in 1981. At this time the Government again rejected the proposed committee and elaborated its arguments.[131] However the Government could not gain a majority for the rejection and the Senate voted to establish the committee.[132]

The important point about this debate was that the Constitutional and Legal Affairs Committee's report responded to the lack of limitations and insufficient safeguards on delegating powers to administrative officials. Another way of understanding this is that the broad understanding of parliamentary democracy that influenced the High Court in the *Dignan* case was regarded as problematic and required an additional parliamentary measure as a check on bills that delegate powers. The Government's response was to resist the additional scrutiny that the Senate would now provide. In its view there were sufficient existing checks on bills that were provided by Cabinet, Parliamentary counsel, and the two houses of Parliament.

The Senate Scrutiny of Bills Committee is now a long established and uncontroversial feature of the Senate. Its annual reports set out its impacts. The most recent annual report at the time of writing, published in 2022, highlights that the committee commented on nearly half of the 223 bills that were introduced in the year and that 34 per cent of its comments related to its criteria regarding delegating legislative power.[133] The report explains that the Committee prompts amendments to bills, influences initial legislative drafting, presses for improved reasons for bills set out in explanatory memorandums, and informs discussion and debate in the Senate and Senate committees.[134]

IV. Conclusions

I started this chapter by setting out Lord Hewart's conspiracy theory and his view that members of Parliament were asleep at the wheel. With the introduction of scrutiny of bills committees, something that Lord Hewart advocated, it is hard to accept that provisions in Acts that delegate regulation-making powers is now unchecked. Government officials may not be able to resist the temptation of adding broad delegations of regulation-making powers but the committees established in the UK and Australia in the 1980s and 1990s provide a check designed to raise concerns about it. There was government resistance to their establishment (to different degrees in each country) but the UK and Australian committees are now firmly established.

[130] Commonwealth, *Parliamentary Debates*, Senate, 22 November 1979, 2796–97 (Ministerial statement).
[131] Commonwealth, *Parliamentary Debates*, Senate, 19 November 1981, 2418–2420 (Senator Durack).
[132] ibid 2427–28.
[133] Senate Scrutiny of Bills Committee, *Annual Report* (March 2022) 8–9.
[134] ibid 9–14.

The scrutiny of bills committees review bills for breadth of regulation-making powers. It is a political matter dealt with through upper house procedures. Although, the Australian High Court has left some small space for litigation challenging overly broad delegation of regulation-making powers, no significant case law has developed since the *Dignan* case in 1931. The conclusion, then, is that in at least these two parliamentary democracies, the safeguards on overly broad delegation of regulation-making powers is primarily a role for Parliament and, more specifically, a review role that suits upper houses given they are not usually controlled by the Government in the UK and Australia.[135]

Nevertheless, the over-reliance on delegations of regulation-making authority is still commonly criticised in the UK by members of the House of Lords[136] and in Committee reports.[137] As we saw in chapter one, in Australia academics have recently raised concerns about the lack of constitutional restrictions on delegating regulation-making powers.[138]

Beyond concerns regarding delegation of regulation-making powers and the introduction of scrutiny of bills committees, this chapter highlights broader features of the debates in the 1920s and 1930s. It was accepted in these debates that the second half of the nineteenth century and beginnings of the twentieth century involved social, political and institutional changes that affected forms of law-making. The expansion of the franchise and development of welfare state policies prompted a shift in the drafting of legislation in which it was common for regulation-making powers to be delegated to administrative officials. The crucial point of the debates and how they were settled in the Donoughmore Committee's report is that this change had occurred and the necessary response was to provide safeguards on it.

The debates highlight a shift in Parliament's role. Whereas Lord Hewart's argument was based on Parliament having a deeper deliberative role than was occurring, John Willis and like-minded commentators acknowledged the reality of changes in its role and set about reconciling a suitable role for Parliament with expansions in administrative functions. The primary measure that was advocated for this reconciliation was the development of safeguards checking administrative officials' exercise of regulation-making powers.

While both Lord Hewart[139] and his opponents largely achieved what they sought from the Donoughmore Committee's report, the important point is that the recommendations required Parliament to adjust so that it continued to have

[135] Russell (n 111) 45 and R Mulgan, 'The Australian Senate as a "House of Review"' (1996) 31 *Australian Journal of Political Science* 191, 201–02.

[136] Lord Judge, 'Ceding Power to the Executive; the Resurrection of Henry VIII' (speech at King's College London, 12 April 2016).

[137] House of Lords, Select Committee on the Constitution (n 137) ch 3.

[138] D Meyerson, 'Rethinking the Constitutionality of Delegated Legislation' (2003) 11 *Australian Journal of Administrative Law* 45; Appleby (n 70).

[139] Due to the Donoughmore Committee publicising the issue and recommending that scrutiny of bills committees be established.

an important role in the new political reality of the administrative state. While it would no longer be the deliberative forum for debates about the detail of all laws, it would be the forum for escalating laws made by administrative officials that were identified as being problematic. These safeguards enabled Parliament to provide a platform in which such concerns could be debated.

In the remainder of part one of this book I examine the particular safeguards developed before and after the Donoughmore Committee's report and the Australian Senate Committee's report in 1930. Whereas this chapter has focused on safeguards developed for Parliament's role in relation to bills, the next chapters focus on the safeguards on the exercise of these powers.

3

Parliamentary Scrutiny of Regulations

The most important contribution made by the 1930s committees was the recommendation to establish parliamentary committees to scrutinise regulations. Prior to then only small steps had been made to establish them, and that step, the House of Lords Special Orders Committee, was at that time very recently established in 1925. Without reference to each other, the Australian Senate Committee recommended in 1930 and the Donoughmore Committee recommended in 1932 that what was missing from regulation-making was systemic checks provided by parliaments.

This aspect of parliaments' role will be the primary focus of this chapter. The scrutiny committees play a crucial role in parliaments' capacity to provide accountability for regulation-making by administrative officials. It is important to recognise that it builds on the prior development of providing powers to houses of parliament to veto regulations. The scrutiny committees' role assumes that parliaments have powers to veto regulations. The committees enable parliaments to deliberate in an informed manner in regard to the exercise of their veto powers. I will briefly examine the development of those powers at the beginning of this chapter.

The issues examined in this chapter can helpfully be framed by comments JAG Griffith made in 1949. He referred to scrutiny committees as an essential element of the response to the constitutional concerns about delegation of regulation-making powers.[1] The parliamentary debates for the establishment of scrutiny committees provides evidence that members of parliament recognise the constitutional significance of parliamentary scrutiny and the committees' function in facilitating that role. The current members of scrutiny committees who identify closely with the parliament's constitutional significance are likely to engage more closely in the committees' scrutiny role. The committees engage directly with ministers, departments and agencies, commonly securing changes to regulations through direct correspondence with departments and ministers that result in correcting the problems identified by the committees.

[1] JAG Griffith, 'Delegated Legislation – Some Recent Developments' (1949) 12 *Modern Law Review* 297, 318.

Examination of the debates in regard to establishing scrutiny committees highlights government resistance to safeguards, an important theme for part one of the book. There is evidence of such resistance to scrutiny of regulations committees but not as much, or as persistent, as we saw for parliamentary committees for scrutinising bills, and as we will see in chapter four in regard to consultation provisions. The parliamentary debates regarding scrutiny of regulations committees reveals that backbenchers and members of upper houses have taken the lead in the development of these committees.

In this chapter, I will primarily focus on examining the inquiry reports that recommended establishing the various scrutiny committees in the UK and Australian parliaments, and the parliamentary debates when those recommendations were implemented. I will focus on two aspects of these materials: the constitutional significance of the committees and the committee's role in raising concerns with regulations directly to ministers and to parliaments. The committees' direct correspondence with ministers and departments continues parliaments' role of questioning legislation and seeking adjustments. The committees' role of informing parliament of problematic regulations exposes governments when they are tempted to deal with politically controversial subject matter in regulations to avoid parliamentary debate.

I. Parliamentary Veto Powers – The Precondition for Parliamentary Deliberation

Parliamentary powers over regulations were well established by legislation by the time of the 1930s debates.[2] There are technical aspects of these powers that I will touch on but not explain in any detail in this chapter. Rather than focusing on them, I will treat parliamentary veto powers as a formal requirement for parliamentary scrutiny that requires supplementation in order for the exercise of parliamentary powers to be effective. The most important, general, issue regarding parliamentary veto powers are the exceptions in which parliament is given no such powers in relation to regulations. This is an important issue and will be dealt with in chapter six.

There are three general types of veto powers.[3] Affirmative resolution is when a regulation requires approval by parliament for it to come into operation.[4] Negative resolution refers to regulations that are subject annulment (in the UK) or disallowance (in Australia) by parliament.[5] It is also possible for legislation to

[2] See C Carr, *Delegated Legislation* (Cambridge University Press, 1921) 38–41.
[3] The more detailed variations of these powers are set out in R Fox and J Blackwell, 'The Devil is in the Detail: Parliament and Delegated Legislation' (Hansard Society, 2014) 76.
[4] See, eg, Financial Services Act 2021 (UK), s 46(3); Health Insurance Act (Cth), s 10B(2).
[5] See, eg, Financial Services Act 2021 (UK), s 46(2); Legislation Act 2003 (Cth), s 42.

grant powers providing for an administrative official to make delegated legislation without provision for parliamentary review.[6] The important difference between the UK and Australia is that parliament's powers and procedure is included in enabling Acts in the UK, and in Australia is included in a generally applicable Act, the Legislation Act 2003 (Cth).

In both countries, the negative resolution procedure is more common.[7] In fact, in Australia the affirmative procedure is rare. The reason for distinguishing the two procedures is to have different levels of parliamentary engagement for different types of regulations and most obviously that regulations dealing with matters of national policy significance are subject to a higher level of general scrutiny. However, reviews of regulation-making procedures indicate that the affirmative resolution procedures do not guarantee substantial parliamentary scrutiny.[8]

As already mentioned, the most fundamental concern relates to exclusion or exemptions from parliamentary scrutiny. That is the feature of the systems in both countries that has the greatest systemic significance. Exclusions from parliamentary veto disable the precondition for parliaments' general control and also the more detailed scrutiny and questioning of regulation-makers by scrutiny committees.

II. Parliamentary Scrutiny Committees – 1930s Reform Debates

As we have just seen, parliamentary veto powers were common prior to the 1930s debates. However, those debates recognised that such powers are far from sufficient. The concerns triggering the 1930s debates started with Lord Hewart raising delegation of law-making power as a problem. The committees examining this problem in both countries in the 1930s recognised parliamentary scrutiny committees to be the necessary additional safeguard that did not yet exist, at least in a broad enough form, at the time. The remaining part of this chapter will examine the debates in regard to the development of the parliamentary committees for scrutinising regulations.

A. United Kingdom

Given the importance of parliamentary scrutiny committees as the additional safeguard as recommended by the Donoughmore Committee, it is surprising

[6] For the UK, see Fox and Blackwell (n 3) 74–76. For Australia, see Legislation Act 2003 (Cth), s 44; Legislation (Exemptions and Other Matters) Regulation 2015 (Cth), ss 9, 10.

[7] House of Commons, *Sessional Returns 2017–19* (30 October 2019) 103–04; Standing Committee on Regulations and Ordinances, *Parliamentary Scrutiny of Delegated Legislation* (3 June 2019) para 8.43.

[8] Fox and Blackwell (n 3) 181–82; Standing Committee on Regulations and Ordinances, *Parliamentary Scrutiny of Delegated Legislation* (3 June 2019) paras 8.62–8.67.

that such committees hardly feature in the contributions of Lord Hewart, John Willis and others. That means that there was no real debate about them in the lead up to the Donoughmore Committee. Their debate focused primarily on the need for delegation of regulation-making powers in the modern era, the function of the courts and, to a lesser extent consultation. It is odd that parliamentary scrutiny of regulations played such a small role in these debates given its potential to mitigate the primary concerns. Nevertheless, it did take that place in the Donoughmore Committee's report.

Lord Hewart recognised that consultation processes and parliamentary veto powers go some way to mitigating against the risk of arbitrary regulation-making.[9] The problems he identified in both of those contexts was the limited operation of the statutory provisions for these safeguards.[10] Lord Hewart did not include in his safeguards a parliamentary committee for scrutiny of regulations, although he did recognise the need for a committee to scrutinise bills.[11] Given that he accepted the benefits of all the other safeguards, it is no stretch to consider that scrutiny of regulations is consistent with his views. He also expressly doubted the capacity of parliamentary review without any such committee. Referring to the limited annulment of regulations by Parliament, Lord Hewart stated: 'It may be that they escape because no member of Parliament has taken the trouble to weigh and consider them'.[12] He therefore recognised the problems of parliamentary review of regulations in the absence of a scrutiny committee but did not expressly advocate for such committees as a potential solution. Cecil Carr, another influential voice in the early debates who was a primary advocate for safeguards on delegation of regulation-making powers, also did not expressly refer to such committees.[13] Like Lord Hewart, he recognised that parliamentary veto powers were dependent on the limited time of members of parliament to review each regulation, but that did not lead him to arguing for a scrutiny committee to carry out that role.[14]

However, other contributors to the 1930s debates did expressly argue that committees for scrutinising regulations should be established. John Willis recognised that they would be a beneficial addition to parliamentary review. He raised questions that would need to be resolved, such as who would conduct the review, would ultra vires review be conducted by the committee, would parliamentary review exclude subsequent judicial review,[15] and whether Parliament would support such a committee.[16] Despite these questions his view was overall

[9] Lord Hewart of Bury, *The New Despotism* (Ernest Benn Ltd, 1929) 86, 89–90.
[10] ibid 88–89, 94–95.
[11] ibid 153–54.
[12] ibid 90.
[13] Carr (n 2) 27–37.
[14] ibid 39.
[15] Willis also referred in the epilogue of his book that establishing a parliamentary committee for scrutiny of regulations could justify the exclusion of judicial review: J Willis, *The Parliamentary Powers of English Government Departments* (Harvard University Press, 1933) 172.
[16] ibid 115.

supportive. In his words, 'the time is ripe for undertaking any experiment which may conduce to more rational methods of control and a greater public confidence'.[17] Willis was not the only contributor to the debates to expressly support scrutiny committees. Frederick Port, a lesser-known administrative law author of the period, also recommended the development of a scrutiny of regulations committee. His view was that such a committee would make parliamentary review 'real and effective', would not involve an onerous workload, and was likely to be conducted with a critical spirit.[18]

The Donoughmore Committee recognised criticisms of the regulation-making system at the time, including the inadequacy of parliamentary control[19] and so it recommended a committee to scrutinise both bills and regulations.[20] This was, as has already been highlighted, an important feature of the Committee's recommendations. Its other recommendations related to adjusting already existing safeguards. The recommendation regarding scrutiny committees was largely a new development. The House of Lords established the Special Orders Committee in 1925 for scrutinising regulations made according to the affirmative resolution procedure. That Committee differed from the committee recommended by the Donoughmore Committee because it was limited to scrutinising regulations made according to affirmative resolution procedures.

The Donoughmore Committee's recommendation was not only significant for recommending a scrutiny committee but also for its recommendations regarding their scope and operation. It included in its report the criteria that the committee would report on:

(1) whether any matter of principle was involved;
(2) whether the regulation or rule imposed a tax;
(3) whether the regulation or rule was (a) permanently challengeable; or (b) never challengeable, i.e., unchallengeable from the commencement; or (c) challengeable for a specified period of time and thereafter unchallengeable and, if so, what was the specified period;
(4) whether it consisted wholly or partly of consolidation;
(5) whether there was any special feature of the regulation or rule meriting the attention of the House;
(6) whether there were any circumstances connected with the making of the regulation or rule meriting such attention;
(7) whether the regulation or rule should be starred, on the grounds that it was exceptional.[21]

The reasons it gave for these criteria was that they were designed not to deal with the 'merits' of reviewed regulations but instead to provide information to members

[17] ibid.
[18] F Port, *Administrative Law* (Longmans, Green and Co, 1929) 356–57.
[19] Committee on Ministers' Powers, Report (1932) ('Donoughmore Committee Report') 53, 63.
[20] ibid 62–63, 67.
[21] ibid 69.

of Parliament. This is made clear in the following important paragraph dealing with the merits of regulations:

> We desire to make it clear that in no case do we contemplate that the Committee should go into the merits of either the Bill or the regulation.
>
> The sole object of the Committee as conceived by us would be to inform the House in the one case of the nature of the legislative powers which it was proposed to delegate and of the general characteristics of the regulation in the other.
>
> In other words the task of the Committee would not be to act as critic or censor of the substantive proposals in either case, but to supply the private Member with knowledge which he lacks at present, and thus enable him to exercise an informed discretion whether to object or criticise himself.[22]

This understanding of the difference between technical scrutiny and review of the merits of particular regulations requires explanation. The scrutiny criteria it recommended made clear that it related to matters of high policy included in regulations; that is, matters of principle, special or exceptional features, and tax. The Donoughmore Committee's point was to inform Parliament of matters that were within its function rather than of the technical detail that is appropriately handled in the modern era by administrators. Its reference to 'merits' seems not to have meant that scrutiny committees avoid examining the substance of particular regulations but was instead a recommendation for them not to provide a critique of particular regulations. The committee's role was to raise Parliament's attention to such regulations rather than argue the defects of particular regulations.

The Donoughmore Committee also made recommendations in regard to managing the workload of the proposed committee. It recommended that the Parliament provide permanent staff assisted by parliamentary counsel in order to manage the high workload.[23] This was an important practical solution to the commonly expressed concern about the number of regulations. For example, Lord Hewart in his melodramatic style stated, 'Does any human being read through this mass of departmental legislation? Is any human brain supposed to have mastered and to retain its contents?'.[24] The development of a committee to scrutinise regulations in a systematic manner with permanent staff and with access to counsel was an important step in ensuring that regulations would not only be read but that steps could be taken to escalate regulations that relate to matters of high policy within the usual function of Parliament to examine.

The Donoughmore Committee's recommendation for such a committee was a crucial step in addressing the concerns raised by Lord Hewart and aligned well with John Willis's preferred solution for managing the increase in law-making by way of regulations. It can be regarded as an uncontroversial measure that is an important

[22] ibid 63.
[23] ibid 63, 69.
[24] Hewart (n 9) 100.

contribution to the constitutional concerns raised about the role of parliaments in parliamentary democracies, such as the UK and Australia. It highlights the Donoughmore Committee's belts-and-braces approach to safeguards. That is, that the safeguards should include all three branches to government: parliament by way of parliamentary veto powers and scrutiny committees; the courts by judicial review; and the administration by consultation.

B. Australia

The 1930 Senate Committee recommended that a senate committee should be established for review of regulations. The Committee stated in regard to senators that, 'the many calls upon their time render it almost impossible for them to make a detailed examination of every regulation'. It referred to submissions to the Committee advocating for a 'systematic check' on the exercise of the delegated powers having a 'very strong case'.[25] The 1930 Committee also referred to the limitations of other safeguards on regulation-making. It referred to the repeal of the consultation provisions in the Australian version of the Rules Publication Act 1903, examined in chapter four, as creating a need 'for the substitution of some other method of protecting the public interest'.[26] It also recognised that judicial review was inadequate for reviewing regulations due to the time and resources it requires,[27] even though the case law indicated that the High Court had found on numerous occasions that particular regulations were ultra vires.

These views led the 1930 Senate Committee to recommend that a scrutiny of regulations committee be established to provide a 'proper and sufficient check on the power to make regulations'.[28] It recommended the following scrutiny criteria for review of regulations:

(a) that they are in accord with the statute;
(b) that they do not trespass unduly on personal rights and liberties;
(c) that they do not unduly make the rights and liberties of citizens dependent upon administrative and not judicial decisions;
(d) that they are concerned with administrative detail and do not amount to substantive legislation which should be a matter for parliamentary enactment.[29]

The 1930 Senate Committee gave minimal explanation for the criteria. Two of the criteria have obvious significance. Principle (a) suggests a systemic check on the legality of regulations, and principle (d) is a check on the content of regulations and in particular whether the regulation deals with matters having political

[25] Senate, *Report from the Senate Select Committee Advising on Establishing Standing Committees*, Parliament of Australia (Report April 1930) paras 14, 15.

[26] ibid para 18.

[27] ibid para 21.

[28] ibid para 22.

[29] ibid para 23.

significance suited to parliamentary deliberation. Principles (b) and (c) are checks on rights and liberties. These principles could have been assumed to be included in principle (d) and more suited to parliamentary enactment. They emphasise that laws affecting rights and liberties are particularly suited to parliamentary consideration rather than be handled by ministers and administrative officials.

The 1930 Senate Committee commented on the distinction between technical scrutiny and review of the merits of regulations, but deliberately did not draw a clear line between the two. The Committee referred to it being desirable for the proposed Standing Committee to bring to the attention of the Senate the merits of particular regulations in exceptional circumstances. However, its general view was for the proposed Committee not to scrutinise regulations in regard to policy grounds as it was concerned it would be less influential if it became a regular critic of government policy.[30]

This highlights that the overall purpose of the scrutiny committee was to inform the Senate of the content of regulations in relation to matters the Senate regarded as being of particular importance; their legality, impacts on rights and liberties, etc. The merits of regulations in regard to those matters should be within the scope of the committee's functions. The limit of the committee's function related to general criticisms of government policy.

There were strong similarities in the concerns that prompted the inquiry into regulation-making, albeit that it came from the Senate rather than the judiciary: the inclusion of broad delegations into legislation, the increased volume of regulations, and the lack of scrutiny by senators in the absence of a committee. The 1930 Senate Committee's recommendations were similar to the Donoughmore Committee's in relation to parliamentary scrutiny, while being made two years prior to it, in that it recommended establishing a parliamentary committee to review both bills and regulations, the need for a systemic check on regulations, and that courts were not adequate in this regard. At the core of both Committees' recommendations was the focus on informing Parliament of matters of concern and that those matters of concern should not be focused on policy generally but on the matters included in the scrutiny criteria.

It is important to recognise that the Australian scrutiny of regulations committee emerged from very similar concerns as those expressed by Lord Hewart in the UK. While the institutional dynamics were different, Lord Hewart's critique was expressed in terms of executive aggrandisement and risks to parliamentary sovereignty while Australia's development came from concern over the Senate's role, the more particular concerns were the same. The quantity of regulations being made was higher than what lawyers and members of parliament expected, and that parliaments lacked capacity to check them. The similarity suggests a fundamental dynamic in the two parliamentary democracies and that scrutiny committees provide a solution that is part of the modern evolution of such systems.

[30] ibid para 24.

III. Parliamentary Scrutiny Committees – Implementation

A. United Kingdom

While the problems that triggered the inquiries in the early 1930s in both countries were similar (as were the recommended solutions), the implementation of scrutiny committees in each country varied to a considerable extent. For one, the Donoughmore Committee recommended that each House of Parliament establish scrutiny committees[31] and this has resulted in the House of Commons having a scrutiny role in the UK while the Australian equivalent, the House of Representatives, does not. The Australian reform debates highlight that the focus was at all times on the Senate being the suitable forum for a scrutiny committee, but that is not the case in the UK where a Commons Committee was established in 1944 but superseded by a joint committee in 1973. Additionally, the committees for scrutinising regulations in the UK developed in a piecemeal manner over decades before settling on the current arrangements involving a joint committee and a Lords committee. We will see in the next part that the Australian scrutiny committee was established soon after the 1930 Senate Committee reported and has remained as a fixture in the Senate's functions.

The following table outlines the developments in the UK. The important themes across all of the developments will then be drawn out.

Table 3.1 Development of UK scrutiny of regulations committees

Committee title	Established	Discontinued	Summary of terms of reference
House of Lords, Special Orders Committee	1925[32]	1972	Scrutinise regulations requiring affirmative resolution. Scrutinise for important matters of policy or principle, precedent, whether the regulations is intra vires.[33]
Commons Committee	1944[34]	1972	Every statutory rule or order laid in the Commons. Scrutinise for whether it imposes a charge, excludes the courts, includes any unusual or unexpected use of statutory powers, has retrospective effect, delay, or requires elucidation.[35]

(continued)

[31] Donoughmore Committee Report, 63, 67.
[32] HL Deb Vol 62 cols 59–67 (14 July 1925).
[33] ibid 59–61.
[34] HC Deb Vol 401 cols 310–11 (21 June 1944).
[35] ibid. For the criteria that was subsequently added, see JE Kersell, *Parliamentary Supervision of Delegated Legislation* (Stevens and Sons Ltd, 1960) 48.

Table 3.1 ***(Continued)***

Committee title	Established	Discontinued	Summary of terms of reference
Joint Committee on Statutory Instruments	1973[36]	Continuing	Scrutinise instruments laid before Houses of Parliament Scrutinise for whether it imposes a charge, excludes challenges to the courts, retrospective effect, delay, ultra vires, unusual or unexpected use of the statutory powers, requires elucidation, defective drafting, other grounds that do not impinge on its merits or policy.[37]
House of Lords Secondary Legislation Scrutiny Committee[38]	2003[39]	Continuing	Scrutinise every instrument laid before Houses of Parliament Scrutinise for whether it is politically or legally important, is inappropriate due to statutory changes, inappropriately implements European Union legislation, imperfectly achieves its policy objectives; explanatory material is insufficient, inadequate consultation, deals inadequately with EU retained law.[40]

The previous chapter explained the way in which governments resisted establishing scrutiny of bills committees in both countries. The development of scrutiny of regulations committees involved similar debates at various stages of the developments. These debates indicate that resistance is stronger in the House of Commons than in the House of Lords. In the House of Commons the parliamentary debate in 1943 and 1944 for the development of a scrutiny of regulations committee was led by a group of members referred to as the 'active backbenchers'.[41] The scrutiny committee was ultimately established by a motion supported by 140 members from all parties.[42] The proponents' primary arguments

[36] HC Deb Vol 850 cols 1217–22 (13 February 1973), HL Vol 339 col 101–04 (20 February 1973).

[37] ibid. The current criteria are included in the Committee's reports.

[38] The Committee was initially named the House of Lords Merits of Statutory Instruments Committee.

[39] HL Deb Vol 655 col 1157 (17 December 2003).

[40] ibid. The Committee's current terms of reference are published on the Parliament's website: committees.parliament.uk/committee/255/secondary-legislation-scrutiny-committee/content/120278/terms-of-reference.

[41] Kersell (n 35) 43–44; John Eaves, *Emergency Powers and the Parliamentary Watchdog* (Hansard Society for Parliamentary Government, 1957) 106.

[42] HC Deb Vol 400 col 212 (17 May 1944) (Commander Bower). For a detailed explanation, see ibid 43–44.

were that Parliament has a duty to protect liberties which were at risk due to the large increase in regulations and that it needed to make changes to ensure powers are 'not being overstepped or overstrained'.[43] This was necessary during World War II and in peace time.[44] One member referred to members' role as representatives required them to control regulations.[45]

The Government initially resisted the proposal. The Secretary of State for the Home Department, Mr Morrison, argued in the House of Commons in May 1943 that the proposal was inappropriate during the war, and would mix executive and legislative functions in a manner that would inevitably involve parliamentary review of the merits of regulations.[46] The Attorney-General added that the scrutiny criteria were unclear and so was the evidence that members would use to review regulations.[47] These views do not seem persuasive now and they did not win out at the time. A year later the Government conceded that a Commons scrutiny of regulations committee should be established.[48]

The proponents accordingly succeeded in establishing the committee against the Government's initial wishes. It may have been the case that the Committee could help the Government achieve its own interest. John Kersell noted in 1960, closer to the time, that it may have helped to minimise the inclusion of affirmative resolution procedures in bills and increase negative resolution procedures.[49] Kersell's point indicates that regulation-making systems are complex, and a long view needs to be taken of the individual developments.

Government resistance was less apparent when the House of Lords established its initial scrutiny of regulations committee in 1925. The Special Orders Committee was established to review regulations made according to special resolution procedures.[50] The debate that did occur related to whether it should be extended to negative resolution instruments. The answer to that question was that any expansion of its scope should be left to later.[51]

The next time the House of Lords developed its own scrutiny of regulations committee occurred in the context of the reforms to the Lords in the early 2000s.[52] In particular, it developed from the Royal Commission into the House of Lords and its recommendation 'for enhanced Parliamentary scrutiny of secondary legislation' and that the 'reformed second chamber should make a

[43] HC Deb Vol 389 cols 1593, 1596 (26 May 1943) (Major Petherick).
[44] ibid col 1639 (Mr Smith).
[45] HC Deb Vol 400 col 211 (17 May 1944) (Mr Molson).
[46] HC Deb Vol 389 cols 1656–62 (26 May 1943).
[47] ibid col 1692.
[48] HC Deb Vol 400 col 260 (17 May 1944) (The Secretary of State for the Home Department, Mr. Herbert Morrison).
[49] Kersell (n 35) 46.
[50] HL Deb Vol 62 col 596 (14 July 1925).
[51] ibid cols 64–5.
[52] See M Russell, *The Contemporary House of Lords: Westminster Bicameralism Revived* (Oxford University Press, 2013).

strong contribution in this area'.[53] This recommendation led to the Committee being established in late 2003.[54] In his speech to the House of Lords proposing the Committee, Lord Williams of Mostyn stated that 'The watchdog must have a louder bark and sharper teeth'.[55] He added:

> A number of your Lordships from all quarters have said that secondary legislation is not properly scrutinised. It is often as complex and detailed as any Bill … Again, without disrespect to the Commons, I suggest that we can do work here that is not presently attempted elsewhere. Since 1980, the number of statutory instruments laid before Parliament has increased by more than a third. It is no exaggeration to say that much secondary legislation may affect the individual more keenly than primary legislation, which we [the House of Lords] scrutinise.
>
> We therefore recommend a Select Committee of your Lordships' House to examine the merits of every statutory instrument subject to parliamentary activity.[56]

The significance to be drawn from these statements is that the House of Lords, in a similar fashion to the Senate in Australia, expressed its scrutiny role in forthright fashion and was able to implement it.

The House of Lords Merits of Statutory Instruments Committee (now the Secondary Legislation Scrutiny Committee) was an important development on prior debates regarding the terms of reference of the various scrutiny committees being limited to technical scrutiny rather than a full policy assessment. As we saw in section II.A above, the Donoughmore Committee recommended restricting scrutiny committees to ensure they do not scrutinise the merits of regulations.[57] There was an unsuccessful attempt in the late 1940s to expand the House of Commons Select Committee on Statutory Instruments to expand its terms of reference to include scrutiny of the merits of regulations.[58] The restriction on scrutiny on the merits remains in operation, albeit obliquely, in the terms of reference for the Joint Committee on Statutory Instruments. It is included as a limit on the breadth of its final criterion, 'or on any other ground which does not impinge on its merits or on the policy behind it'.[59]

It is important to recognise that a fundamental issue is at stake in these debates. The merits review limit suggests that the committees subject to it are not able to inform the relevant house of big picture policy issues being dealt with in regulations. If that were the case the committees would be disabled from carrying

[53] Royal Commission on the Reform of the House of Lords, 'A House for the Future' (The Stationery Office, 2000) 69.

[54] HL Deb Vol 655 cols 1156–57 (17 December 2003). The Committee was established following consideration and recommendations of a series of committees. These developments are explained in the Committee's first report: Merits of Statutory Instruments Committee, *Special Report: Inquiry into Methods of Working* (2003–04, HL Paper 18) App 2.

[55] HL Deb Vol 635 col 642 (21 May 2002).

[56] ibid col 645.

[57] Donoughmore Committee Report, 69.

[58] See Griffith (n 1) 298–99; Kersell (n 35) 49–52.

[59] House of Commons Standing Order No 151(1)(B) and House of Lords Standing Order No 74(2).

out one of their primary functions – escalating controversial issues dealt with by administrative officials by way of regulations to the houses of Parliament.

However, limiting scrutiny committees from reviewing the merits of regulations, is not as clear as it initially seems and does not necessarily restrict committees from carrying out their escalation function. The terms of reference for the committees in which the distinction applies includes criteria that would enable the escalation function to operate to some degree. The terms of reference for the House of Commons committee established in 1944 included a criterion 'that it appears to make some unusual or unexpected use of the powers conferred by the Statute under which it is made'.[60] This scrutiny criterion was accepted by the Home Secretary in the parliamentary debates once the Government accepted that a Commons committee should be established and it seems to have been justified as a kind of parliamentary adaptation of the ultra vires principle.[61] An equivalent provision is now included in the Joint Committee on Statutory Instruments' terms of reference.[62]

The 'unusual or unexpected use of powers' criterion has long been recognised as an exception to the limit on merits scrutiny. In 1960 John Kersell referred to it as 'marginal authority … to draw the attention of the House to alleged political sins of departments'.[63] Sir Cecil Carr, the adviser to the Commons committee established in 1944, commented that in using that criterion the Committee 'has often found itself peeping over the fence at questions of policy, merits, and vires'.[64] These references to this criterion being marginal is confirmed in the work of the Joint Committee on Statutory Instruments, the current committee that applies it. The Committee's statistics indicate that the 'unusual or unexpected use of powers' criterion and 'other grounds' were the two least used criteria in recent sessions of Parliament for which statistics have been provided.[65] This suggests that the Joint Committee on Statutory Instruments remains constrained in its ability to carry out the escalation function.

Accordingly, the establishment of the House of Lords Committee in 2003 is particularly important for informing Parliament on policy-based matters. Its terms of reference make this crystal-clear. Ground (a) states it is to draw to the special attention of the House an instrument that is 'politically or legally important or gives rise to issues of public policy likely to be of interest to the House' and ground

[60] HC Deb Vol 401 cols 310–11 (21 June 1944).

[61] HC Deb Vol 400 col 274 (17 May 1944) (The Secretary of State for the Home Department, Mr. Herbert Morrison).

[62] House of Commons Standing Order No 151(1)(B)(vi) and House of Lords Standing Order No 74(2)(f).

[63] Kersell (n 35) 50.

[64] C Carr, 'Parliamentary Supervision in Britain' (1955) 30 *New York University Law Review* 1045, 1050.

[65] House of Commons, *Sessional Returns 2017–19*, (20 January 2020, HC (2019) 1) 104; House of Commons, *Sessional Returns 2016–17* (13 July 2017, HC 1) 55; House of Commons, *Sessional Returns 2015–16* (20 July 2016, HC 1) 52. The statistics for previous sessions of Parliaments are provided in Fox and Blackwell (n 3) 201.

(c) adds that it should do so for any instrument that 'imperfectly achieves its policy objectives'.[66] These criteria are similar to the Lords Special Orders Committee established in 1925 whose first scrutiny criteria was 'whether the provisions raise important questions of policy or principle'.[67]

It is therefore important to recognise that the implementation of the Donoughmore Committee's recommendation to establish scrutiny committees has been mixed in terms of enabling the committees to inform the Houses of Parliament of controversial policy matters that are included in regulations. That may be related to the Donoughmore Committee's reference to such committees not dealing with the merits of regulations. However, the Donoughmore Committee also recommended scrutiny committees review regulations for 'whether any matter of principle was involved' and 'whether there was any special feature of the regulation or rule meriting the attention of the House'.[68] This suggests the Donoughmore Committee was ambivalent. In any case, there is no doubt that the scrutiny committees with membership drawn from the House of Commons have had limited ability to raise such policy matters. The fact that this limitation is not now included for the current House of Lords committee highlights the greater role of the House of Lords in scrutiny of regulations.

While the merits restriction has been an important aspect of the establishment of scrutiny committees, it is also necessary to recognise that these committees' escalation function, which it tends to restrict, is not the only aspect of the design and practice of scrutiny committees that relates to parliamentary deliberation. There is also a long history of scrutiny of regulations committees corresponding directly with ministers and departments to raise questions and require explanations of particular regulations. This aspect of the committees' function was included in the terms of reference of the Commons Committee established in 1944 and the Joint Committee on Statutory Instruments[69] and has been conducted as a matter of practice by the House of Lords Committees.[70] This is an additional process for questioning executive officials about regulations made by them and it enables regulations and the accompanying explanatory documents to be corrected. This is a feature of scrutiny committees that is not commonly discussed in the scholarship, but when it is discussed it is usually to point out that it is an effective aspect of their work.[71] It can be regarded as a process that

[66] HL Deb Vol 655 cols 1157 (17 December 2003). The Committee's current terms of reference are published on the Parliament's website: committees.parliament.uk/committee/255/secondary-legislation-scrutiny-committee/content/120278/terms-of-reference.

[67] HL Deb Vol 62 cols 59–61 (14 July 1925).

[68] Donoughmore Committee Report, 69.

[69] House of Commons Standing Order No 151(9), HC Deb Vol 401 cols 310–11 (21 June 1944).

[70] Secondary Legislation Scrutiny Committee, *Accessing the Scrutiny Work of the Committee and Information Resources Relating to Secondary Legislation* (2017–19, HL Paper 312) 4. For the Lords Special Orders Committee, see Kersell (n 35) 30.

[71] See G Ganz, 'Delegated Legislation: A Necessary Evil or a Constitutional Outrage?' in P Leyland and T Woods (eds), *Administrative Law Facing the Future: Old Constraints and New Horizons*

supports Parliament's deliberation function: questioning executive officials and requiring justification for their regulations.

The implementation of the Donoughmore Committee's recommendations regarding parliamentary scrutiny committees highlights three points in relation to the UK's parliamentary democracy. First, there was evidence in the parliamentary debates of government resistance to scrutiny committees being established but that resistance did not prevail. Secondly, each of the committees have had powers sufficient to raise matters of policy for the attention of the Houses of Parliament; however, this role has been marginalised for the committees with membership drawn from the House of Commons. All the committees have directly engaged with departments, a process that replicates Parliament's traditional deliberation functions but on the small stage of scrutiny committees.

B. Australia

The implementation of the 1930 Senate Committee's recommendations to establish a scrutiny committee in Australia was settled much more quickly and comprehensively than the implementation that occurred in the UK. The Regulations and Ordinances Committee (now the Scrutiny of Delegated Legislation Committee) was established in 1932.[72] Although the period was relatively short, the 1930 Senate Committee reporting in the mid-1930s and the scrutiny committee being established in March 1932, the period was particularly dramatic for the Senate and review of regulations. The parliamentary conflict occurring at this time provides background to its implementation. It also explains the fact that the Government proposed implementing the 1930 Senate Committee's recommendation. That is an important difference to the development of other safeguards requiring parliamentary approval in which governments have been fairly consistent in their opposition and resistance.

The period coincided with the two *Dignan* cases,[73] one of which (as we saw in chapter two) being the primary Australian case on the constitutional significance of delegating regulation-making powers to administrative officials. The regulations in that case were made under the Transport Workers Act 1928 (Cth) and the High Court determined that the enabling provision in the Act was valid. Yet through 1930 and 1931 the Senate disallowed 17 regulations made according to the enabling provision in that Act.[74] In late 1931 the Labor Government was

(Blackstone Press Ltd, 1997) 60, 74. See also SA de Smith, 'Delegated Legislation in England' (1949) 2 *The Western Political Quarterly* 514, 521–21 and Kersell (n 35) 54–55.

[72] Commonwealth, *Parliamentary Debates*, Senate, 4 March 1932, 648.

[73] *Dignan v Australian Steamships Proprietary Limited* (1931) 45 CLR 188; *Victorian Stevedoring and General Contracting Co Pty Ltd and Meakes v Dignan* (1931) 46 CLR 73.

[74] See eg Transport Workers (Waterside) Regulations, No 38 of 1931 disallowed by the Senate, Commonwealth, *Parliamentary Debates*, Senate, 15 May 1930, 1779, 1802; Transport Workers (Waterside) Regulations No 158 of 1931 and No 159 of 1931 and Transport Workers (Waterside

removed in an election and replaced by the United Australia Party Government, a precursor to the current Liberal Party.[75]

A minister in the new government, George Pearce, proposed that the Senate adopt the 1930 Senate Committee's recommendation.[76] Senator Pearce's speech focused on the proposal being a recommendation of the 1930 Senate Committee and on the representation of senators of different parties in the proposed Committee. He closed his primary speech by stating the proposed Committee was supported by the Government as 'an innovation in the Federal Parliament, and the result will be watched with interest. There is scope for much useful work to be performed by the committee'.[77] The proposal was supported by the Senate. The debate did not focus on whether or not the new Committee was an appropriate development. It related to the rules for appointing senators to the Committee and representation on the Committee of the various political parties.

The Regulations and Ordinances Committee was established in March 1932 by an amendment to the Senate Standing Orders. The Standing Orders provided the committee with authority to 'consider and, if necessary, report on' regulations tabled in the Senate.[78] The standing orders also did not initially include scrutiny principles by which it would assess regulations. In its initial report the new Committee expressed concerns about one regulation in terms of escalating matters of policy not suited to being included in regulations. The regulation was made under customs legislation that included provisions for censorship of films. The Committee referred to this being subject matter of the 'highest public importance, and that it involves to a very large extent the rights and privileges of many individuals' and went on to say that 'determination of public policy on a matter of such moment should not be accomplished by departmental regulation'.[79] In its fourth and fifth reports it adopted the scrutiny criteria that were set out by the 1930 Senate Committee in its report and that were referred to in section II.B above.[80]

Workers) Regulations No 10 of 1931 disallowed by the Senate, Commonwealth, *Parliamentary Debates*, Senate, 20 March 1931. For the full list of regulations disallowed, see GS Reid, 'Parliament and Delegated Legislation' in JR Nethercote (ed), *Parliament and Bureaucracy: Parliamentary Scrutiny of Administration – Prospects and Problems in the 1980s* (Hale and Iremonger, 1982) 149, 154 fn 11 and table p 342.

[75] The United Australia Party was made up of previous members of the Labor Party and members of numerous non-Labor parties: G Souter, *Acts of Parliament: a Narrative History of the Senate and House of Representatives Commonwealth of Australia* (Melbourne University Press, 1988) 274–80.

[76] Commonwealth, *Parliamentary Debates*, Senate, 4 March 1932, 648.

[77] ibid 648.

[78] Senate Standing Order 36A(4) set out in Commonwealth, *Parliamentary Debates*, Senate, 4 March 1932, 648.

[79] Senate Regulations and Ordinances Committee, *First Report* (Parliament of Australia, 18 May 1932) paras 3–4.

[80] Senate Regulations and Ordinances Committee, *Fourth Report* (Parliament of Australia, 23 June 1938) para 2; Senate Regulations and Ordinances Committee, *Fifth Report* (Parliament of Australia, 17 September 1942) para 5.

At the same time, the Regulations and Ordinances Committee emphasised, consistently with views expressed by both the Donoughmore Committee and the 1930 Senate Committee, that it was not a policy-focused committee. On the one hand, it regarded its role as including identifying regulations that were not suited to that form of law and needed to be escalated, such as the regulation dealing with the censorship of films referred to in the previous paragraph. However, it also referred to the Committee itself not reviewing such policy issues within those regulations. Accordingly, it prefaced its comment on the customs legislation dealing with censorship by stating: 'Your Committee expresses no opinion as to the wisdom or otherwise of the particular changes that were made by the regulations'.[81] It regularly expressed concerns in its initial reports that particular regulations dealt with subject matter that should have been included in an Act rather than a regulation. Additional to this concern regarding censorship, the Committee also referred to a regulation providing for state law regarding transport workers to have no effect[82] and a regulation dealing with trade policy.[83]

The early reports of the Regulations and Ordinances Committee also made clear its processes for engaging with ministers and departments. It stated that ministers and departments should directly make changes to regulations in which issues have been raised by the Committee rather than when a disallowance motion has been made.[84] This statement was made in the context of regulations that it regarded as being ultra vires, but it also noted that its more general recommendations in earlier reports had been corrected by departments, apparently without resort to recommending formal disallowance of the regulations.[85] This approach of making recommendations about particular regulations without extending to recommending disallowance became a common practice. In the Committee's fifth report it explained that it had conducted most of its work since its prior report directly with ministers' departments.[86]

The main features of the Regulations and Ordinances Committee established in its early years continue. Its name has changed to the Senate Committee for the Scrutiny of Delegated Legislation and most of the guidelines and practices that it developed have been transformed from practices and guidelines to being included in the Senate Standing Orders. The scrutiny criteria were expanded in

[81] Senate Regulations and Ordinances Committee, *First Report* (Parliament of Australia, 18 May 1932) para 4.

[82] Senate Regulations and Ordinances Committee, *Second Report* (Parliament of Australia, 8 December 1933) para 8.

[83] Senate Regulations and Ordinances Committee, *Fourth Report* (Parliament of Australia, 23 June 1938) para 13.

[84] Senate Regulations and Ordinances Committee, *Third Report* (Parliament of Australia, 31 October 1935) paras 6–7.

[85] Senate Regulations and Ordinances Committee, *Third Report* (Parliament of Australia, 31 October 1935) para 10.

[86] Senate Regulations and Ordinances Committee, *Fifth Report* (Parliament of Australia, 17 September 1942) para 1. See also Senate Regulations and Ordinances Committee, *Ninth Report* (Parliament of Australia, 21 October 1954) paras 5–9.

2019 and 2021.[87] Informing the Senate of 'significant issues, or otherwise gives rise to issues that are likely to be of interest to the Senate' is now a discrete function included in the Standing Orders.[88] While the Committee's processes have varied, much of its work is now conducted by correspondence with ministers, departments and agencies that regularly leads to changes being made and undertakings to make changes.[89] This process is supported by a practice in which the chair of the committee lodges notices of disallowance for regulations in which the Committee is engaged in correspondence and the notice remains in place until the committee's concerns are satisfied.[90]

There are a number of points to draw from the implementation of the 1930 Senate Committee's recommendation. It was a relatively simple process due to the Government initially proposing the Committee. Much of the more detailed implementation in terms of scrutiny criteria and processes were established by the Committee itself through guidelines and practices, at least initially, rather than the Senate as a whole. Part of that implementation was to establish a line between policy review (excluded from its role) and policy escalation (within its role). The distinction seeks to enable the Committee to avoid criticism of the micro-policy decisions that underpin the provisions of a regulation and instead focus on informing the Senate of regulations having macro-political significance. The distinction may not have a sharp line, but it is important to protect its role of escalating matters of macro-political significance that administrative officials have attempted to include in regulations.

IV. Parliamentary Scrutiny and Veto in Practice – Effectiveness

Scrutiny committees provide an answer to concerns that arose in the 1930 reform debates regarding whether anyone in parliaments read regulations. The reform recommendations were for scrutiny committees to be established to review all regulations and inform the houses of parliaments of particular problems identified in them. This solution provides a systemic check on regulations that could not be provided by parliaments without such committees or by courts. It had practical benefits in terms of informing the houses of parliaments of matters relevant to the exercise of their affirmative and negative resolution powers.

[87] Commonwealth, *Parliamentary Debates*, Senate, 27 November 2019, 4382; 16 March 2021, 1972–74 and 16 June 2021, 106.

[88] Senate Standing Orders 23(4).

[89] Standing Committee for the Scrutiny of Delegated Legislation, *Annual Report 2020* (23 June 2021) 16–21. See also Stephen Argument, 'Legislative Scrutiny in Australia: Wisdom to Export?' (2011) 32 *Statute Law Review* 116, 138.

[90] H Evans, *Odgers Senate Practice*, 14th edn (Department of the Senate, 2016) 440.

However, this is also the area in which most concern has been expressed in recent years about regulation-making systems. As we saw in chapter one, concerns have been expressed in the UK and Australia in regard to the effectiveness of parliamentary scrutiny of regulations and the work of scrutiny committees. The concerns regarding parliamentary scrutiny in the UK are wide-ranging, extending from the rareness of the exercise of veto powers, the minimal time given to parliamentary deliberation of regulations, to the weaknesses of parliamentary scrutiny committees. In Australia the concerns have focused more on restricting committee scrutiny to technical matters as opposed to the merits of the regulation.

These concerns have come to the fore in recent years, but they are not new. In the 1970s Jack Beatson made the point that strong forms of parliamentary review would defeat Parliament's initial purpose of delegating regulation-making.[91] Susan Rose-Ackerman in her analysis of parliamentary scrutiny concluded that the UK Parliament is unable to provide an effective democratic check on regulations and dismisses its relevance for providing democratic legitimacy.[92]

In this section, I will examine these concerns by highlighting the rarity of the exercise of veto powers by the UK and Australian Parliaments. I agree that it is rare in both countries, but in Australia it occurs numerous times each year. Since the veto power is only ever employed in Australia by the Senate, a question arises over the different characteristics of the Senate to the House of Lords. This is an important comparative difference between the two parliamentary democracies.

A. Exercise of Veto Powers

It is important to appreciate that while parliamentary veto powers are recognised to be a fundamental feature of regulation-making systems in both countries, the powers are rarely exercised to defeat regulations, particularly in the UK. The rareness of the use of the veto powers has been recognised by the Hansard Society and UK public law scholars as supporting views that parliamentary scrutiny is a weak safeguard.

It is clearly apparent that the use of veto powers by the houses of the UK Parliament is rare. There are some variations in the figures reported, but all indicate they are very low. The House of Commons library reports that since World War II the House of Commons has annulled eight regulations subject to negative resolution procedures and not approved only one regulation subject to the affirmative procedure.[93] In the same period the House of Lords has annulled only one

[91] J Beatson, 'Legislative Control of Administrative Rulemaking: Lessons from the British Experience?' (1979) 12 *Cornell International Law Journal* 199, 212.

[92] S Rose-Ackerman, *Democracy and Executive Power: Policymaking Accountability in the US, the UK, Germany, and France* (Yale University Press, 2021) 49–53.

[93] R Kelly, *Statutory Instruments* (Commons Briefing Paper, Number 06509, 15 December 2016) 24. See also Fox and Blackwell (n 3) 6, 186, 233.

regulation subject to the negative procedure and not approved four regulations subject to affirmative resolution procedures.[94]

These figures are commonly referred to as a sign of the weakness of parliamentary scrutiny. Adam Tucker and Jeff King, in separate articles regard the rareness of the exercise of veto powers as evidence of the inadequacy of parliamentary scrutiny.[95] The Hansard Society's, 2014 report into parliamentary scrutiny, 'The Devil is in the Detail', examined the complex processes in the UK and concluded that one reform that could be implemented is for the House of Lords to consider making greater use of its veto power.[96]

While the veto power is rarely used in the UK, Parliament does take other types of action in relation to regulations. We will see below that scrutiny committees regularly criticise particular regulations. It also must be recognised that the House of Lords makes 'non-fatal' motions of 'regret' in regard to regulations in order to express dissatisfaction with them. The House of Lords Library has reported that from 1950 to the end of 2015, 85 non-fatal motions were made in the Lords, and 27 of those motions were successful, resulting in a 'government defeat'.[97] While these motions express criticisms of a regulation and may prompt their reconsideration, they do not require the Government to change it.

The concerns regarding the rare use of veto powers are often supplemented by concerns about the small amount of time given to debating regulations in the Houses of Parliament in the UK. Jeff King has calculated from statistics provided by the House of Commons Library that on average the House of Commons devotes 4.3 per cent of its time to debating legislation to regulations.[98] The Hansard Society's 'The Devil is in the Detail' report has also highlighted statistics that reveal that the debating time in the House of Commons is far less – in most years less than half – of the time allocated to debating regulations in the House of Lords.[99]

Parliamentary veto is more common in Australia. While both houses have power to disallow regulations according to section 42 of the Legislation Act 2003, in practice it is only exercised by the Senate. The Australian Parliament keeps

[94] H Evennett, *Delegated Legislation in the Lords since 1997* (House of Lords Library Note, LLN 2016/001, 5 January 2016) 6; Fox and Blackwell (n 3) 186, 233.

[95] A Tucker, 'Parliamentary Scrutiny of Delegated Legislation' in A Horne and G Drewry (eds) *Parliament and the Law* (Hart Publishing, 2018) 368–69; King, 'The Province of Delegated Legislation' in E Fisher, J King, AL Young, *The Foundations and Future of Public Law* (Oxford University Press, 2020) 161–66.

[96] Fox and Blackwell (n 3) 187–89.

[97] Evennett (n 94) 35, 37. Records of government defeats in relation to regulations subsequent to this report can be found at the Constitution Unit's website, *Government Defeats in the House of Lords*, www.ucl.ac.uk/constitution-unit/research-areas/parliament/changing-role-house-lords/government-defeats-house-lords.

[98] King (n 95) 163, drawing on statistics provided in V Apostolova, *Acts and Statutory Instruments: The Volume of UK Legislation 1950 to 2016* (House of Commons Library, Commons Briefing papers CBP-7438 2017) 12.

[99] Fox and Blackwell (n 3) 175, 177–80.

statistics on disallowance from 1991,[100] which show that the Senate has vetoed 119 regulations in that time. This is clearly far more than equivalent figures of the UK Parliament. Although the statistics for the exercise of veto powers prior to 1991 are not provided by the Australian Parliament, we saw in section III.B above the famous historical example of numerous successful disallowances in the Senate for regulations made under section 3 of the Transport Workers Act 1928 (Cth). That episode in Australia's public law history confirms that disallowance of regulations by the Australian Parliament, more particularly the Senate, is not as rare as it is in the UK.

B. Comparative Differences in Relation to Upper Houses

The very low use of veto powers in the UK compared to Australia supports the view of scholars and the Hansard Society that parliamentary scrutiny in the UK is weak. The Hansard Society's 'The Devil is in the Detail' report examined the contribution of practices and processes to the weaknesses in detail. The point of interest for this book is the difference between the UK and Australia in this regard, and in particular the difference between the House of Lords and the Australian Senate. The Hansard Society's report recognised that the House of Lord has stronger procedures for scrutiny of regulations and is better suited to such scrutiny than the House of Commons.[101] Similar points have been made in the past. In the 1980s, JD Hayhurst and Peter Wallington researched the Joint Committee on Statutory Instruments in a period in which there was no separate House of Lords scrutiny committee. They commented that Parliament's ineffectiveness in relation to scrutiny of regulations is largely due to the Government's effective control of the House of Commons.[102]

As we have just seen, however, there is relatively little debate in the House of Lords in relation to particular regulations, and it rarely vetoes them. But, of course, there must regularly be regulations that raise concerns. A question arises as to what explains that House's reluctance to veto regulations. Unlike the House of Commons, the Government will not have a majority in the House of Lords.[103] It is also important to recognise that unlike its powers regarding primary legislation,

[100] For statistics from 1991 to 2011, see Senate Statsnet Classic, available at www.aph.gov.au/Parliamentary_Business/Statistics/Senate_StatsNet_Classic/Consolidations/Notices_of_motion_for_disallowance_1991–2011. From 2011, see New Senate Statsnet, available at www.aph.gov.au/Parliamentary_Business/Statistics/Senate_StatsNet#/motions?from=2011-01-01&to=2022-12-31&type=Disallowance.

[101] Fox and Blackwell (n 3) 222.

[102] JD Hayhurst and P Wallington, 'The Parliamentary Scrutiny of Delegated Legislation' [1988] *Public Law* 547, 573. See also Ganz (n 71) 60, 74 'it is nevertheless surprising how little the [Joint Committee on Statutory Instruments] has done to curb the worst excesses of delegated legislation within its terms of reference'.

[103] See Russell (n 52) 44.

the House of Lords has equal power to the House of Commons to veto regulations. The Parliament Acts that limit the powers of the House of Lords for primary legislation do not apply to regulations.[104] Yet the two houses are not regarded as equal in relation to scrutiny of regulations. The House of Commons is often referred to as having primacy due to it being elected.[105] There is sometimes discussion of conventions in regard to exercise of the House of Lords' powers regarding regulations, but they are not clear. In a report published in 2006, the Joint Committee on Conventions concluded that the House of Lords should only exercise its veto powers in 'exceptional circumstances'.[106] The Joint Committee rejected the Government's view that the House of Lords should never exercise its veto powers, but did recognise that there would be a 'serious problem' if the House of Lords frequently used them.

The complexity regarding the exercise of the House of Lords' powers can be seen in a conflict that arose between it and the Government in 2015. This arose when the House of Lords voted to decline to consider a draft of the Tax Credits (Income Thresholds and Determination of Rates) (Amendment) Regulations 2015, which required approval of both Houses of Parliament. The House of Lords withheld its approval until the Government had reviewed particular policy issues and reported back.[107] The Government responded soon after by holding a review into the House of Lords' powers regarding scrutiny of regulations, the 'Strathclyde Review: Secondary Legislation and the Primacy of the House of Commons'.[108] The report recommended that the House of Lords' powers be reduced from a veto power to a power enabling the House of Lords to require the House of Commons reconsider regulations that the House of Lords regards as problematic.[109] This recommendation was not adopted and numerous House of Lords committees disagreed with it.[110]

A similar dynamic can be seen in subsequent developments. In 2021 two House of Lords Committees – the Delegated Powers and Regulatory Reform Committee and the Secondary Legislation Scrutiny Committee – held reviews into the Government's use of regulations during the COVID-19 pandemic and in prior years. The reports of both Committees were critical of Government

[104] D Natzler and M Hutton, *Erskine May's Treatise on The Law, Privileges, Proceedings and Usage of Parliament* Part 4, Ch 31, available at erskinemay.parliament.uk/section/5639/practice-of-the-house-of-lords-on-delegated-legislation; Russell (n 52) 84, 140–41.

[105] See eg Fox and Blackwell (n 3) 78.

[106] Joint Committee on Conventions, *Conventions of the UK Parliament* (HL 2005–06, 265-I) para 227.

[107] HL Deb Vol 765, col 1038–42 (26 October 2015).

[108] (CMD 9177, 2015).

[109] *Strathclyde Review: Secondary Legislation and the Primacy of the House of Commons* (CMD 9177, 2015) 18.

[110] See Select Committee on the Constitution, *Delegated Legislation and Parliament: A Response to the Strathclyde Review* (2015–16, HL 116); Delegated Powers and Regulatory Reform Committee, *Special Report: Response to the Strathclyde Review* (2015–16, HL 119); Secondary Legislation Scrutiny Committee, *Response to the Strathclyde Review: Effective Parliamentary Scrutiny of Secondary Legislation* (2015–16, HL 128).

practices regarding regulations and made proposals.[111] These reports will be considered again in chapter nine regarding emergency laws. The relevant aspect of this flare-up between the Government and the House of Lords for the current chapter is the Government's response to the reports.[112] In the House of Lords debate, Lord True, the Minister for State for the Cabinet Office, restated the Government's view as in the Strathclyde Review in 2015, emphasising the primacy of the House of Commons and a potential legal mechanism that provides for it in relation to regulations. His contribution to the debate included the following: 'as we go forward, we will keep that situation under review, and we remain prepared to act if the primacy of the Commons is threatened'.[113] These recent debates in the House of Lords reveal the ongoing nature of the tensions between the legal powers of the House of Lords and the conventions regarding its exercise.

The constitutional context is much clearer in Australia. As already stated, the Senate is provided with veto powers over regulations by section 42 of the Legislation Act 2003. There are no conventions that limit its exercise to exceptional circumstances. Section 53 of the Commonwealth Constitution sets out the relationship between the House of Representatives and the Senate by stating that generally the Senate has 'equal power with the House of Representatives in respect of all proposed laws'. The exceptions relate to laws relating to taxation. The constitutional context in Australia indicates that generally for law-making, the Senate has equal powers and since the Government usually does not have a majority in the Senate, there is no government control of it. The result is that Senate veto of regulations is more common in Australia.

These differences between the UK and Australia in relation to upper house veto powers can be explained by recent developments in comparative political science that have begun to influence comparative constitutional law scholars. This scholarship is influenced by the Senate's equal status to the House of Representatives and its different electoral system, proportional representation in the Senate rather than the majoritarian system used for the House of Representatives. These aspects of the Australian Senate are understood to involve a separation between the executive and legislature that is unusual for parliamentary democracies. The development in political and legal scholarship is to recognise this form of parliamentary democracy as 'semi-parliamentarism'; the term coined by Steffen Ganghof[114] and adopted by constitutional law scholars.[115] Ganghof recognises

[111] Delegated Powers and Regulatory Reform Committee, *Democracy Denied? The Urgent Need to Rebalance power between Parliament and the Executive* (HL 2021–22, 106); Secondary Legislation Scrutiny Committee, *Government by Diktat: A Call to Return Power to Parliament* (HL 2021–22).

[112] HL Deb Vol 817, cols 759–94 (6 January 2022).

[113] ibid col 788.

[114] S Ganghof, *Beyond Presidentialism and Parliamentarism: Democratic Design and the Separation of Powers* (Oxford University Press, 2022).

[115] See T Khaitan, 'Balancing Accountability and Effectiveness: A Case for Moderated Parliamentarism' (2021) 7 *Canadian Journal of Comparative and Contemporary Law* 81, 123–27; S Gardbaum,

the Commonwealth level in Australia, Japan, and most of the Australian states as being closest to the ideal of semi-parliamentarism. In this governmental system, lower houses in parliamentary systems provide the function of providing confidence for the Government while the Upper House provides for control of legislation, but not for dismissal of the Government.[116] While the constitutional context in Australia generally reflects Ganghof's conception of semi-parliamentarism, the UK does not as the members of the House of Lords are not elected. As we have seen in this section, this creates doubts as to the legitimacy of the House of Lords vetoing regulations, or at least indicates that it should be minimised, in a manner that just does not arise in Australia.

C. Committee Effectiveness

The concerns about parliaments' infrequent exercise of veto powers and the small amount of time given to debates are supplemented by concerns about the work of scrutiny committees. In the UK, this has continued after the House of Lords established its separate committee in 2003 specifically designed for scrutiny of regulations on their merits.[117] In Australia, doubts about the effectiveness of parliamentary scrutiny committees have in recent years focused on the Senate Delegated Legislation Committee's function being limited to technical scrutiny.[118]

This is not the place to address these concerns in a systemic or comprehensive manner. That kind of analysis would require different methodology to the research for this book. Instead, I want to make three points about the strengths and weaknesses of parliamentary scrutiny committees by reference to their contribution to the system of safeguards and more generally their contribution to parliamentary deliberation.

The first is that the weaknesses analysed in this chapter regarding parliamentary scrutiny should be understood in the context of the other two safeguards examined in this book: consultation and judicial review. The safeguards operate differently and have different democratic purposes. The concerns with the effectiveness of parliamentary scrutiny of regulations can be tempered when public consultation and administrative committees have effective input into the substance

'Democratic Design and the Twin Contemporary Challenges of Fragmented and Unduly Concentrated Political Power' in T Ginsburg, Aziz Huq and T Khaitan (eds), *The Entrenchment of Democracy: The Comparative Constitutional Law of Elections, Parties, and Voting*, available at papers.ssrn.com/sol3/papers.cfm?abstract_id=4225070.

[116] Ganghof (n 114) 2–3.

[117] See, eg, Fox and Blackwell (n 3) ch 11; Tucker (n 95) 363–70; King (n 95) 161–63.

[118] D Pearce, 'Legislative Scrutiny: Are the Anzacs Still the Leaders?' (Paper presented at Australia–New Zealand Scrutiny of Legislation Conference, Scrutiny and Accountability in the 21st Century, Canberra Australia, 6–8 July 2009), available at www.aph.gov.au/About_Parliament/Senate/Whats_On/Conferences/sl_conference/papers/pearce; M Aronson, 'Subordinate Legislation: Lively Scrutiny or Politics in Seclusion' (2011) 26 *Australasian Parliamentary Review* 4, 11–15. For doubts about such concerns, see S Argument (n 89) 137–38.

of particular regulations. This is examined in chapter four. While Parliamentary scrutiny committees were the main development resulting from the 1930s debates, it is important to recognise that they provide a systemic check: a functionally necessary addition to the then established safeguards, but a safeguard that is likely to be weaker than others simply due to the high workload. The high number of regulations that are made, the range of matters that demand members' time and the technical nature of most regulations without connection to current political controversies limit the ability of scrutiny committees to be a strong accountability mechanism.

The second point is that the effectiveness concerns tend not to deal in any detail with scrutiny committees' regular practice of raising questions directly with departments, agencies and ministers. When this is addressed, it is usually referred to as a secondary function of parliamentary scrutiny.[119] However, this aspect of the committees' role is an important means for achieving parliaments' deliberative function. The committees' concerns and correspondence are included in published reports, exposing the problems with the processes, design and drafting of particular regulations. The reports also include administrative officials' justifications, sometimes persuasive or plausible, at other times, weak. It is important to understand that this correspondence occurs with the possible, even if rare, risk of veto in the background.[120] It is a risk that cannot be dismissed when upper houses in which the Government does not have a majority can veto regulations. Parliamentary scrutiny committees' general reports often make clear that they secured many changes to regulations as part of this work.[121]

The remaining concern is whether the scope of the various scrutiny committees' role is sufficient to carry out the function intended for them in the 1930s reform debates, ie informing the Houses of Parliament of controversial policy matters included in regulations. Scrutiny committee reports provide statistics on the issues brought to the attention of particular Houses of Parliament according to their scrutiny criteria.[122] However, concerns are still sometimes raised as to whether that is sufficient when the scrutiny committee's criteria are limited to technical matters. As we saw in section III, the distinction between merits and technical scrutiny should be regarded as not being as restrictive as it may initially seem. It operates most clearly for the Joint Committee on Statutory Instruments and the Senate Committee on Delegated Legislation. Nevertheless, the terms of reference for those committees are broad enough to provide some scope for raising concerns about policy matters.

[119] See eg Fox and Blackwell (n 3) 208; King (n 95) 153–54, 163.

[120] See Argument (n 89) 138; Fox and Blackwell (n 3) 209; Evans (n 90) 440.

[121] Joint Committee on Statutory Instruments, *Government Response to Parliamentary Scrutiny of Statutory Instruments* (2017–19, HL 311, HC 2057); Secondary Legislation Scrutiny Committee, *Work of the Committee in Session 2019–21* (2019–21, HL 276) 4, 11; Senate Standing Committee for the Scrutiny of Delegated Legislation, *Annual Report 2020* (23 June 2021) 16–22.

[122] See eg House of Commons, *Sessional Returns 2017–19* (20 January 2020, HC (2019) 77; Senate Standing Committee for the Scrutiny of Delegated Legislation, *Annual Report 2021* (28 September 2022) paras 2.8–2.24.

The escalation function is clearer for the Lords Secondary Legislation Scrutiny Committee 'that it is politically or legally important or gives rise to issues of public policy likely to be of interest to the House'. There is no directly equivalent scrutiny power in Australia but there is a scrutiny power that approximates it. The Senate Committee's scrutiny powers include the ability to draw the attention of the Senate to regulations that raise 'significant issues, or otherwise gives rise to issues that are likely to be of interest to the Senate'.[123] This power was added to the Senate Standing Orders following an inquiry in 2019 seeking to address concerns regarding the lack of policy review.[124]

It is helpful and necessary for parliaments and commentators to reflect at regular intervals on whether scrutiny of regulations committees conduct their role effectively or not. There are aspects of their institutional location and function that raise risks in regard to their effectiveness. For example, there are many regulations to review, and regulations often deal with technical detail that is unlikely to be within the particular interests of members of the committees. More generally, Members of Parliament may be more interested in the general macro-policy issues of the time and their work on other committees, rather than holding departments and agencies accountable for the regulations they make.

However, it is important to recognise that scrutiny committees fill an important gap in the safeguards that was recognised in the 1930s debates. The committees can escalate important issues and can engage directly with departments and agencies. It may be that in the future additional powers and procedures are recognised to be necessary for them to carry out the scrutiny role more effectively. Such changes would most likely involve incremental developments. Scrutiny committees' systemic role is established and plays a fundamental role in the safeguards. They not only support parliaments' constitutional role in providing a process to ensure that parliamentary accountability is in place, but also enable parliamentary deliberation through their regular engagement with departments raising questions, exposing problems and requiring answers. In this way, departments and agencies are aware that their regulations are reviewed and that ministers may be drawn into committee correspondence to provide answers.

V. Conclusions

The development of parliamentary scrutiny committees since the 1930s debates has involved important contributions to parliamentary democracy in the UK and Australia. They provide processes and personnel that enable parliaments to conduct their scrutiny functions. They do this through informing parliament of

[123] Senate Standing Order 23(4).

[124] Senate Standing Committee on Regulations and Ordinances, *Parliamentary Scrutiny of Delegated Legislation* (3 June 2019) paras 6.33–6.37.

regulations that have problems or have particular significance and through direct correspondence with Ministers and departments. These developments should be recognised as being major achievements, given the resistance we have seen by governments to safeguards on regulation-making. It is particularly important to recognise that it was upper houses that established committees with the broadest scope to scrutinise regulations and it took particularly active backbenchers to provide the catalyst for the House of Commons scrutiny committee in the 1940s.

As we have seen, concerns have been expressed in recent years about the effectiveness of parliamentary scrutiny of regulations more generally. These concerns are important and require additional research to determine the extent of the problems and to offer solutions. However, it is also important to recognise that the three safeguards on regulation-making should not be understood on a rigid, separate basis. History highlights that they were intended to be a collection of checks on regulation-making. Scrutiny committees provide for a parliamentary form of deliberation for regulations. This should be recognised as operating alongside administrative forms of deliberation through consultation processes and administrative committees, to be examined in the next chapter.

4

Administration – Consultation, Advisory Committees and Regulatory Impact Assessments

Delegation of regulation-making powers often comes with procedural requirements. The enabling Act, a generally applicable Act, or government-imposed procedures are likely to include additional, deliberative obligations. These deliberative obligations come in different forms. Consultation is likely to be the most well known as it is often included in legislation and enforced by the courts. There are additional forms of process that are designed to enhance administrative deliberation. The two that will be discussed in this chapter are the inclusion of advisory committees in the decision-making process and regulatory impact assessments.

These aspects of regulation-making processes can be regarded as contributing to deliberative democracy in administrative forums, in contrast to the parliamentary forums that we have examined so far in this book. These forms of democratic safeguard can be regarded as a form of direct democracy as they involve contributions by those affected by the proposed regulation and by interest groups representing those who will benefit from the regulation by reduced pollution, public health benefits, etc. Members of the public with competing interests can debate the merits of the proposed regulation usually through making written submissions, and regulation-makers can respond to those arguments in their written explanations of the final form of the regulation.

The focus of this book is on the legal implementation of the safeguards on regulation-making. This chapter will examine the patchy statutory implementation of administrative procedures. Consultation is often understood in the scholarship quite pragmatically. It is regarded as a good practice but is rarely regarded as providing a democratic process in substitution for the relative lack of parliamentary engagement. It is referred to in this pragmatic way in Edward Page's well-known empirical research into regulation-making.[1] He explains the civil servant's perspective of consultation as being to make sure that the proposed regulations will operate as expected and without unintended consequences. Testing

[1] EC Page, *Governing by Numbers: Delegated Legislation and Everyday Policy-Making* (Hart Publishing, 2001).

draft regulations through consultation processes is thought to help avoid the regulated industry and other interest groups making a 'fuss about it in public' and the regulation being challenged in Parliament or the courts.[2] This – civil servants' experience of consultation processes – recognises consultation as a way of heading off escalation of problems with particular regulations to the primary accountability institutions. The civil servant's perspective on consultation processes presented in Page's work is to avoid 'difficulty and embarrassment'[3] rather than provide a substitute democratic procedure.[4]

Legal scholarship and administrative law doctrine presents a different reason for consultation. Concerns are often expressed about administrative decision-making and regulation-making regarding their potential for arbitrariness. As is examined in chapter five, administrative law-making can be reviewed by the courts for a degree of rationality. Consultation and other forms of administrative process are intended to support decision-making rationality. This was recognised in the 1930s reform debates and some of the subsequent scholarship.

When consultation processes are recognised as a safeguard, among others, of mitigating the risk of arbitrary administrative decision-making, we can see that it provides a substitute for parliamentary forms of deliberation, such as committee inquiries and question time, based on parliamentary rules enabling debate. Consultation, advisory committees and potentially regulatory impact assessment provide an administrative form of deliberation that supplements parliamentary deliberation of regulations by scrutiny committees.

It is also important to recognise the resistance by governments in the UK and Australia to consultation being a legal requirement, or at least as a generally applicable legal requirement. We will see in this chapter that this was a major theme of the reform debates for the implementation of consultation processes. Accordingly, one of the major themes of this chapter is the tension between the generally accepted recognition of consultation processes being a beneficial addition to regulation-making and the government resistance to its implementation as a general legal requirement.

I. The 1930s Debates – Consultation Consensus

Consultation was one of the three safeguards emphasised by the Donoughmore Committee. It was also accepted by Lord Hewart and John Willis, and other contributors in the 1920s as a beneficial process for regulation-making. The primary problem that was raised related to the design of the then current legislation. The 1930 Senate Committee did not address consultation directly but as we

[2] ibid 148.
[3] ibid.
[4] ibid 154.

will see in this sub-part there is brief reference to it that is critical to its general recommendation for establishing parliamentary committees. In this sub-part I will examine the participants' views as to the significance of administrative deliberative procedures.

Lord Hewart's attack on delegating regulation-making powers was partly based on the exercise of those powers. He referred to the exercise of these powers as involving 'Administrative Lawlessness', which was the heading of the relevant chapter in his book.[5] In this chapter he developed his concern regarding the arbitrary exercise of delegated powers. He referred to the laws being made by 'anonymous' officials rather than Ministers, there are no procedural requirements or rules of evidence for information gathering and that reasons are not usually required to be provided.[6] He concluded in the following manner:

> To employ the terms administrative 'law' and administrative 'justice' to such a system, or negation of system, is really grotesque. The exercise of arbitrary power is neither law nor justice, administrative or at all. The very conception of 'law' is a conception of something involving the application of known rules and principles, and a regular course of procedure. There are no rules or principles which can be said to be rules or principles of this astonishing variety of administrative 'law' nor is there any regular course of procedure for its application.[7]

Yet at the time Lord Hewart was writing there was a general statute, the Rules Publication Act 1893, dealing with numerous features of regulation-making, including a provision requiring public consultation. Public consultation is of course a form of administrative procedure. Hewart addressed public consultation in a subsequent chapter, chapter 6. He referred to it there as a 'valuable security against hasty and unreasonable legislation',[8] in other words a process that mitigates the risk of arbitrary law-making. While Lord Hewart recognised in this way the contribution of public consultation to mitigating the primary problem to which he sought to draw attention, he also explained in some detail the limitations on the consultation provisions included in the Rules Publication Act. These were the regulations that were exempted from being subject to public consultation; some due to the use of terminology such as 'statutory order' and their exclusion from regulations made by particular departments and agencies.[9] Accordingly for Hewart the overarching problem was the risk of arbitrary law-making. Consultation processes mitigated that risk, but he criticised the laws relating to it as being too confined.

John Willis made clear in the first paragraph of his book that his general purpose was to investigate the claims made by Hewart of administrative lawlessness and of

[5] Lord Hewart of Bury, *The New Despotism* (Ernest Benn Ltd, 1929) ch 4.
[6] ibid 43–44.
[7] ibid 44.
[8] ibid 86.
[9] ibid 88–9. See also CT Carr, *Delegated Legislation* (Cambridge University Press, 1921) 34–35.

the arbitrary methods of government departments.[10] He denied that administrative decision-making was necessarily arbitrary[11] and regarded the consultation provisions of the Rules Publication Act as a measure providing for administrative procedures.[12] He also made the point, which was repeated in subsequent decades,[13] that administrators are likely to consult even when not required to do so. He stated that departments are most likely 'in the habit of asking for advice' as they have to 'act through human beings, and even the most hostile critics of the Civil Service must admit that the civil servant likes to tread softly'.[14] Willis seemed to be making a similar point to the civil servants in Edward Page's empirical research many decades later that I referred to in the introduction to this chapter. Their incentive in conducting consultation processes on draft regulations is to head off the risk of escalation to Parliament and the courts.

Willis included in his response to Lord Hewart's 'administrative lawlessness' critique an additional feature of consultation processes at the time and that continue in current legislation. This is the inclusion in legislation of the requirement to consult with advisory committees usually made up of experts and persons representing affected interests.[15] He pointed to the inclusion of these committees in legislation as a method to ensure that regulations were based on 'facts rather than conjecture'.[16] Their function was to provide relevant information based on their expertise and to enable public confidence in the rules made by administrative officials.[17]

The general point to draw from Willis's response to Lord Hewart's arbitrariness critique was that Willis sought to recognise the processes and methodologies that facilitate administrative deliberation. These were partly by legislation that imposed consultation requirements and advisory committees and also due to administrative incentives such as to 'tread softly'. Most importantly, Willis's analysis seeks to counter Lord Hewart by highlighting the administrative procedures that provide a substitute for parliamentary deliberation. As we saw in Chapter Two, Willis regarded administrative regulation-making as a critical feature of the shift to democratic government in the nineteenth century. It was administrative officials that were required to do the detailed work of implementing social welfare laws.[18] For Willis, the administrative implementation role was not necessarily arbitrary. It involved different deliberative methods to courts and

[10] J Willis, *The Parliamentary Powers of English Government Departments* (Harvard University Press, 1933) 3.

[11] ibid 35.

[12] ibid 26.

[13] See eg, B Schwartz and HWR Wade, *Legal Control of Government: Administrative Law in Britain and the United States* (Clarendon Press, 1972) 98–99; JAG Griffith, 'Delegated Legislation – Some Recent Developments' (1949) 12 *Modern Law Review* 297, 306.

[14] Willis (n 10) 26.

[15] ibid 36.

[16] ibid 35.

[17] ibid 37.

[18] ibid 49–51.

parliaments, but they were methods that fitted the specialist nature of the task and the methods for supporting the legitimacy of administrative activities.

The Donoughmore Committee agreed in a qualified manner with Lord Hewart's arbitrariness critique; administrative law-making had the potential for arbitrariness when not subject to safeguards.[19] The Committee (reporting prior to Willis's book being published) did not see the range of administrative procedures and practices facilitating administrative deliberation, as Willis had argued. Instead, it concluded its review of the then current regulation-making process as lacking a system. They explained this in the following manner:

> The practice of delegating legislative powers to Ministers of the Crown grew without system. The result is such as must always be expected from unsystematic growth.
>
> We believe that the dangerous tendencies, which we observe, and desire to see restrained, are due to the absence of system and the lack of direction. While we are of opinion that Parliament has been right to delegate legislative powers to Ministers of the Crown, we are equally of opinion that the methods by which those powers have been delegated are open to serious criticism.[20]

The Donoughmore Committee's contribution to laws regarding regulation-making was therefore to focus on a system of generally necessary, but not individually sufficient, safeguards including, public consultation, judicial review, and parliamentary scrutiny committees. It regarded consultation as 'a safeguard of the highest value'.[21] The main difficulty was with the exceptions in the Rules Publication Act and it recommended reforms that would broaden its application.[22]

The situation in Australia had some differences and similarities. The 1930 Senate Committee referred to Lord Hewart's critique of over-reliance on administrative law-making at the expense of parliament but not to his arbitrariness critique. As the Committee reported in 1930, it could not refer to the Donoughmore Committee's report which was published in 1932. Nevertheless, the 1930 Senate Committee used similar terminology and made a similar recommendation. As we saw in Chapters Two and Three, it agreed that a systemic check on regulation-making was required and that a Senate committee was best suited to providing it.[23] The regulation-maker's engagement with members of the public was considered in coming to those findings. The Senate Committee referred to the fact that generally applicable statutory public consultation requirements, equivalent to the Rules Publication Act 1893 (UK), were repealed in 1916.[24] It regarded this as establishing the need for a different method, in the Committee's words, 'of protecting the

[19] Committee on Ministers' Powers, Report (London, 1932) ('Donoughmore Committee report') 19.
[20] ibid 58.
[21] ibid 44.
[22] ibid 45–46, 62, 66.
[23] Senate, *Report from the Senate Select Committee Advising on Establishing Standing Committees*, Parliament of Australia (Report, April 1930) ix–x.
[24] The repeal of this provision is explained in section II.B of this chapter.

public interest'.[25] The Senate Committee recommended that the Senate scrutiny committee to be established should include processes enabling persons affected by a regulation to make submissions to it.[26]

The 1930 Senate Committee's recommendation for establishing a scrutiny committee can therefore be understood as correcting what was lost by the repeal of the Commonwealth's public consultation statutory provisions in 1916. The Senate could establish its own process enabling members of the public to raise concerns about regulations.

The result is that the main contributors to the 1930s reform debates recognised the relevance of public consultation. The outcome in the UK was to recommend reforming the consultation provisions to broaden their application. The outcome in Australia was for the Senate to provide a substitute process to counter the repeal of the general consultation provisions. Public consultation was therefore accepted by all as being a necessary and beneficial process for regulation-making. John Willis went slightly further and recognised the additional benefits of advisory committees being legislated and playing an important role in regulation-making.

II. Consultation Provisions – Government Resistance

While there was apparent consensus in the 1930s debates and reports that consultation was necessary and that the relevant legislative provisions for consultation were inadequate, the broader history makes it clear that governments and parliaments were reluctant to enact statutory provisions for administrative procedures applying to regulation-making generally. The result is that there are now no generally applicable, mandatory public consultation requirements in either country. Other related forms of administrative procedure for regulation-making, such as advisory committees and regulatory impact assessment are also not general and mandatory. The reform discussions subsequent to the Donoughmore Committee and the 1930 Senate Committee make it clear that governments have been consistently reluctant to propose legislation that includes general, mandatory public consultation requirements. The result in both countries is a patchwork of different rules providing for administrative procedures.

A. United Kingdom

There was a general Act in the UK dealing with publication of regulations and public consultation at the time of the 1930s debates. The Act was the Rules Publication Act 1893. Its public consultation provisions required a notice to

[25] n 23, ix.
[26] ibid x.

be published 40 days before the rules were to be made providing for where the draft regulations could be obtained. In that 40-day period members of the public were permitted to make 'representations or suggestions' for consideration by the regulation-maker.[27] The Rules Publication Act also provided for printing regulations, as well as for numbering them and the places where they could be purchased.[28] Both the consultation and publication provisions of the Rules Publication Act were important contributions to the development of regulation-making. Commentators during the 1930s debates referred to the consultation provisions as making administrative procedures that had been required by earlier sector-specific legislation applicable generally.[29] Cecil Carr referred to it as an 'attempted standardisation of procedure'.[30] The publication provisions were equally as important. It was said that prior to the enactment of those provisions, regulations were 'almost undiscoverable'.[31]

It is worthwhile mentioning, as it is a common theme for the development of legislation proposing general consultation provisions, that there was governmental resistance to enacting the Rules Publication Act 1893. CK Allen stated that 'strong opposition was offered by a number of Departments' to it.[32] The text of the Act suggested that such opposition was successful as it expressly excluded regulations made by the Local Government Board for England and Ireland, the Board of Trade and other departments and agencies.[33] As referred to in Part I of this Chapter, both of the main contributors to the 1930s reform debates, Lord Hewart and John Willis, argued that the consultation provisions of the Rules Publication Act were too restricted.[34] The Donoughmore Committee recommended that the exclusions should be removed[35] but this recommendation was not implemented.

In fact, in the decade after the Donoughmore Committee's report the Rules Publication Act 1893 was repealed by the Statutory Instruments Act 1946[36] which deliberately excluded the public consultation provisions in the 1893 legislation. The government explained in Parliament that this was to reduce duplication of engagement by government departments when making regulations. The duplication was due to departments consulting with members of the public prior to a regulation being drafted as a matter of practice. The requirement to make the draft

[27] Rules Publication Act 1893 (56–57 Vict c 66), s 1(1), (2).

[28] ibid s 3.

[29] Willis (n 10) 26; Griffith (n 13) 307–8 tracing the consultation provisions to the early factory legislation.

[30] Carr (n 9) 33–34.

[31] ibid 44. See also CK Allen, *Law and Orders: An Inquiry into the Nature and Scope of Delegated Legislation and Executive Powers in English Law*, 3rd edn (Steven & Sons, 1965) 98; JE Kersell, *Parliamentary Supervision of Delegated Legislation* (Stevens and Sons, 1960) 6.

[32] Allen (n 31) 98.

[33] Rules Publication Act 1893 (56–57 Vict c 66), s 1(4).

[34] Hewart (n 5) 88–89; Willis (n 10) 26–27. See also Carr (n 9) 34–35 and Allen (n 31) 99.

[35] Donoughmore Committee Report (n 19) 66.

[36] Statutory Instruments Act 1946 (9 & 10 Geo 6), s 12.

order available for public consultation was regarded as unnecessary duplication. In an important explanation in parliament, the Solicitor-General, Major Sir Frank Soskice, stated:

> In substance, what would happen if you retained it is this: You would get the Department discussing the matter with interested parties. The Department, already having discussed it fully and having come to the stage at which they can prepare the instrument, prepare it and publish it. Then 40 days have to elapse, during which nothing takes place. It is a complete blank and a complete waste of time, because the discussions with the interested persons have already been completed and the instrument has been fashioned as a result of those discussions. You have 40 days, during which you must notify it in the 'Gazette,' but nothing takes place. Practice and experience have shown that only in the very rarest cases has it been brought about that, during the 40 days in which an Instrument has been notified in the 'Gazette' any further point of view has been advanced by any person, any member of the public, as a result of the publication, which has not already been completely traversed and discussed in the preliminary talks with the interested parties. Therefore, the scheme is to jettison all that antecedent publicity as not being worth while retaining.[37]

The Lord Chancellor, Lord Jowitt, repeated the point in the House of Lords stating that the 1893 public consultation requirement was 'quite obsolete to-day, having regard to the modern practice of discussion with trades associations and so on and the association of local government authorities'.[38]

The parliamentary debates reveal that the government's position explained in these quotations was challenged, albeit unsuccessfully. Excluding public consultation provisions was referred to as shifting it from being a legally, mandated requirement to a 'voluntary discussion'.[39] Concerns were raised that the removal of general, public consultation would result in governments consulting with a narrow range of stakeholders.[40] There was also criticism of the particular argument the government used to support the exclusion. Lord Balfour of Burleigh argued that there seemed to be little reason offered by the government against having preliminary informal consultation and then later a formal, legally required, formal consultation period.[41] In the House of Commons, Mr Proctor argued that the concern about the time taken for consultation could simply be mitigated by reducing the public consultation period to less than 40 days.[42]

The current general framework for public consultation in the UK has more recently been provided by a series of consultation codes, developed since 2000.[43] The current code was made in 2012 and updated in 2018.[44] Their implementation

[37] HC Deb Vol 415 col 1096 (6 November 1945).

[38] HL Deb Vol 139 col 11 (29 January 1946).

[39] HC Deb Vol 415 col 1140 (6 November 1945) (Sir John Mellor).

[40] HL Deb Vol 139 col 16 (29 January 1946) (Lord Addington) and HL Deb Vol 139 col 332 (7 February 1946) (Lord Balfour of Burleigh).

[41] HL Deb Vol 139 col 333 (7 February 1946).

[42] HC Deb Vol 415 col 1138 (6 November 1945).

[43] Cabinet Office, Code of Practice on Written Consultation (November 2000).

[44] Cabinet Office, Consultation Principles 2018 (19 March 2018).

as a code rather than as a regulation indicates that they do not have legal status.[45] That has been confirmed in each iteration of them, as each version has expressly stated that they do 'not have legal force'.[46] The consultation codes developed from the Blair Government's 'Modernising Government' initiative that included extending public participation in policy-making.[47] Concerns were raised in Parliament as to the Cabinet Office's capacity to ensure departmental compliance with the initial Consultation Code and the Select Committee on Public Administration recommended that the government consider introducing legislation with one overarching consultation process.[48] However the government did not propose legislation to implement the recommendation and consultation remains being dealt with generally through the Cabinet Office codes.

The developments explained so far have all related to general consultation requirements. There are mandatory public consultation provisions included in primary legislation relating to particular areas of regulation. Such Acts were referred to in the 1930s reform debates[49] and remain common.[50] The consultation provisions in these Acts are commonly enforced by the courts.[51] In Chapter Five we will see that the UK courts have a highly developed set of case law principles for enforcing these provisions and for supervising consultation processes when there are no statutory requirements for it.

The result is that the developments regarding public consultation are not what was recommended in the 1930s by the Donoughmore Committee – generally applicable, judicially enforceable statutory provisions. The question then is whether the combination of an unenforceable general consultation code and sector-specific statutory consultation provisions provide sufficiently broad coverage. It may be regarded as acceptable given the commonly expressed view that government departments and agencies tend to consult on proposed regulations with or without statutory requirements. These views are supported by Edward Page's empirical research highlighting institutional incentives to conduct consultation processes.[52] There may now be a non-statutory norm that government departments and agencies will consult on proposed regulations and that not

[45] A Blick, *The Codes of the Constitution* (Hart Publishing, 2016) 68.

[46] Cabinet Office, *Code of Practice on Written Consultation* (2000) 3; Cabinet Office, *Code of Practice on Consultation* (2004) 3; Better Regulation Executive, *Code of Practice on Consultation* (2008) 5; Cabinet Office, *Consultation Principles: Guidance* (2012) 3; Cabinet Office, *Consultation Principles 2016* (2016) 2; Cabinet Office, *Consultation Principles 2018* (19 March 2018) 2.

[47] R Manwaring, *The Search for Democratic Renewal: The Politics of Consultation in Britain and Australia* (Manchester University Press, 2014) 88.

[48] Committee on Public Administration, *Innovations in Citizen Participation in Government* (HC 2000–01, Sixth Report, 26 March 2001) paras 19, 37.

[49] Donoughmore Committee Report (n 19) 47–48.

[50] See, eg, Consumer Protection Act 1987, s 11(5); Food Standards Act 1999, ss 27(6), 30(5); Financial Services and Markets Act 2000, ss 138I, 138J; Communications Act 2003 s 403(4); Energy Act 2004, s 111(5).

[51] See, eg, *R (Moseley) v Haringey London Borough Council* [2014] UKSC 56, [2014] 1 WLR 3947; *R (Article 39) v Secretary of State for Education* [2020] EWCA Civ 1577, [29], [33], [83].

[52] Page (n 1) 148.

consulting exposes them to a potent line of criticism when unintended consequences arise. Notwithstanding the lack of general enforceable consultation provisions, a general norm that lack of consultation for regulations is a challenge to their legitimacy may nevertheless apply.

B. Australia

The Australian developments follow a similar path to the UK. The Rules Publication Act 1893 (UK), including its consultation provisions, was replicated in Australia in the first years after Federation. However, the consultation provisions were soon after repealed. There were also developments at the beginning of the twenty-first century, but rather than a non-legislative code, the Australian reform involved enacting consultation provisions that were deliberately unenforceable. As the primary steps in the developments are similar in Australia to the UK, I will focus closely on the reasons for each step and the counter-arguments expressed in the debates.

The starting point is the enactment of the Rules Publication Act 1903 (Cth). This Act that was rightly referred to as a 'copy' of the 1893 UK Act by the responsible minister in his second reading speech in the House of Representatives.[53] However, there were some differences. There were no exceptions from the consultation provisions for particular government departments and agencies[54] and the consultation period was increased to 60 days to accommodate delays in the mail to Western Australia from the eastern states.[55] The debates for the bill indicate that the consultation provisions were regarded favourably. The minister referred to the consultation provisions in the 1893 UK Act as having 'been found very useful in England' and referred to them as enabling 'public criticism' of proposed regulations.[56]

This starting point soon fell out of favour with the Government and it brought legislation to Parliament for its repeal in 1916.[57] The reasons offered by the Government for the repeal were based on the urgency provision[58] being generally relied on to enable provisional regulations to become effective immediately and then subsequently confirmed after the public consultation period. The explanation was that few changes were made to such provisional regulations so there was little need for the confirmation stage and there was expense in reprinting

[53] Commonwealth, *Parliamentary Debates*, House of Representatives, 20 October 1903, 6264 (Mr Deakin, Minister for External Affairs).

[54] Rules Publication Act 1903, s 3.

[55] ibid s 3(1); Commonwealth, *Parliamentary Debates*, House of Representatives, 20 October 1903, 6266–67 (Mr Deakin, Minister for External Affairs).

[56] Commonwealth, *Parliamentary Debates*, House of Representatives, 20 October 1903, 6264 (Mr Deakin, Minister for External Affairs).

[57] Rules Publication Act 1916 (Cth).

[58] ibid s 4.

the confirmed regulations.[59] This explanation was very similar to the equivalent repeal in the UK in 1946. The consultation process in practice involved duplications that raised resource issues. The main difference is that the UK justification referred to consultation occurring voluntarily. There was no such explanation in the Australian Parliament.

It is important to highlight the reliance in the Government's explanation on the urgency provision being commonly used as a means for avoiding delays in making regulations operative. That was likely to have been understandable and acceptable in 1916, in the middle of World War I. In other periods such a general explanation would likely have been subjected to criticism. The parliamentary debates for the repeal reveal that there was little resistance to it. One senator requested the government provide notice of proposed regulations as a matter of practice and another was concerned that repealing the consultation provisions would grant overly broad power to government departments.[60]

The Rules Publication Act 1903 (Cth) continued operating without the consultation provisions until 2005[61] when a new, generally applicable, Act commenced dealing with regulations. The Act was the Legislative Instruments Act 2003 (Cth), now named the Legislation Act 2003 (Cth), and it includes consultation provisions. The changes were prompted by a report of the Administrative Review Council in 1992 recommending that a mandatory public consultation provision be enacted subject to some exceptions.[62]

The consultation provisions enacted in 2003, that remain in operation with some minor changes, do not refer to general, public consultation, as was the case for the Rules Publication Acts but for consultation with persons with expertise and persons affected by the proposed regulation.[63] The consultation provisions were deliberately made to be discretionary and unenforceable by courts. The provisions expressly state that the form of consultation is to be determined by the regulation-maker.[64] The fact that they are unenforceable by courts is made clear by section 19, which states, 'The fact that consultation does not occur does not affect the validity or enforceability of a legislative instrument'. If there is no consultation for a particular regulation, reasons for that decision must be included in the explanatory statement.[65] The accountability for a department or agency's consultation processes is conducted by the Senate Delegated Legislation

[59] Commonwealth, *Parliamentary Debates*, House of Representatives, 23 May 1916, 8371; Commonwealth, *Parliamentary Debates*, Senate, 11 May 1916, 7828.

[60] Commonwealth, *Parliamentary Debates*, Senate, 11 May 1916, 7829 (Senator Keating); Commonwealth, *Parliamentary Debates*, Senate, 12 May 1916, 7877–78 (Senator Senior).

[61] It was repealed by the Legislative Instruments (Transitional Provisions and Consequential Amendments) Act 2003 (Cth).

[62] Administrative Review Council, *Rule Making by Commonwealth Agencies* (Report No 35, 1992) 33, 35 recommendation 9.

[63] Legislation Act 2003 (Cth), s 17(2).

[64] ibid s 17(1).

[65] ibid s 15J(2)(e).

Committee which can raise questions about the adequacy of the regulation-maker's consultation process.[66] It is therefore clear that these provisions were designed to be largely discretionary and unenforceable in the courts.

The Government's explanation for these provisions was that it sought to encourage regulation-makers to engage in consultation and that the check on that consultation is to be through explanations in the explanatory statement for the regulation.[67] The explanatory memorandum for the Bill referred to the consultation provisions 'sending a clear message about the importance of consultation'.[68] As in other reforms concerning consultation processes there was criticism of the provisions. The criticism focused on the discretionary and unenforceable form of the provisions. Opposition members of Parliament argued that it was adopted due to the concerns of government agencies rather than members of Parliament.[69] The important point is that while there was consensus on the importance of consultation as a procedure for regulation-making, differences developed as to whether the provisions should be enforceable in the courts.

As in the UK, the unenforceable nature of the consultation provisions is mitigated by the inclusion of enforceable sector-specific consultation provisions.[70] The courts have enforced these provisions, at times commenting on their significance. In the High Court's decision in *Scurr v Brisbane City Council*[71] Stephen J emphasised the importance for administrative officials to be informed of a range of views and objections to proposed government actions.[72] The courts have regularly enforced the different stages of consultation processes when the provisions are mandatory: in particular that the notice of proposed action is sufficiently informative[73] and administrative officials are to give genuine consideration to written submissions.[74]

The developments in each country make clear the modern reluctance to enact general, *enforceable* public consultation requirements. The development is very similar in the UK and Australia. The initial legislation, the consultation provisions included in the Rules Publication Acts of each country were repealed in the first half of the twentieth century for practical reasons, primarily inefficiency.

[66] Senate Standing Order 23(3)(d).

[67] House of Representatives, 26 June 2003, 17626 (Mr Williams). See also the Explanatory Memorandum to the Legislative Instruments Bill 2003, 2.

[68] Explanatory Memorandum to the Legislative Instruments Bill 2003, 2.

[69] Commonwealth, *Parliamentary Debates*, House of Representatives, 21 August 2003, 19281 (Mr McClelland); Commonwealth, *Parliamentary Debates*, Senate, 2 December 2003, 18626 (Senator Ludwig).

[70] See, eg, Veterans' Entitlements Act 1986 ss 196F–196G; Food Standards Australia New Zealand Act 1991 (Cth), ss 58–63; Broadcasting Services Act 1992 (Cth) s 126; Environment Protection and Biodiversity Conservation Act 1999 (Cth), ss 275–76.

[71] (1973) 133 CLR 242.

[72] ibid 251–2.

[73] See, eg, *Tickner v Chapman* (1995) 57 CLR 451, 456–59 (Black CJ); *Visa International Service Association v Reserve Bank* [2003] FCA 977, (2003) 131 FCR 300, [548]–[554].

[74] *Tobacco Institute of Australia v National Health and Medical Research Council* (1996) 71 FCR 265, 280–81.

Both countries looked again at general, enforceable provisions in the early twenty-first century but did not enact them. The text of the UK codes and the Australian Legislation Act 2003 reveal that the primary concern is judicial review of regulations on the basis of breach of consultation requirements.

III. Advisory Committees

While public consultation provisions have been the primary focus of the reform debates, provisions establishing and requiring engagement with advisory committees were included in legislation prior to the 1930s debates and continue to be included now.

John Willis regarded them as particularly important. We saw in section I that he highlighted these committees in his response to Hewart's argument that administrative regulation-making was necessarily arbitrary.[75] He pointed to examples in legislation starting at the turn of the twentieth century[76] and noted that they proliferated during World War I. He supported them on the ground that they enable administrative officials to be informed by experts and representatives of persons affected. He also stated that if more was known publicly of their contributions there might be more public confidence in administrative forms of law-making and acceptance of it.[77] That is, he regarded such provisions and their operation as a legitimacy-enhancing measure. However, he also made it clear that he was aware of criticisms that they could draw responsibility away from ministers and that such committees may lack power.[78]

The inclusion of advisory committees in regulatory legislation enables a more controlled form of deliberative engagement than general public consultation. The latter involves notice to the public and submissions by self-selecting persons and groups. There was wider recognition of the inclusion of advisory committees in Acts that delegate regulation-making powers in the 1930s debates period. Harold Laski, a famous political scholar of the time and a member of the Donoughmore Committee, also recognised them as having this role. He argued for governments to engage more broadly with experts in its regulatory functions and particularly recognised their benefit as a form of formal and focused consultation in regulation-making.[79] Departmental officials were regarded as having insufficient expertise for making regulations without the input of committees of experts and representatives of affected persons.

[75] Willis (n 10) 35–38.

[76] ibid 35–36. He gave the following examples: Board of Education Act 1899 (62 & 63 Vic c 33), s 4, Census of Production Act 1906 (6 Ed 7 c 49), s 9; Merchant Shipping Act 1906 (6 Ed 7 c 48), s 79(1).

[77] ibid 37–38.

[78] ibid 39.

[79] HA Laski, *A Grammar of Politics* (George Allen & Unwin Ltd 1941) 371–75, 385–87, 391.

However, the 1930s committees inquiring into regulation-making did not focus on advisory committees. The Donoughmore Committee did not refer to them as a general safeguard even though it recognised their inclusion in legislation.[80] They were not referred to at all by the 1930 Senate Committee as its focus was on the need for a systemic parliamentary check on regulation-making. The result is that they were either on the periphery of the 1930s debates or not included at all. However, they are still included as a form of administrative procedure in legislation in the UK[81] and Australia.[82]

The establishment and use of advisory committees is related to the inclusion of public consultation provisions in legislation. The statutory provisions enable a process managed by administrative officials with formal contributions from experts and stakeholder representatives. The contribution of these committees is often not clearly visible in explanatory materials that are made public for regulations. The exception is in emergency periods, as members of advisory committees can become highly visible and their interactions with government officials can become controversial.[83] As John Willis recognised, advisory committees can help to mitigate against arbitrary regulation-making. Reference to them can support the information base from which regulations are made and, in so doing, can help to ensure that regulations are not necessarily arbitrary. On the other hand, their contributions can be opaque, thus contributing to one of the difficulties of administrative law-making.

IV. Regulatory Impact Assessment

The administrative procedures examined so far in this chapter were established prior to the 1930s debates and, despite changes to the legal form of public consultation provisions, have retained their general significance since then. In the late twentieth century they were supplemented by regulatory impact assessment as an addition to administrative procedures for regulation-making. Regulatory impact assessment is different to the other forms of administrative process examined in this book due to it not generally being included in legislation. It is established by administrative policies and guidance. Its purpose is related to the general purposes of public consultation and of advisory committees; to alleviate the risk of arbitrary administrative decision-making, Lord Hewart's primary concern with

[80] Donoughmore Committee Report (n 19) 47–48, 124–26.

[81] See, eg, Social Security Administration Act 1992, s 170; Merchant Shipping Act 1995, s 301; Medicines and Medical Devices Act 2021, s 20.

[82] See, eg, National Health Act 1953 (Cth), s 100A, 110; Health Insurance Act 1973 (Cth), ss 66–67; Carbon Credits (Carbon Farming Initiative) Act 2011, ss 106(10), 256.

[83] See eg, L Trueblood: '"Following the Science": a Legal and Democratic Challenge' (UK Constitutional Law Blog, 21 September 2020), available at ukconstitutionallaw.org/2020/09/21/leah-trueblood-following-the-science-a-legal-and-democratic-challenge; EL Windholz (2020) 'Governing in a Pandemic: From Parliamentary Sovereignty to Autocratic Technocracy' (2020) 8 *The Theory and Practice of Legislation* 93.

administrative law-making. My analysis of regulatory impact assessment is brief due primarily to it being a safeguard that lacks legal status. That means there is little parliamentary debate, case law or legal scholarship discussing its contribution to regulation-making safeguards.

The requirements for regulatory impact assessments in both countries involve similar features.[84] They require administrative officials to work through an evaluation considering the reasons for government action, the relevant policy options, the likely impacts of the proposed action and a cost–benefit analysis.[85] Regulatory impact assessment requirements in both countries also make clear that public consultation remains an important feature of the process.[86] This very general overview is sufficient to make clear that regulatory impact assessment is a modern measure for ensuring non-arbitrary, deliberative law-making.[87] The combination of considering governmental purposes, implementation options and impacts, as well as public consultation facilitates an administrative process by which relevant factors in a law-making process are considered and resolved. It is arguably democratic because it is a formalised way of collecting information regarding the social and economic benefits of the proposed regulation and the effect on those who have to comply with it.

The initial steps in the implementation of regulatory impact assessment occurred in the 1980s in both countries. In the UK it developed from the deregulatory policies of the Thatcher Government which were subsequently transformed into regulatory impact-assessment processes in the late 1990s by the Blair Government.[88] This transformation involved a shift from an anti-regulation approach to one that sought to improve regulatory laws.[89] The current, generally applicable, regulatory impact assessment requirements are included in government documents,[90] which is consistent with it being recognised as a form of internal, administrative requirement.[91] However, there are some provisions in sector-specific legislation imposing obligations on agencies

[84] Department of Business, *Better Regulation Framework – Interim guidance* (March 2020), available at assets.publishing.service.gov.uk/government/uploads/system/uploads/attachment_data/file/916918/better-regulation-guidance.pdf; Department of Prime Minister and Cabinet, *Australian Government Guide to Policy Impact Analysis* (17 February 2023), available at oia.pmc.gov.au/resources/guidance-impact-analysis/australian-government-guide-policy-impact-analysis.

[85] Department of Business (n 84) para 1.2.4; Department of Prime Minister and Cabinet (n 84) 25–31.

[86] Department of Business (n 84) 17; Department of Prime Minister and Cabinet (n 84) 32–37.

[87] T Prosser, *The Regulatory Enterprise – Government, Regulation, and Legitimacy* (Oxford University Press, 2010) 214.

[88] R Baldwin, 'Is Better Regulation Smarter Regulation?' [2005] *Public Law* 485, 485–86; Colin Jacobs, 'The Evolution and Development of Regulatory Impact Assessment in the UK' in C Kirkpatrick and D Parker (eds), *Regulatory Impact Assessment: Towards Better Regulation?* (Edward Elgar, 2007) 106, 107.

[89] Baldwin (n 88) 486.

[90] Department of Business (n 84); HM Treasury, *The Green Book: Central Government Guidance on Appraisal and Evaluation* (2022), available at www.gov.uk/government/publications/the-green-book-appraisal-and-evaluation-in-central-governent.

[91] Jacobs (n 88) 112.

for conducting regulatory impact assessment.[92] The development of regulatory impact assessment procedures at the Commonwealth level in Australia is very similar to the UK. It was first established by the Hawke Government in the 1980s as part of its 'new managerialist' reforms and then re-established in the 1990s due to government initiatives for regulatory reform based on economic pressures.[93] Like its implementation in the UK, it is imposed by a government document[94] rather than by generally applicable legislation.

As is common with institutional procedures, regulatory impact assessment has been subject to criticism. In both countries there has been strong criticism that regulatory impact assessment has been poorly implemented by government departments and agencies.[95] In particular, there is concern that cost–benefit analysis attempts to monetise impacts and benefits,[96] and that the difficulty of quantifying social benefits of a regulatory proposal[97] can result in the cost–benefit analysis having a poor understanding of the purposes that are to be achieved.

While these concerns are important for the ways in which regulatory impact assessment are factored into regulation-making processes and how they are conducted, these issues are beyond the scope of this chapter. The relevant point is that regulatory impact assessment provides a formalised administrative procedure aimed at supporting a particular form of administrative deliberation and reducing the risk of arbitrariness.

V. Conclusions

In this chapter we have seen three related forms of administrative process, designed to counter the issue of administrative arbitrariness raised by Lord Hewart. Public consultation and advisory committees were in place prior to the 1930s debates and regulatory impact assessment is a more recent addition. Each of the contributors to the 1930s debates recognised that public consultation played an important role as a safeguard for regulation-making. However, the focus at that time was establishing parliamentary scrutiny rather than analysing the contribution of administrative deliberation processes. For the Donoughmore Committee, that was understandable as the Rules Publication Act 1893 included

[92] See, eg, Utilities Act 2000 (UK), s 5A; Communications Act 2003 (UK), s 7; Health and Social Care Act 2012 (UK), s 69.

[93] B Morgan, *Social Citizenship in the Shadow of Competition* (Routledge, 2003) 61–62.

[94] Department of Prime Minister and Cabinet (n 84).

[95] See, eg, Baldwin (n 88) 491–92; CM Harrison, 'Assessing the Impact of Regulatory Impact Assessment' (2009) 16 *Agenda* 41; P Carroll, 'Australia and New Zealand' in C Dunlop and C Radaelli (eds), *Handbook of Regulatory Impact Assessment* (Edward Elgar Publishing, 2016) 347, 358–59; Lords Secondary Legislation Scrutiny Committee, *Losing Impact: why the Government's Impact Assessment System is Failing Parliament and the Public* (HL 2022–23, 62).

[96] See, eg, Prosser (n 87) 215–16.

[97] Baldwin (n 88) 492; Jacobs (n 88) 119–20.

general public consultation procedures and was operating at the time. In that context, it is understandable that there was no great need to examine how public consultation specifically, and administrative procedures more generally, contribute to providing democratic legitimacy for regulation-making. The Donoughmore Committee's focus was on the exceptions in the Rules Publication Act enabling no consultation to be conducted. The 1930 Senate Committee's starting point was the repeal of the Commonwealth public consultation processes and so it focused on what the Senate could do to make up for that.

The result to be drawn from the 1930s debates is that administrative procedures play an important but not sufficient role in the safeguards on delegating regulation-making powers. That helps us to understand the ways in which these administrative deliberation processes can be regarded in the system of safeguards for regulation-making. Judicial review and parliamentary scrutiny are close to being fully, and legally, implemented safeguards. Administrative deliberation processes have been implemented in a more limited manner.

That does not necessarily make them less significant for the safeguard system. Lack of, or poor, consultation processes or engagement with advisory committees may not always be challengeable in the courts. However, they are circumstances in which persons affected, experts, academics and public interest groups can make a strong case that particular regulations lack democratic legitimacy. That may lead to regulated organisations resisting compliance or it may strengthen the arguments of interest groups raising concerns politically. The important point is that although there may not be general implementation of these administrative processes in legislation, they remain influential as a norm of regulation-making in the UK and Australia.

5

Judicial Review of Regulations

Judicial review can be a form of escalation for regulations as it enables debate about the terms and operation of a regulation in a public forum. It requires the government to provide a justification for the legality of the challenged regulation. Accordingly, judicial review is commonly recognised as an important safeguard on regulation-making. Joe Tomlinson, Lewis Graham and Alexandra Sinclair have stated that in the UK the most thorough form of scrutiny of regulations is by courts rather than Parliament.[1] That may be the case, but judicial review also has important limitations. This chapter examines the role of the courts in terms of the safeguards on delegating law-making power to administrative officials. How do the courts contribute to the democratic legitimacy of regulations?

I will argue that the developments in the twentieth century regarding judicial review of regulations are largely similar in each country. Understandings of parliamentary democracy have been a major influence on the scope and function of judicial review in both countries in relation to standing, the standards applied by the courts to review regulations, and the remedies applied. The primary difference is that the Human Rights Act 1998 (HRA 1998) has prompted changes to judicial review in the UK. The equivalent legislation at the Commonwealth level in Australia, the Human Rights (Parliamentary Scrutiny) Act 2011 (Cth), establishes (as its name indicates) parliamentary scrutiny of regulations rather than judicial review.[2] Judicial review of regulations according to the HRA 1998 has required the UK courts to review the process for making regulations to a greater extent than would generally be the case. The judicial review methodology in these cases focuses on administrative deliberation, similar to the forms that were examined in chapter four. There is no clear example of this being developed by the Australian courts.

[1] J Tomlinson, L Graham and A Sinclair 'Does Judicial Review of Delegated Legislation under the Human Rights Act 1998 Unduly Interfere with Executive Law-Making?' (UK Constitutional Law Blog, 22 February 2021), available at ukconstitutionallaw.org/2021/02/22/joe-tomlinson-lewis-graham-and-alexandra-sinclair-does-judicial-review-of-delegated-legislation-under-the-human-rights-act-1998-unduly-interfere-with-executive-law-making.

[2] There is enforceable human rights legislation in the Australian states and territories: Human Rights Act 2004 (ACT); Charter of Human Rights and Responsibilities Act 2006 (Vic); Human Rights Act 2019 (Qld).

I. Courts in the 1930s Debates

The issues raised in the 1930s debates in relation to judicial review focused primarily on whether it could legitimately be excluded by statutory provisions. There was relatively little debate as to the standards and methodologies applied by the courts. The recommendations on that issue were that statutory attempts to exclude judicial review should be narrowed down to exceptional circumstances relating to emergencies. The secondary issue that arose in Willis's contributions and in Australia raised concerns that judicial review is not a sufficient safeguard and recommended that it should be supplemented by parliamentary scrutiny. The main point being that the availability of judicial review is necessary, but judicial review is not a sufficient safeguard. It needs to be supplemented by a more systemic, parliamentary safeguard.

Lord Hewart focused on legislative attempts to limit judicial review of regulations. He sought to raise awareness that Parliament would pass laws including such limits.[3] He did not focus on the substantive function of the courts as a safeguard on regulation-making. It was assumed to be an important role in terms of the rule of law. When he did refer to its function he explained it in simple terms: to ensure that the statute authorised the regulation and that no irrelevant factors were considered.[4] His focus was on what exclusion meant for administrative officials: that it risked administrative officials over-reaching the parameters of their powers delegated by Parliament.[5] For Lord Hewart, the fact that judicial review is not systemic (the courts do not review all regulations) was not a weakness. The threat of judicial review was sufficient to make administrative officials realise that regulations are potentially exposed to judicially scrutiny.[6]

Willis, on the hand, was sceptical of judicial review. His concerns related to incoherence of the case law, its sporadic nature, and the formalist reasoning of the judges.[7] Cases were determined by statutory interpretation that in practice involved the judge's personal views on the scope of discretion granted to administrative officials: views developed by the judges primarily in their private law, rather than governmental, backgrounds.[8] Harold Laski made a similar point in his 1926 critique of the House of Lords' decision in *Roberts v Hopwood*: that judicial review of administrative action required the judges to exercise forms of restraint to ensure that their political views did not influence their reasoning.[9]

[3] Lord Hewart of Bury, *The New Despotism* (Ernest Benn Ltd, 1929) 73, 79–80.

[4] ibid 64.

[5] ibid 73.

[6] ibid 160–61.

[7] J Willis, *The Parliamentary Powers of English Government Departments* (Harvard University Press, 1933) 47–48.

[8] ibid 112.

[9] *Roberts v Hopwood* [1925] AC 528. H Laski, 'Judicial Review of Social Policy in England: A Study of Roberts v Hopwood' (1926) 39 *Harvard Law Review* 832, 833, 847–48.

While Willis's scepticism of judicial review related to substantive aspects of judicial reasoning, he also made an important systemic point: that judicial review litigation is 'sporadic'; it is dependent on the 'accident' of an applicant bringing proceedings.[10] He elaborated this concern by stating that regulations that are beyond power could operate for years without challenge due to the persons affected lacking resources, and that other regulations that are apparently within power can be invalidated by an 'uninformed or unsympathetic' court.[11] Such views led Willis to being sympathetic to limited and restrained forms of judicial review[12] and that parliamentary scrutiny by a committee was a better solution to the need for checks on regulation-making than judicial review.[13]

The Donoughmore Committee's view was that judicial review was one of the necessary safeguards for regulation-making powers. Its report focused on statutory attempts to exclude or limit judicial review. The Committee regarded some forms of these provisions as being ineffective and the potentially effective forms were referred to as 'objectionable'.[14] The Committee regarded judicial review as being fundamental for the rule of law and should be limited only in exceptional circumstances where finality is particularly relevant.[15] Where that is the case, the appropriate measure is a three to six-month time limit on judicial review rather than attempts to exclude it.[16]

The Australian debates in the late 1920s and early 1930s were less developed in relation to judicial review in Australia than in the UK. The 1930 Senate Committee regarded judicial review as an insufficient safeguard on regulation-making. It regarded judicial review as not being efficient or cost-effective for persons seeking to criticise particular regulations.[17] This led the Committee to recommend establishing a standing Senate committee to scrutinise regulations in which such criticisms could be made.[18]

What comes out of the 1930s debates is that judicial review of regulations is firmly accepted as one of the safeguards on regulation-making. Exclusions and restrictions of it are generally regarded as being illegitimate. Yet, more interestingly, there was also recognition of its weaknesses and limitations. Willis and the 1930 Senate Committee made clear that judicial review was not systemic. It depends on a person or organisation being willing to bring proceedings – something that may be regarded as unlikely due to the associated costs. Both Willis and the 1930 Senate Committee recognised parliamentary scrutiny as a

[10] Willis (n 7) 112.
[11] ibid 172–73.
[12] ibid 82.
[13] ibid 114–15.
[14] Committee on Ministers' Powers, Report (London, 1932) ('Donoughmore Committee Report') 40–41.
[15] ibid 61–62, 64.
[16] ibid 62, 65.
[17] Senate, *Report from the Senate Select Committee Advising on Establishing Standing Committees*, Parliament of Australia (Report, April 1930) para 21.
[18] ibid para 22.

necessary supplement to judicial review. This is an important point to recognise in the 1930s debates. The safeguards on regulation-making were regarded as necessarily multifaceted. They are better understood systemically – each being necessary and any exclusion or limit of one requires justification. Moreover, the fact that parliaments have a scrutiny role does not prevent or limit the courts from their review role. This is recognised by the courts in both countries.[19]

II. Judicial Review and Democratic Legitimacy of Regulations

The issues raised in the 1930s debates regarding attempts to exclude and limit judicial review of regulations have been largely resolved. Such exclusions and limits are now rare and would be largely ineffective due to judicial methods of avoiding and minimising them. As we saw in the previous chapters, the introduction of parliamentary scrutiny committees has added a systemic level of review to the other safeguards. There are nevertheless questions that arise from the 1930s debates regarding judicial review that are within the scope of this study. They relate to the scope of judicial review given that it is sporadic, being dependent on an applicant bringing proceedings. How have the courts shaped their function now that the safeguards recommended in the 1930s debates have largely been implemented? How can the courts' role be understood in terms of parliamentary democracy and administrative forms of deliberation? What changes have affected the courts' role in review of regulations?

I will argue that the core function of judicial review remains as it was recognised in the 1930s debates. Courts ensure that a challenged regulation is consistent with the statutory provisions delegating regulation-making power to administrative officials. This has a direct and accepted relationship with parliamentary democracy. The courts are enforcing the scope of delegation granted by Parliament. There is, however, much additional complexity to this apparently simple, formal framework for judicial review of regulations. I will examine in this part the additional features and how they have developed.

It should be recognised that even prior to the 1930s debates, courts had extended the core function. They sought to ensure that regulations are considered legal solutions to the problem they were directed to resolving. The terminology used in nineteenth-century cases was that regulations could not be 'unreasonable', a concept filled out by reference to synonyms such as 'oppressive', 'capricious'

[19] *F Hoffmann-La Roche & Co v Secretary of State for Trade and Industry* [1975] AC 295, 365 (Lord Diplock); *R (Javed) v Secretary of State for the Home Department* [2001] EWCA Civ 789, [2002] QB 129 [51]; *R (BAPIO Action Limited) v Secretary of State for the Home Department* [2007] EWCA Civ 1139 [30]–[32]; *R (Public Law Project) v Lord Chancellor* [2016] UKSC 39, [2016] AC 1531 [22]; *Clark v Vanstone* [2004] FCA 1105, (2004) 211 ALR 412 [117].

or 'lacking justification'.[20] Modern cases have focused on proportionality. In the UK this has primarily been due to developments relating to enforcing the HRA 1998. These are forms of substantive review of regulations. There have been developments in this form of review that focus on administrative deliberation and democratic participation. It can be understood as drawing on the deliberative underpinnings of parliamentary law-making to seek a comparable form of deliberation in administrative law-making.

A. Standing

Standing rules are recognised to be a strong indication of the function of judicial review.[21] When this point is made it is usually elaborated by setting out different understandings of the function of judicial review inherent in the rules of standing. Traditional standing rules are designed to ensure administrative officials comply with the terms of the delegation of power in order to protect the applicant's liberty or property. A related but expanded version of this idea is that enforcing compliance with the statutory terms of delegation is to protect the rule of law. There is an additional, and further expanded, basis for standing focusing on democratic participation. In this form, the courts' function includes reviewing administrative action to ensure that the decision-making process enabled participation by interest groups and individuals.

It is worthwhile examining these models in more detail. The traditional model starts with standing being limited to persons whose rights are affected or are personally harmed by administrative action in relation to their property or financial interests.[22] The scholarship on this form of standing have connected them to the development of judicial review from private law litigation.[23] The purpose of such standing tests is to ensure that the plaintiff has a personal stake in the litigation which is to be confirmed by their interests being harmed by the decision that they want to challenge. This model of judicial review was explained by Carol Harlow and Richard Rawlings using their drainpipe metaphor: the narrow approach to who can bring proceedings is matched by the narrow standards the

[20] *Slattery v Naylor* (1888) 13 App Cas 446, 453; *Kruse v Johnson* [1898] 2 QB 91, 99–100.

[21] SM Thio, *Locus Standi and Judicial Review* (Singapore University Press, 1971) 2–5; R Stewart 'The Reformation of American Administrative Law' (1975) 88 *Harvard Law Review* 1669, 1723; PP Craig, *Public Law and Democracy in the United Kingdom and the United States of America* (Clarendon Press, 1990) 28–29; P Cane, 'Administrative Law as Regulation' in C Parker, C Scott, N Lacey and J Braithwaite, *Regulating Law* (Oxford University Press, 2004) 207, 219.

[22] For the UK, see, eg, *Boyce v Paddington Borough Council* [1903] 1 Ch D 109; *Gouriet v Union of Post Office Workers* [1978] AC 435. For Australia, see, eg, *Victorian Chamber of Manufactures v The Commonwealth (Prices Regulations)* (1943) 67 CLR 335, 343 (Starke J); *Real Estate Institute of NSW v Blair* (1946) 73 CLR 213, 224 (Rich J), 226 (Starke J), 228 (Dixon J); *Australian Conservation Foundation v Commonwealth* (1980) 146 CLR 493, 526–27, 530 (Gibbs J); *Argos Pty Ltd v Corbell, Minister for the Environment and Sustainable Development* (2014) 254 CLR 394, 408–09 (French CJ and Keane J), 417 (Hayne and Bell JJ), 423 (Gageler J).

[23] M Allars, 'Standing: The Role and Evolution of the Test' (1991) 20 *Federal Law Review* 83, 93–94.

courts would apply to test challenged administrative action.[24] This limited role of the courts seems to have heightened Willis's scepticism of the courts' input to the safeguards on regulation-making in his contribution to the 1930s debates. His view seemed to be that the courts' role is limited to being concerned about personal liberty and property in a manner that restricts governments from welfare-based reforms.[25]

The obvious problem with the traditional model is that it is narrow. It necessarily results in unauthorised administrative actions being allowed to remain effective when the only likely applicant is not recognised to have standing.[26] The primary alternative emphasises that the court's role is to enforce the law by ensuring that governmental institutions operate within legal boundaries.[27] The courts commonly justify this expanded version of standing by reference to the rule of law.[28] Its primary significance is that it allows broader scope for standing – usually focusing on the applicant's qualifications and capacity to bring the proceedings.[29] Jason Varuhas has argued that this approach to standing in the UK developed from the 1970s procedural reforms to judicial review.[30] It is often pointed out that this form of broadened standing does not necessarily invoke a change to the standards applied by the courts to test decisions and regulations. Accordingly, Harlow and Rawlings's metaphor for the model of judicial review when this form of broadened standing applies is a funnel.[31]

The extension of standing has also been regarded as having the potential for, or at least suggesting the need for, developments in the standards applied by courts in judicial review cases. Courts in this model not only ensure that administrative officials comply with the statutory terms of the delegation of power, but also ensure that administrators use participatory procedures and make regulations according to requirements of administrative rationality. The rationale for these expansions was to enhance public participation in administrative decision-making, in line with developments in the United States.[32] It has been regarded

[24] C Harlow and R Rawlings, *Pressure Through Law* (Routledge, 1992) 311. See also R Rawlings, *Modelling Judicial Review* (2008) 61 *Current Legal Problems* 95, 98–100.

[25] Willis (n 25) 30. See also JA Corry, 'Administrative Law and the Interpretation of Statutes' (1936) 1 *University of Toronto Law Journal* 286, 287–88.

[26] *Inland Revenue Commissioners v National Federation of Self-Employed and Small Businesses Ltd* [1985] AC 617, 644 (Lord Diplock).

[27] Thio (n 21) 2; P Cane, L McDonald and K Rundle, *Principles of Administrative Law*, 3rd edn (Oxford University Press, 2018) 213–14.

[28] *Inland Revenue Commissioners* (n 26) 644 (Lord Diplock)); *AXA General Insurance Limited v HM Advocate* [2011] UKSC 46; [2012] 1 AC 868, 952 [169] (Lord Reed); *Walton v Scottish Ministers* [2012] UKSC 44 [94] (Lord Reed).

[29] Cane, McDonald and Rundle (n 27) 213–14.

[30] JNE Varuhas, 'The Public Interest Conception of Public Law: Its Procedural Origins and Substantive Implications' in J Bell, M Elliott, JNE Varuhas and P Murray (eds), *Public Law Adjudication in Common Law Systems: Process and Substance* (Hart Publishing, 2016). 45, 57–60.

[31] Harlow and Rawlings (n 24) 311–12. See also Rawlings (n 24) 100–02. See also TT Arvind and L Stirton, 'The Curious Origins of Judicial Review' (2017) 133 *Law Quarterly Review* 91, 108–14.

[32] See, eg, Stewart (n 21) 1670, 1722, 1756–60.

as the basis for a deliberative model of judicial review.[33] Harlow and Rawlings' metaphor for this model is the 'American freeway' or 'British Motorway'.[34]

Harlow and Rawlings referred to the participation model of standing as being 'an ideal type' and 'imaginary' rather than an actual basis for standing and a model of judicial review.[35] However, there are signs of it in practice in both the UK and Australia. It was clearly a relevant factor in Lord Reed's consideration of standing in *Walton v Scottish Ministers*. He understood the fact that the applicant participated in an inquiry and sought to challenge the manner in which the consultation process was managed as being sufficient for him to have standing.[36] I will examine below how judicial review of regulations on the basis of human rights principles in the UK can include methodologies having deliberative significance. The courts in Australia have applied a similar approach to Lord Reed in *Walton v Scottish Ministers*.[37] However, it usually does not extend to participation in public consultation,[38] which means that it has no real significance for judicial review of regulations. The primary Australian cases relate to participation in a mining warden's hearing[39] and an administrative conference with a small number of participants.[40]

The trajectory of standing rules has been towards expansion. While the starting point is that standing in judicial review cases is to enable the courts to ensure administrative officials make decisions and regulations in accordance with the empowering legislation, this is qualified by reference to the applicant's rights or personal interests being affected by the decision or regulation. Without changing the rationale of judicial review to a great extent, the test was liberalised to facilitate the rule of law function of judicial review. Yet, there is also a trace, in the scholarship and in the case law, of a different understanding of judicial review that affects the principles of standing. That is, to review administrative action to protect participation and ensure a minimum level of deliberation in administrative processes. This recognises that administrative decision-making requires a form of legitimacy based on participatory deliberation and that protecting Parliament's qualifications on delegation of regulation-making authority is not sufficient.

[33] S Fredman, 'New Horizons: Incorporating Socio-Economic Rights in a British Bill of Rights' [2010] *Public Law* 297, 297–98; Rawlings (n 24) 103.

[34] Harlow and Rawlings (n 24) 311. See also Rawlings (n 24) 102–07.

[35] Harlow and Rawlings (n 24) 311. See also Rawlings (n 24) 102.

[36] *Walton* (n 28) [86]–[88].

[37] Allars (n 23) 101–04.

[38] *Australian Conservation Foundation* (n 22) 531–32 (Gibbs J), 542 (Stephen J), *cf* 556–57 (Murphy J dissenting). See also *North Coast Environmental Council Inc v Minister for Resources* (1994) 55 FCR 492, 512.

[39] *Sinclair v Maryborough Mining Warden* (1975) 132 CLR 473.

[40] *United States Tobacco Company v Minister for Consumer Affairs* (1988) 20 FCR 520.

B. Statutory Authority

The role of the courts when reviewing regulations for their compliance with enabling legislation is more complex than might be initially expected. There is an initial, relatively simple explanation for the role, ie that the courts are enforcing the limits on the delegated power provided by statute. However, Willis was right to say that this legal issue is ripe with complexities that arise due to the need for judicial interpretation. In particular, those complexities relate to the court's ability to draw on statutory purposes and judicially recognised interpretive presumptions. It is in these interpretive presumptions, in particular, that an additional role for the court and for parliamentary democracy arises. The courts now recognise the operation of these presumptions as creating incentives for parliaments to deliberate more carefully and transparently on matters that provide the basis for the presumptions.

Courts recognise their review power as being a matter of ensuring that administrative officials make regulations within the scope of the authority granted to them by legislation. The basic question, as the Supreme Court stated in *R (Public Law Project) v Lord Chancellor*,[41] is whether the challenged regulation 'has an effect, or is made for a purpose, which is ultra vires, that is, outside the scope of the statutory power pursuant to which it was purportedly made'. The High Court in *Shanahan v Scott*[42] elaborated on what this involves. The majority judgment stated that regulation-making powers:

> [A]uthorise the provision of subsidiary means of carrying into effect what is enacted in the statute itself and will cover what is incidental to the execution of its specific provisions. But such a power will not support attempts to widen the purposes of the Act, to add new and different means of carrying them out or to depart from or vary the plan which the legislature has adopted to attain its ends.[43]

The basic review function is sometimes referred to as involving a three-step interpretive exercise: interpreting the enabling provision of the Act; interpreting the regulation for its scope and operation; and establishing whether the regulation is within the scope of the enabling provision in the Act.[44] This is expressly recognised by the courts as a matter of the supremacy of parliament over the executive.[45] That is, the court enforcing the legislation against administrative officials exercising those powers.

Judicial review of regulations is made more complex by the courts interpreting enabling provisions by reference to their purpose. That is a key feature of

[41] *Public Law Project* (n 19) [23].
[42] *Shanahan v Scott* (1957) 96 CLR 245.
[43] ibid 250.
[44] *McEldowney v Forde* [1971] AC 632, 658 (Lord Diplock); *South Australia v Tanner* (1989) 166 CLR 161, 173 (Brennan J).
[45] *Public Law Project* (n 19) [23].

administrative law in the UK and Australia generally,[46] and it plays an important role in judicial review of regulations. Reference to the purpose has been used to confirm the breadth of the enabling provisions and that the enabling provision supports harsh regulations. This is particularly apparent in war-related national security regulations.[47] Reference to the purpose of the Act has also been used to limit the scope of enabling provisions.[48] While this highlights that judicial review of regulations can have additional complexity, the rationale does not change. Drawing on the purposes of the Act is a familiar advanced form of enforcing the enabling Act against regulation-makers.

The rationale of judicial review of regulations shifts when courts employ the principle of legality methodology for testing regulations against the enabling statute. This interpretive methodology involves presuming that the delegation of regulation-making power does not extend to affecting fundamental rights or the general legal system unless the intention to do so is made very clear in the Act. It has been recently applied to regulations made according to Henry VIII clauses,[49] provisions restricting access to courts and tribunals,[50] regulations involving communications with lawyers,[51] and regulations that affect political communication.[52]

The modern justification for the principle of legality has been explained by the courts as being based on a particular understanding of parliamentary democracy. The most well-known explanation of this principle was expressed by Lord Hoffmann in *R v Secretary of State for the Home Department, ex p Simms*:

> Parliamentary sovereignty means that Parliament can, if it chooses, legislate contrary to fundamental principles of human rights …. The constraints upon its exercise by Parliament are ultimately political, not legal. But the principle of legality means that Parliament must squarely confront what it is doing and accept the political cost. Fundamental rights cannot be overridden by general or ambiguous words. This is because there is too great a risk that the full implications of their unqualified meaning may have passed unnoticed in the democratic process.[53]

[46] See, eg, *Padfield v Minister for Agriculture* [1968] AC 997, 1030 (Lord Reid) and *Water Conservation and Irrigation Commission (NSW) v Browning* (1947) 74 CLR 492, 504 (Dixon J).

[47] See, eg, *R (Zadig) v Halliday* [1917] AC 260, 269–70 (Lord Finlay LC); *Attorney-General for Canada v Hallet & Carey Ld.* [1952] AC 427, 449–50; *Adelaide Company of Jehovah's Witnesses v Commonwealth* (1943) 67 CLR 116, 138–39 (Latham CJ).

[48] *Hotel and Catering Industry Training Board v Automobile Proprietary Ltd* [1969] 1 WLR 697, 700–01 (Lord Reid); *Public Law Project* (n 19) [37]; *Brownwells Ltd v Ironmongers' Wages Board* (1950) 81 CLR 108, 119–20 (Latham CJ); *R v Toohey, ex p Northern Land Council* (1981) 151 CLR 170, 186–87 (Gibbs CJ).

[49] *Public Law Project* (n 19) [25]–[28].

[50] *R (UNISON) v Lord Chancellor* [2017] UKSC 51, [2020] AC 869 [65]–[85] (Lord Reed).

[51] *R v Secretary of State for the Home Department, ex p Leech* [1994] QB 198, 214–17.

[52] *R v Secretary of State for the Home Department, ex p Simms* [2000] 2 AC 115, 131–32 (Lord Hoffmann); *Attorney-General (SA) v Adelaide City Corporation* [2013] HCA 3, (2013) 249 CLR 1 [42]–[46] (French CJ); *Evans v New South Wales* [2008] FCAFC 130, (2008) 168 FCR 576 [68]–[79].

[53] *Simms* (n 52) 131.

A very similar statement was made in Australia by the High Court a few years earlier in *Coco v The Queen*:

> [C]urial insistence on a clear expression of an unmistakable and unambiguous intention to abrogate or curtail a fundamental freedom will enhance the parliamentary process by securing a greater measure of attention to the impact of legislative proposals on fundamental rights.[54]

These passages highlight that the terminology and purposes of the interpretive principle is the same in both countries, suggesting that it is a feature of judicial review of regulations in parliamentary democracies. Legal scholars regard these statements as being the modern rationale for an old interpretive technique.[55] As a matter of general statutory interpretation, the reasoning accepts parliamentary supremacy but raises concerns about its deliberation practices in regard to matters of fundamental rights, and the political and legal systems. Understood in that way, it is consistent with Lord Hewart's concerns regarding delegating regulation-making powers to administrative officials. For both Lord Hewart and the modern rationale of the principle of legality expressed in these passages, there is a risk of insufficient parliamentary deliberation. When the principle of legality is applied to broad delegations of regulation-making power, the concern is that administrative officials are purportedly enabled to regulate matters that are recognised by courts as being particularly sensitive: fundamental rights and the basic features of the political and legal system.

The principle of legality has particular relevance for regulation-making. It seems to distinguish technical matters relating to matters such as public health and product safety, that are regarded as appropriate for administrators, from subject matters with enhanced legal significance. The latter require clear and detailed authority to be provided by the enabling statute. If not, there is a risk that courts will determine that the statute does not authorise it to be made by regulations. The legislation needs to make it very clear that the delegation of regulation-making authority extends to such matters. This form of review can be justified for judicial review of regulation-making on the basis that making laws dealing with fundamental rights or affecting the legal and political structure, are not well suited to administrative officials. The usual, accepted function of regulation-making is limited to implementing statutory purposes and matters that have micro-policy significance.

The principle of legality is relatively uncontroversial when applied to fundamental rights and the structural aspects of political and legal systems. In these contexts it can be understood as having particular relevance for judicial review

[54] *Coco v The Queen* (1994) 179 CLR 427, 437–38.

[55] See, eg, B Lim, 'The Normativity of the Principle of Legality' (2013) 37 *Melbourne University Law Review* 372, 389–93; D Meagher, 'The Principle of Legality as Clear Statement Rule: Significance and Problems' (2014) 36 *Sydney Law Review* 413, 415–22; B Chen, 'The Principle of Legality: Issues of Rationale and Application' (2015) 41 *Monash University Law Review* 329, 336–39; JNE Varuhas, 'The Principle of Legality' (2020) 79 *Cambridge Law Journal* 578, 604.

of regulations to ensure that powers that affect such matters are clearly authorised. However, it becomes controversial when applied outside of those contexts. One example from Australia of applying beyond such boundaries occurred in *Brett Cattle Company Pty Ltd v Minister for Agriculture, Fisheries and Forestry*.[56] In that case the Federal Court treated 'the right to carry on business in one's own way within the law' as something to be protected by the principle of legality when reviewing a regulation dealing with export of live cattle to Indonesia.[57] The difficulty is that rather than being a matter of systemic significance to the political and legal system, the manner in which exporters carried out their business was at the core of the discretionary judgments to be made by administrative officials. Modern legislation is commonly designed to regulate the manner in which businesses operate, in particular in relation to public health, consumer safety and the environment. The principle of legality arguably provides a helpful function for modern judicial review of regulations by separating out matters that are particularly sensitive as requiring particular clarity in the statutory enabling provisions. However, in practice the line between sensitive and non-sensitive can be unclear and may not always be well understood.

This examination of judicial review of regulations to ensure that they are within the scope of the delegation of power highlights that the courts have a primary principle on which they carry out their task. The primary task is to enforce legislation made by Parliament. That simple, primary principle is supplemented by the courts' use of purposive reasoning when assessing the scope of the enabling provision in the relevant Act and the principle of legality. These are general features of administrative law in each country that have particular relevance for review of regulations. The principle of legality is a particularly vigilant form of judicial review when regulations deal with subject matters that the courts have traditionally found to be sensitive, for example access to the courts and political communication. The modern rationale of the principle of legality creates incentives for parliaments to deliberate on such matters and provide very clear authority for them to be dealt with by regulations. Understood in this way, both the primary principle and its supplementation by the principle of legality are directly within the parliamentary democracy model. Both recognise fundamental features of parliamentary democracy – parliamentary supremacy and its deliberative methodology.

C. Procedural Review

Judicial review of regulations on process grounds is quite different to judicial review of administrative decisions. When parliaments enact mandatory consultation provisions the courts enforce them against regulation-makers. However,

[56] *Brett Cattle Company Pty Ltd v Minister for Agriculture, Fisheries and Forestry* [2020] FCA 732, (2020) 274 FCR 337.

[57] ibid [292].

as we saw in chapter four, in the UK and Australia the general statutory provisions applying to regulation-making do not include enforceable consultation requirements. More interestingly, the courts in both countries have not developed general procedural fairness principles for regulation-making. However, there have been specific developments in the law of procedural fairness in the UK that support public consultation. This has developed in particular through application of the *Gunning* principles,[58] by which courts ensure that public consultation processes are conducted in a manner that enables fair participation. The *Gunning* principles are:

> First, that consultation must be at a time when proposals are still at a formative stage. Second, that the proposer must give sufficient reasons for any proposal to permit of intelligent consideration and response. Third, … that adequate time must be given for consideration and response and finally, fourth, that the product of consultation must be conscientiously taken into account in finalising any statutory proposals.[59]

The *Gunning* principles were confirmed by the UK Supreme Court in *R (Moseley) v Haringey London Borough Council*,[60] with Lord Wilson adding that public consultation reflects 'the democratic principle at the heart of our society'.[61]

Yet these consultation principles do not apply generally for regulation-making. They apply when there are consultation requirements required by the Act empowering the administrator,[62] when an administrator's policy, promise or practice raises a legitimate expectation that consultation will occur,[63] or if the administrator has employed a public consultation process notwithstanding there is no statutory requirement to do so.[64] The Court of Appeal confirmed that the consultation principles do not have general application in *R (BAPIO Action Limited) v Secretary of State for the Home Department*,[65] where it refused to extend them to the Immigration Rules in the absence of the factors set out above. This aspect of the *BAPIO* case was confirmed by the Supreme Court in *Moseley*.[66] That means that there are no general, procedural fairness-based consultation requirements for courts to apply in regard to regulations.

Australian procedural fairness law is more straightforward. It does not extend to regulations[67] or other kinds of government action that affect the public generally.[68] There is also no realistic possibility of such an extension when general

[58] *R v Brent London Borough Council; ex p Gunning* (1985) 84 LGR 168.
[59] ibid 189.
[60] *R (Moseley) v Haringey London Borough Council*, [2014] 1WLR 3947, 3957–58 [25].
[61] ibid 3957 [24].
[62] ibid 3951 [8].
[63] *R (Niazi) v Secretary of State* [2008] EWCA Civ 755, [29], [50]; *BAPIO* (n 19) [39]–[40].
[64] *R v North and East Devon Health Authority; ex p Coughlan* [2001] QB 213, 258 [108].
[65] *BAPIO* (n 19) [41]–[47].
[66] See *Moseley* (n 60) 3961 [35], [37]–[38]; *Bank Mellat v Her Majesty's Treasury (No 2)* [2014] AC 700, 781–82 [44]–[45].
[67] *Re Gosling* (1943) 43 SR (NSW) 312, 318.
[68] *Kioa v West* (1985) 159 CLR 550, 582, 584 (Mason J), 620 (Brennan J), 632 (Deane J).

regulation-making legislation in Australia imposes procedures for commencement, publication and tabling of regulations in Parliament, but deliberately stops short of establishing enforceable public consultation requirements.

Accordingly, enforceable public consultation duties are not imposed in Australia by general regulation-making legislation or common law. Consultation requirements are broader in the UK than Australia, but the *BAPIO* case makes clear that procedural fairness does not extend to a general duty to consult in regard to regulations.

D. Substantive Review

UK courts have developed substantive review in human rights cases to include consideration of the administrator's deliberative process. The courts have increasingly utilised deliberative forms of judicial review in cases involving challenges to regulations. Most interestingly, in the cases I examine, public consultation provisions did not control the regulation-making power exercised by administrators, indicating that this form of judicial review has developed in the absence of statutory public consultation requirements. By these indirect means regulations made by administrative officials are reviewed for their deliberative processes.

The clearest examples of these developments are UK human rights cases. In these cases, UK courts have examined whether interference with human rights are justified according to a proportionality analysis. The cases reveal that the courts commonly test whether such regulations are justified or not by examining consultation processes in great detail. Using proportionality review in this way must prompt administrators who make regulations that touch on human rights to conduct public consultation processes, even when they are not required by law, and to conduct them in a thorough manner. While the significance of review of deliberations relating to the making of primary legislation has been subjected to considerable scholarly analysis,[69] its significance for review of regulations has not.

In these cases, the courts test whether a regulation that prima facie interferes with a particular human right is nevertheless necessary in a democratic society by satisfying a proportionality test. The general principle in the human rights proportionality cases is that the court's focus has to be on the substance of the

[69] See HJ Hooper, 'The Use of Parliamentary Materials by Courts in Proportionality Judgments' in H Hooper, M Hunt and P Yowell (ed), *Parliament and Human Rights: Redressing the Democratic Deficit* (Oxford University Press, 2015) 363; A Kavanagh, 'Proportionality and Parliamentary Debates: Exploring Some Forbidden Territory' (2014) 34 *Oxford Journal of Legal Studies* 443; L Lazarus and N Simonsen, 'Judicial Review and Parliamentary Debate: Enriching the Doctrine of Due Deference' in M Hunt (ed), *Parliament and Human Rights: Redressing the Democratic Deficit* (Oxford University Press, 2015) 385.

decision rather than the administrator's process.[70] Nevertheless, in the *Denbigh High School* case Lord Bingham gave weight to the administrator's substantive judgment as there was evidence of their engagement with the relevant human right in the process leading to the making of the particular decision being challenged. The evidence of engagement was that the school had consulted with stakeholders in a manner that informed its decision.[71] In later cases Supreme Court judges have said they will 'give weight' to the judgment of those with responsibility for the particular decision due to their 'access to special sources of knowledge and advice'.[72] This is a form of deference to the judgment made by the administrator which, in practice, can involve assessment of the steps taken by the decision-maker to engage those most affected by the decision in their deliberations leading to the decision.

While reviewing Parliament's deliberative processes for making primary legislation in human rights cases raises constitutional concerns, such concerns do not generally arise for review of regulations. In recent cases, courts have trawled through public consultation and parliamentary materials to examine the justification for the regulation. The courts have also made clear that the fact that regulations have been laid in Parliament is not a sufficient reason for the courts to give weight to the regulation-maker; although they will when there has been 'active debate'.[73] This is consistent with deliberative forms of democratic legitimacy.

In some cases the courts' examination of public consultation and parliamentary materials has led to the conclusion that the deliberative process was thorough and that the challenged regulation was proportionate. Lord Reed's judgment in *R (SG) v Secretary of State for Work and Pensions*[74] is a good example of this. Lord Reed conducted an extensive review of the process leading to the regulation that was challenged.[75] His review included examining the public consultation process, debate of the regulations in Parliament, and the parliamentary debate on the broader legislative system of which the regulations were a part.[76] He referred to the policy underpinning the Act and the regulations as being 'subjected to detailed and vigorous scrutiny by both Houses of Parliament, over a period of more than 12 months'.[77]

[70] *R (Begum) v Headteacher and Governors of Denbigh High School* [2007] 1 AC 100, 116–17 [29]–[34] (Lord Bingham of Cornhill), 125–26 [68] (Lord Hoffmann); *Belfast City Council v Miss Behavin' Ltd* [2007] 1WLR 1420, 1430 [31].

[71] *Denbigh High School* (n 70) 108 [7]–[8], 117 [34].

[72] *Huang v Secretary of State for the Home Department* [2007] 2 AC 167, 185 [16]–[17] (Lord Bingham of Cornhill). See also *R (Aguilar Quila) v Secretary of State for the Home Department* [2012] 1 AC 621, 643–44 [46] (Lord Wilson); *Bank Mellat* (n 66) 771 [21]; *R (SG) v Secretary of State for Work and Pensions* [2015] 1WLR 1449, 1478 [92] (Lord Reed).

[73] *Huang* (n 72) 185–6 [17] (Lord Bingham of Cornhill); *R (SG) v Secretary of State for Work and Pensions* [2015] 1 WLR 1449, 1479 [95] (Lord Reed).

[74] *R (SG)* (n 72).

[75] ibid 1458–67 [16]–[56], 1478–79 [94]–[95].

[76] ibid 1458–59 [18], 1466 [49]–[51], 1467 [55].

[77] ibid 1461 [27].

The significance of Lord Reed's consideration of the process for making the challenged regulation was to show that it was subjected to a great deal of debate and criticism, and that adjustments had been made to it. He referred to giving 'due weight' to the assessments made by government and Parliament when concluding that the regulations were relevantly proportionate.[78] This form of legal reasoning is an example of a court regarding the deliberative process as relevant to review of the substance of the regulation. In the *SG* case the extensive deliberations provided support for upholding the challenged regulation. On the other hand, the administrator's judgment will not be given weight by the court when there is no evidence that the administrator has addressed their mind to the relevant rights raised in the review proceedings.[79]

Examination of public consultation and parliamentary materials can expose problems with the administrator's justification for their regulation. That can lead judges to conclude that the challenged regulation fails the proportionality test. In *Bank Mellat*, Lord Sumption set out the Government's justification for the challenged regulation in an explanatory statement, a written ministerial statement to Parliament, and correspondence provided by government officials with the claimant in the case.[80] He drew from these materials that the officials' reasoning was 'arbitrary and irrational', which led directly to his conclusion that the regulations were disproportionate and unlawful.[81] This reasoning highlights that the minister was required to justify their regulation by reference to the materials used in discussions by which it is made.[82]

The courts' examination of evidence of deliberation can therefore have different results: it can reveal that the particular issue was examined thoroughly by institutions with processes specifically designed for debate of moral, economic and policy issues (and thus provide a reason for deference); and it can also expose lack of consideration of the essential issue or flawed deliberation. The significance of these developments for judicial review of regulations more generally is that process-based issues can be reviewed by the courts by way of proportionality review. This goes some way to alleviating the lack of judicial review on procedural grounds due to there being no requirement for public consultation in the Statutory Instruments Act 1946, and in the rules of procedural fairness.

This is particularly clear in cases involving the Immigration Rules.[83] Recall that in section II.C above, we saw that the Court of Appeal in the *BAPIO* case would not extend common law procedural fairness requirements to the Immigration Rules. In the human rights cases however, the Supreme Court has thoroughly examined the deliberative processes used for making them. For example, in

[78] ibid 1479 [96].
[79] *R (Tigere) v Secretary of State for Business, Innovation and Skills* [2015] 1 WLR 3820 [32].
[80] *Bank Mellat* (n 66) 766–68 [12]–[13].
[81] [2014] AC 700, 773–74 [27]. See also *In re Brewster* [2017] 1 WLR 519, 532 [34]–[37], 540–41 [64]–[67].
[82] Note that the burden of justification is on the Minister: *Quila* (n 72) 643 [44].
[83] Authorised by the *Immigration Act 1971* (UK), s 3(2).

R (Aguilar Quila) v Secretary of State for the Home Department[84] the Supreme Court focused closely on the process leading to amendments to the Immigration Rules that were aimed at deterring forced marriages. This included a report prepared by academics, a House of Commons Committee report, a consultation process, and a ministerial statement evaluating submissions in the consultation process.[85] The Court's assessment of these procedural steps highlighted that the minister had failed to directly engage with questions concerning how the amendment would relate to the right to respect for private and family life.[86] The significance is that despite procedural fairness not generally being applicable for regulation-making, review by the courts on human rights grounds can nevertheless provide a basis for review of deliberative processes. This is especially the case in an area such as immigration that is susceptible to human rights challenges.

This form of reasoning is not limited in the United Kingdom to human rights cases. It can also arise in traditional forms of judicial review such as irrationality review.[87] Proportionality review is much less developed in Australia where there is no judicially enforceable Commonwealth human rights legislation.[88] While the unreasonableness ground of judicial review has evolved in recent years in Australia to accept forms of proportionality review,[89] it is not apparent that it includes deliberative review as is apparent in the UK regulations cases.

The UK cases indicate that the courts can use proportionality review to test the deliberative processes conducted in regulation-making. The lack of general statutory and common law procedural rules that provide the framework for deliberative administrative decision-making reduces in significance due to the courts seeking in proportionality review of regulations evidence of justification of the primary judgments administrators make and their engagement with stakeholders. The approach taken to proportionality review in the United Kingdom creates incentives for administrators to not only conduct deliberative processes but to do so in a thorough manner.

[84] *Quila* (n 72).

[85] ibid 636–39 [22]–[29].

[86] ibid 648 [58].

[87] See, eg, *R (London Criminal Courts Solicitors' Association) v Lord Chancellor* [2015] EWCA Civ 230, [2016] 3 All ER 296 [102]–[105]; *R (Ben Hoare Bell Solicitors) v Lord Chancellor* [2015] 1 WLR 4175, 4186 [31], 4189–95 [40]–[62]; C Sheldon QC, 'Consultation: Revisiting the Basic Principles' [2012] *Judicial Review* 152, 159.

[88] The relevant Commonwealth legislation, the *Human Rights (Parliamentary Scrutiny) Act 2011* (Cth), establishes a parliamentary committee to scrutinise legislation on human rights grounds. It provides no role for the courts.

[89] *Minister for Immigration and Citizenship v Li* (2013) 249 CLR 332, 352 [30] (French CJ); 364 [68], 366 [73]–[74] (Hayne, Kiefel and Bell JJ]); *Attorney-General (SA)* (n 52) [56] (French CJ), [117] (Hayne J), [199] (Crennan and Kiefel JJ).

E. Restrictions, Timing and Remedies

We saw in section I that John Willis had doubts about judicial review as a safeguard on regulation-making due to its sporadic nature and the variability of the judges' interpretation of Acts. He was therefore sympathetic to restrictions on judicial review. However, the Donoughmore Committee regarded general exclusions of judicial review to be in conflict with the rule of law,[90] but that time limits of between three and six months were appropriate when the subject matter of the regulation, such as when they relate to property or marriage, raises a particular need for finality.[91]

These are important concerns, and two points can be made about them. Willis's concern leads to a more general point: that judicial review is not a sufficient safeguard. The 1930 Senate Committee made the same point. Part of its reason for recommending the establishment of a standing committee to scrutinise regulations was that judicial review is expensive and is delayed.[92] The more specific issue raised in the 1930s debates is that judicial review can raise difficulties when the challenged regulation that is determined to be invalid by the courts has been relied on by individuals and businesses. There is an obvious inconvenience and potential disruption when regulations that have been relied on are determined to have been made without statutory authority, are invalid and are quashed retrospectively. The Donoughmore Committee's recommendation to alleviate such disruption was that a time limit on bringing judicial review proceedings can be appropriate.

The concerns raised by the Donoughmore Committee continue to be relevant. They are now mitigated by a number of techniques. There is a three-month time limit in the Civil Procedure Rules on bringing judicial review.[93] This provision may help to reduce the concern regarding the impact on non-parties, but it is not a complete solution. However even if applications are made within the three-month period, litigation, judgment writing and, potentially, appeals can extend the time in which a potentially invalid regulation remains operative. The courts have developed remedies that are more limited than retrospective quashing, such as by granting declarations that there has been a particular failure by the Government,[94] that particular sections of a regulation are invalid,[95] and reading

[90] Donoughmore Committee Report (n 14) 40–41, 61.

[91] ibid 62.

[92] Senate, *Report from the Senate Select Committee Advising on Establishing Standing Committees*, Parliament of Australia (Report, April 1930) x.

[93] CPR 54.5(1).

[94] See, eg, *R (Hurley) v Secretary of State for Business, Innovation and Skills* [2012] EWHC 201 (Admin) [99]–[100]; *Tigere* (n 79) [48]–[49]; *Re Gallagher* [2019] UKSC 3; [2020] AC 185 [66]. See also *Project Blue Sky v Australian Broadcasting Authority* [1998] HCA 28, (1998) 194 CLR 355 [97]–[100].

[95] See, eg, *Evans* (n 52) [83], [88]; *R (Rights of Women) v Lord Chancellor* [2016] EWCACiv 91, [2016] 1 WLR 2543, [51].

down provisions of regulations to confirm their validity.[96] It is also possible for courts to refuse to grant a remedy on the basis of inconvenience to others.[97]

The same concerns have been raised by judges and in government reports. Sir John Laws suggested in an article that such disruption could be mitigated by enabling applicants and government officials to bring cases prior to regulations commencing in order to test that they are within power and by the court, if necessary, issuing an 'advisory declaration'.[98] The issue also arose in the Faulks Committee's review of judicial review in 2021.[99] The Committee regarded a case in which the High Court declined to suspend orders to quash a regulation[100] as being unsatisfactory. The Committee recommended that courts be empowered to grant 'suspended quashing orders'.[101] The Government's response to the Committee was to suggest a more radical approach to remedies that would require courts to quash government actions, such as regulations, on a prospective basis only.[102] However, the amendments that were ultimately made provide for courts to determine whether quashing orders be suspended or to limit the retrospectivity of a quashing order.[103]

This is not the place to analyse these contributions. My concern is how judicial review fits into the safeguards for regulation-making. The relevance of the recent analysis of remedies for judicial of regulations is that they raise practical concerns that are consistent with the concerns raised by both Willis and the Donoughmore Committee. The more recent analysis and recommendations indicate the timing of judicial review can involve practical difficulties that are hard to resolve. They highlight the recurring nature of the concerns in relation to operationalising the rule of law and its potential impacts in practice.

III. Conclusions

Judicial review of regulations has a traditional function and an additional potential function. The traditional function is to enforce parliamentary laws. In this chapter I have shown that key features of this function remain in operation and that there have been some developments. The first is by reference to the principle of legality so that regulations that restrict fundamental rights or affect political and

[96] See, eg, *Evans* (n 52) [84].

[97] Senior Courts Act 1981 (UK), s 31(6).

[98] J Laws, 'Judicial Remedies and the Constitution' (1994) 57 *Modern Law Review* 213, 217–18. *cf* PC, 'The Constitutional Basis of Judicial Remedies in Public Law' in P Leyland and T Woods (eds), *Administrative Law Facing the Future: Old Constraints and New Horizons* (Blackstone Press Ltd, 1997) 242, 267–68.

[99] Faulks Committee, 'The Independent Review of Administrative Law' (March 2021).

[100] *Hurley* (n 94).

[101] n 99 paras 3.53–3.54.

[102] Ministry of Justice, 'Judicial Review Reform: The Government Response to the Independent Review of Administrative Law' (March 2021) para 60.

[103] Senior Courts Act 1981 (UK), s 29A(1).

legal structures require clear statutory authority. The rationale for this approach to judicial review is to enhance parliamentary deliberation on sensitive subject matters. This is an interesting and important development. It operates clearly within the framework of parliamentary democracy – parliaments are to play their traditional deliberative role for laws dealing with these fundamental matters. The second are indications of judicial review shifting to overseeing forms of administrative deliberation. This is not directly but through the courts managing the scope of substantive judicial review according to the HRA 1998.

The more general conclusion is that Willis's and the 1930 Senate Committee's concerns remain. Judicial review may be a necessary safeguard for rule of law purposes, but its primary weakness is its dependence on applicants. Once engaged, it is a relatively intense form of review on the legal authorisation of the regulation (protecting parliament's role) and potentially reinforcing administrative forms of deliberation. However, it is not a systemic check. Analysing judicial review as one of three safeguards on regulation-making highlights the need recognised in the 1930s reform period for multiple safeguards on regulation-making. Parliamentary scrutiny of bills and regulations is intended to be the primary systemic check and public consultation, and other forms of administrative deliberation, enable stakeholders to influence and contribute to the design and drafting of regulations. Judicial review contributes to the democratic legitimacy of regulations, but it is important to recognise its limitations.

As this is the final chapter of this part of the book, it is worth summarising how the main argument has been substantiated in chapters two to five. The 1930s debates raised concerns about delegation of law-making powers and increases in the use of those powers in the UK and Australia. The immediate result of those debates was to recognise the need for the three safeguards: parliamentary scrutiny; public consultation; and judicial review. Parliamentary scrutiny was the primary addition to the safeguards in the twentieth century. It was a crucial addition due to it providing for a systemic check. However, it is also recognised as being one of three primary safeguards and that each of them is necessary. We have also seen that there has been much debate over the inclusion and exclusion, at least as an enforceable legal requirement, of particular safeguards. We have also seen each safeguard's particular inherent weaknesses. However, we should also recognise their individual contributions to democratic legitimacy of regulations and that collectively they add up to a sufficient system.

PART II

Circumventing and Minimising the Safeguards

6

Excluding Parliamentary Scrutiny

In this part of the book, I move from examining the contributions of the three main safeguards to democratic legitimacy, to examining exceptions to these safeguards. My primary focus is on excluding regulations, either wholly or partially, from exposure to parliamentary scrutiny and potential veto. Some of the techniques examined in this part of the book are complex and often hidden under administrative technicality. Nevertheless, they can be regarded as forms of executive aggrandisement that raise fundamental questions about the democratic legitimacy of regulations. The primary systemic measures for connecting administrative law-making to parliamentary deliberation are removed or limited. When parliamentary scrutiny is removed, the democratic legitimacy of regulations is left to consultation, or similar processes, if they have occurred, and judicial review, a non-systemic measure designed to ensure regulations are authorised and have some degree of rationality.

Some of the exemptions examined in this chapter and chapters seven to nine were known in the 1920s and 1930s, the main period in which modern systemic safeguards were debated and designed. For example, it was recognised that Henry VIII clauses, an exception to the norm that parliaments enact and amend primary legislation, risked the integrity of legislation-making in parliamentary systems and should be permitted only in limited circumstances. However, the issues that are addressed in the following chapters were generally not engaged with any detail in the 1930s debates. Additional practices have arisen which result in parliamentary scrutiny being circumvented.

The themes addressed in this part are significant for the overall arguments made in the book. They address a different general issue from the primary concerns arising in the 1930s debates. At the forefront of those debates were parliamentary attempts to exclude judicial review.[1] The current issues focus on parliamentary democracy and in particular the increased parliamentary capacity to exercise its review powers through scrutiny committees in the decades after the 1930s debates. I will highlight that the modern attempts to exclude checks have involved a shift of focus from measures to exclude the courts to measures to

[1] Lord Hewart of Bury, *The New Despotism* (Ernest Benn Ltd, 1929) 64–80; J Willis, *The Parliamentary Powers of English Government Departments* (Harvard University Press, 1933) ch 3; Committee on Ministers' Powers, Report (London, 1932) ('Donoughmore Committee Report') 40–41.

exclude or minimise parliamentary scrutiny. This suggests that the political and administrative officials instructing legislative drafters do not see the democratic checks in the manner commonly expressed by public lawyers, ie as a minimal, tokenistic form of review.[2]

In this chapter, I address practices in which regulations are allowed to avoid parliamentary scrutiny and veto. This is clearly an exception to the norms developed for ensuring that parliaments have scrutiny powers and the capacity to effectively exercise them. Exceptions to this squarely raise legitimacy questions for regulations made without being exposed to systemic parliamentary review. While it was largely assumed in the 1930s debates that regulations are subject to parliamentary review according to negative or affirmative resolution processes, excluding parliamentary review is a fundamental exception to the safeguards on regulation-making and raises questions about democratic legitimacy of regulations. The analysis in this chapter highlights that it should now be recognised as a problem.

There are a number of layers to the problem. The first is the most important: that lack of parliamentary veto powers diminishes the democratic supporting structure for regulations. Lack of parliamentary veto means that parliamentary scrutiny may be generally avoided or, if parliamentary scrutiny committees can review these regulations, it is without the threat of veto. That has particular practical consequences. Parliamentary scrutiny committees identify a range of potential problems, including drafting errors and concerns about whether regulations are authorised. The committees provide an independent check on regulations that bring to light problems that may not have been seen or understood by administrative officials during the drafting of the regulation. Limiting parliament's powers over regulations can mean that such problems are not picked up and corrected.

The second layer is the difficulty of developing principles for identifying rule-like government action that should be subject to parliamentary veto powers and scrutiny. That engages a more fundamental concern regarding the characteristics of legislative laws. Government actions with the characteristics of legislative law should be subject to parliamentary oversight. Given the range of governmental actions; that is, decisions, declarations, orders, bylaws and regulations, it would be expected that some principles would have developed by now as to the characteristics that give particular actions legislative characteristics and are therefore suited to parliamentary control. However, this remains unclear and underdeveloped.

The third layer is the more general relationship between the executive and Parliament. As an exemption from the most systemic of the three safeguards, it is important for it to be contained and understood as justifiable only on principled grounds. Without that, there is a risk that executive officials' interests in removing

[2] See ch 3.

the general checks become more widespread and, at worst, that the exception swallows the norm. The decisions for removal of parliamentary scrutiny need particular monitoring to ensure that they can be plausibly justified.

This chapter examines these problems. I will show that no specific norms were generated in the 1930s debates to address them. I will then examine the nature and extent of the legislative practices that enable avoiding parliamentary scrutiny and veto. Finally, I will examine potential principles that could be developed for this aspect of regulation-making to influence legal developments and administration of current systems.

I. Parliamentary Veto Powers in the 1930s Debates

Parliamentary veto powers over regulations had been included in legislation that delegates regulation-making powers for decades prior to the 1930s debates.[3] However, they were given minimal attention in those debates. Lord Hewart referred to parliamentary powers being likely to make administrative officials more careful than would the case if such provisions are not included.[4] His main concern was when there are no powers provided for parliamentary control.[5] Willis also did not address parliamentary powers and procedures in any detail. His discussion of Parliament's review role, expressed at a high level of generality, indicate his view that his concern was with their variety and the 'haphazard' drafting of the provisions.[6] The Donoughmore Committee recognised the role of such provisions for providing a parliamentary safeguard, but raised its concern that there was no parliamentary procedure ensuring scrutiny.[7] It recommended a standardised procedure for parliamentary consideration of its annulment powers.[8]

Parliamentary veto powers remained largely uncontroversial in the processes for making the current general Acts – the Statutory Instruments Act 1946 and the Legislation Act 2003 (Cth). The parliamentary debates for the Statutory Instruments Act 1946 were largely based on the assumption that parliamentary powers were necessary. The focus was instead on procedural details such as the time periods in which parliament can take action and public consultation provisions.[9] The concern raised in the committee report prompting the changes to the regulation-making framework also raised the concern that there were no

[3] See C Carr, *Delegated Legislation* (Cambridge University Press, 1921) 38–41.
[4] Hewart (n 1) 89–90.
[5] ibid 94–95.
[6] Willis (n 1) 186–87. See also Carr (n 3) 40–41.
[7] Donoughmore Committee Report (n 1) 41–44, 63.
[8] ibid Recommendation XII, 67.
[9] See, Select Committee on Statutory Rules and Orders, *Special Report* (HC, 31 October 1944) 1031; HC Deb Vol 415 col 1097 (6 November 1945); HL Deb Vol 139 col 10 29 January 1946).

principles for deciding between parliamentary veto by negative or affirmative resolutions,[10] but this was deliberately not addressed in the bill that became the Statutory Instruments Act 1946. The explanation provided by the Government was that it was best dealt with in legislation delegating regulation-making powers.[11]

While a standardised procedure has not been implemented in the UK, such a procedure was established in Australia by section 10 of the Acts Interpretation Act 1904 (Cth). It was a negative resolution procedure by which regulations commence when published in the *Gazette*, and when tabled in Parliament either house had 15 sitting days to disallow it. The parliamentary debates for this Act indicate that it was explained as standardising then current practice.[12] The parliamentary veto powers were discussed in more detail for the current Legislation Act 2003. The report of the Administrative Review Council prompting the reforms leading to its enactment sought to establish a general system for making, publishing and parliamentary scrutiny of regulations.[13] That led the Council to consider general principles for determining the governmental action that should be classified as 'legislative instruments' that would be caught by the system for controlling the making and scrutiny of regulations.[14] The Council's recommendation was that all instruments made under delegated powers that had a legislative character would be caught unless they were specifically identified as exempted from the system.[15] This framework was implemented in the Legislation Act 2003 (Cth). It provides another example of Australia relying more heavily on generally applicable legislation for controlling regulation-making but with flexibility, in this case by providing a formal process for making exemptions to the general system.

The important point to draw from this brief historical exposition is that direct parliamentary control of regulations is a long-established, primary feature of the system. It has been included in legislation in different ways in the two countries and is generally accepted as being fundamental. The debates in the reform periods focus on regulating parliamentary review rather than whether parliamentary review is necessary or worthwhile. This indicates that it is beyond debate that parliamentary veto powers are a fundamental feature of parliamentary democracies, at least in the UK and Australia. In terms of comparative administrative law, this feature of regulation-making processes sets the UK and Australia apart from at least the United States, where Congressional review plays a very limited role.[16]

[10] Select Committee on Statutory Rules and Orders, *Special Report* (HC, 31 October 1944) 1031, para 4.

[11] HC Deb Vol 415 col 1099.(6 November 1945).

[12] Commonwealth, *Parliamentary Debates*, House of Representatives, 14 April 1904, 1037; Commonwealth, *Parliamentary Debates*, Senate, 16 March 1904, 547–48.

[13] Administrative Review Council, *Rule Making by Commonwealth Agencies* (Report No 35, 1992) para 1.29.

[14] ibid para 3.2–3.10.

[15] ibid para 3.17.

[16] See A Edgar, 'The Westminster Model in Comparative Administrative Law: Incentives for Controls on Regulation-Making' (2019) 38 *University of Tasmania Law Review* 47, 58.

The lack of direct engagement with the parliamentary veto powers in the 1930s period has contributed to the lack of norms emerging in regard to two relevant aspects of regulation-making systems. The first is what kinds of government action should be recognised to be regulations. Statutes grant powers to government officials to do many kinds of action. Which ones should be treated as regulations and therefore subject to parliamentary scrutiny and veto powers? The second is that for the government actions that are recognised as regulations, what are the circumstances in which it would be acceptable to determine that parliaments should have no scrutiny and veto role?

While these questions were not subject to attention in the 1930s debates, concerns have been raised more recently in both the UK and Australia.

II. Nature and Extent of the Problem

A. United Kingdom

It is commonly stated that many regulations are made without being subject to parliamentary oversight. For example, the UK Government's Cabinet Manual states that 'Much secondary legislation is made without being subject to any Parliamentary proceedings; it is simply approved and signed by the relevant minister'.[17] The same point has been made by the Hansard Society's report into delegated legislation except that its terminology was 'the majority' rather than 'much'.[18] This point is not new. Cecil Carr stated in 1955 that 'Perhaps more than half the instruments registered in the year (including in particular the large contingent of orders having only local application) are not required to be laid at all'.[19]

It is concerning if it is true that many regulations are made each year without being subject to parliamentary scrutiny and potential veto. The concern is that such regulations are defined in the enabling Act as 'statutory instruments' but the enabling provision will not include a parliamentary procedure.[20] Regulations made according to such powers are included in the UK Legislation database but without systemic scrutiny by Parliament. The exception from parliamentary scrutiny clashes, at least in a prima facie sense, with the democratic norms developed in the 1930s debates. It will be an even deeper clash if there is also no consultation requirement. Accordingly, statutory instruments not subject to parliamentary review can be recognised as an ongoing tension rather than a recently developed problem. They prompt questions as to whether other forms of administrative rules, commonly

[17] UK Government, 'Cabinet Manual' (October 2011) [5.28].

[18] R Fox and J Blackwell, *The Devil is in the Detail: Parliament and Delegated Legislation* (Hansard Society, 2014) 74.

[19] C Carr, 'Parliamentary Supervision in Britain' (1955) 30 *New York University Law Review* 1045, 1048.

[20] Note that 'statutory instruments' are defined in the Statutory Instruments Act 1946 as being determined by the enabling Act.

referred to as 'guidance' in the UK, are given legal effect without any parliamentary review. Both forms of administratively made rules will be examined in this part.

There is no substantive guidance on the kinds of statutory instruments that are appropriately exempted from parliamentary scrutiny. The Cabinet Office's 'Guide to Making Legislation' simply states 'Some instruments are not even laid before Parliament. This is commonly the case with commencement orders or regulations'.[21] The House of Lords Constitution Committee's report on the delegation of power also recognised the provisions in statutes that do not provide scrutiny procedure but did not address norms for when it is appropriate or not.[22] The most one can find is in guidance provided by the House of Lords Delegated Powers Committee that enabling provisions that do not provide for a parliamentary procedure require justification.[23]

This is particularly concerning when such a large proportion of statutory instruments are not subject to parliamentary review. The House of Lords Delegated Powers and Regulatory Reform Committee reported in 2016 that approximately 2,200 of 3,250 statutory instruments made per year are not subject to parliamentary procedures.[24] The Committee referred to this category as a 'complete' form of delegation by which a 'Minister can make law on his own authority' and gave as examples the closing of roads and commencement orders. The number of statutory instruments that are not subject to parliamentary scrutiny since then can be seen in the following table.

Table 6.1 Statutory instruments laid and not laid in UK Parliament

Year	Statutory instruments laid in Parliament[25]	Statutory instruments not laid in Parliament[26]	Total statutory instruments[27]
2015	950	1,107	2,057
2016	620	623	1,243
2017	650	639	1,289

(continued)

[21] (July 2017) 140.

[22] Select Committee on the Constitution, *The Legislative Process: The Delegation of Powers* (2017–19, HL Paper 225) 25.

[23] Delegated Powers and Regulatory Reform Committee, *Guidance for Departments on the Role and Requirements of the Committee* (July 2014) 9–10.

[24] Lords Delegated Powers and Regulatory Reform Committee, *Special Report: Response to the Strathclyde Review* (2015–16, HL Paper 119) App C. See also J King, 'The Province of Delegated Legislation' in E Fisher, J King and AL Young, *The Foundations and Future of Public Law* (Oxford University Press, 2020) 145, 153.

[25] These figures were drawn from the Lords Secondary Legislation Scrutiny Committee 'Work of the Committee' reports in 2015–16, 2017–19 and 2019–21. They are approximate due to the source information being provided in charts. More precise figures are included in House of Commons sessional returns reports but provided per session rather than by year.

[26] The numbers in the column were calculated by subtracting the number of laid statutory instruments each year from the total of statutory instruments made in each year.

[27] The numbers in this column were taken from the UK Legislation site and checked, when available, against V Apostolova, 'Acts and Statutory Instruments: the Volume of UK legislation 1950 to 2016' (Commons Library Briefing Paper CBP 7438, 21 April 2017) 7.

Table 6.1 ***(Continued)***

Year	Statutory instruments laid in Parliament	Statutory instruments not laid in Parliament	Total statutory instruments
2018	859	529	1,387
2019	604	806	1,410
2020	926	691	1,617
Average	**768 (51.2%)**	**732 (48.8%)**	**1,500**

The UK Legislation website confirms that many statutory instruments that are not subject to tabling in Parliament often have local significance[28] or provide for commencements.[29] There are also statutory instruments that are included in the overall total of UK statutory instruments but are Welsh instruments and are laid before the Senedd Cymru rather than the UK Parliament.[30] These are apparently common forms of statutory instruments not subject to scrutiny by the UK Parliament, but seem to have been accepted as unproblematic. It may be the case that a full review of the instruments not subject to parliamentary review would reveal some problematic examples.

Concerns have arisen when statutes provide for administrative guidance to have legal effect without parliamentary review. The Delegated Powers and Regulatory Reform Committee has raised concerns about provisions of bills that give administrative guidance or administrative codes of practice legal effectiveness without making them statutory instruments or providing for a parliamentary procedure.[31] For example, the Committee raised concerns in regard to four provisions of the Police, Crime, Sentencing and Courts Bill that provided for making guidance and for that guidance to be a mandatory consideration in the exercise of discretionary powers.[32] The justification provided was that the guidance was to be a consideration rather than a discrete standard. This was not accepted by the Committee which emphasised that it had raised this concern in previous reports.[33] It regarded it as influencing the exercise of statutory powers both administratively and by the courts. The justification that some of the guidance

[28] See, eg, Air Navigation (Restriction of Flying) (Windsor Castle) (Restricted Area EG R156) Regulations 2021.

[29] See, eg, Financial Services Act 2021 (Commencement No 3) Regulations 2021; Digital Economy Act 2017 (Commencement No 8) Regulations 2021.

[30] See, eg, Senedd Cymru (Representation of the People) (Amendment) Order 2021; Trade in Animals and Related Products (Wales) (Amendment) (EU Exit) (No 3) Regulations 2021).

[31] Delegated Powers and Regulatory Reform Committee, *Democracy Denied? The Urgent Need to Rebalance power between Parliament and the Executive* (HL 2021–22, 106) paras 91–100. See also Secondary Legislation Scrutiny Committee, *Government by Diktat: A Call to Return Power to Parliament* (HL 2021–22, 105) paras 47–59.

[32] Delegated Powers and Regulatory Reform Committee, *Police, Crime, Sentencing and Courts Bill; Public Service Pensions and Judicial Offices Bill* (2020–21 HL 65) 3–4.

[33] ibid 4.

would be subject to consultation was also not accepted by the Committee, which stated that consultation 'cannot be a reason for denying Parliament any scrutiny role'.[34] The Committee concluded that some of the guidance referred to in the bill should be subject to the negative procedure and others should be subject to the affirmative procedure.

The Delegated Powers and Regulatory Reform Committee's scrutiny of statutory provisions enabling the making of such guidance highlights that there are forms of delegation of rule-making powers beyond statutory instruments. Although guidance could be seen as not having the kind of legal effect that regulations generally have (that is, a legal norm that must be complied with by members of the public), they have an effect that is important to recognise. Guidance directs the general exercise of discretionary powers to be exercised in ways that may have great significance for members of the public. It is overly formalistic to refer to it as a guide for administrative officials exercising discretionary powers. The consideration of the guidance by those officials effects the members of the public who are subject to the decisions. As recognised by the Delegated Powers and Regulatory Reform Committee, the guidance will generally control the exercise of the power in practice and will only not be applied when there are cogent reasons that support an exception.[35] We will come back to the over-reliance on guidance in chapter nine on administrative law-making in emergency periods.

The problem that becomes apparent when reviewing the Government's guidance documents such as the Cabinet Manual and the Delegated Powers and Regulatory Reform Committee's guidance material, is that there is a lack of principles developed as to when statutory instruments and other administrative rules with legal effect are appropriately not subject to parliamentary scrutiny. The more specific problem that we have seen in regard to regulations not subject to parliamentary scrutiny is with providing legal effect to guidance. Bills are drafted to provide for administrative officials to make a form of law that will affect members of the public without that law being subject to parliamentary review. This is a similar concern to that raised in the 1930s debates: empowering law-making by administrative officials without parliamentary scrutiny.

B. Australia

Very similar problems arise in Australia. Administrative officials commonly seek to make regulations exempted from parliamentary scrutiny. The key difference is that the statutory scheme controlling regulation-making processes, as seen in chapter three, have a general, trans-substantive effect. This results in a different focus in relation to how the exceptions, legislative instruments not subject to parliamentary scrutiny, are managed.

[34] ibid 5.
[35] ibid 4.

The Legislation Act 2003 includes a definition of 'legislative instruments', which is similar to the UK approach in that it includes instruments defined as such by their enabling Act. However the definition extends to a functional understanding of regulations by defining them as instruments with provisions that determine or alter the content of the law and have direct or indirect effects on rights, privileges or interests.[36] This Act then provides generally for legislative instruments to be tabled in the Commonwealth Parliament and to be subject to disallowance by either house of Parliament.[37] These provisions set out the general position for the status, and parliamentary scrutiny, of Commonwealth regulations.

The important question becomes how exceptions to parliamentary scrutiny and veto are managed. The Legislation Act expressly provides for exemptions from disallowance to be stated in an enabling Act or by regulations.[38] The Government has exercised the power to make regulations, the Legislation (Exemptions and Other Matters) Regulations 2015. These regulations exempt particular classes of legislative instruments and legislative instruments made under particular primary Acts from disallowance.[39]

In contrast to the UK approach to providing for parliamentary scrutiny, the Australian statutory provisions are based on some relatively clear general norms defining legislative instruments. The Legislation Act is clear that regulations that determine the content of law are legislative instruments and are generally subject to parliamentary scrutiny. The exemptions are also relatively transparent – particularly when included in the Legislation (Exemptions and Other Matters) Regulations 2015. That regulation provides a repository for instruments that are exempted from the status of legislative instruments[40] and exempted from the disallowance provisions.[41] It is not however the only place in which regulations are exempted from parliamentary review. Primary Acts can include exemptions from parliamentary scrutiny in the provisions granting powers to make regulations.[42]

The statistics for legislative instruments made per year highlight that there are a smaller number of legislative instruments that are exempt from parliamentary scrutiny than in the UK.[43]

[36] Legislation Act 2003 (Cth), s 8(4).
[37] ibid ss 38, 42.
[38] ibid s 44.
[39] Legislation (Exemptions and Other Matters) Regulations 2015, ss 9–10. At the time of writing (June 2023) these provisions exempt legislative instruments made under 33 Acts.
[40] ibid ss 6–7.
[41] ibid ss 9–10.
[42] See, eg, Competition and Consumer Act 2010 (Cth), s 44AH(3)); Migration Act 1958 (Cth), s 9A(7).
[43] Statistics sourced from the Senate Standing Committee for the Scrutiny of Delegated Legislation, *Annual Report 2020* (23 June 2020) 10 Table 1: Instruments exempt from disallowance 2013–2020.

Table 6.2 Disallowable and non-disallowable legislative instruments in Australia

	Disallowable legislative instruments	Legislative instruments exempt from disallowance	Total legislative instruments
2015	1,840	361 (16.4%)	2,201
2016	1,698	347 (17%)	2,045
2017	1,436	265 (15.6%)	1,701
2018	1,630	256 (13.6%)	1,886
2019	1,345	330 (19.7%)	1,675
2020	1,415	299 (17.4%)	1,715
Averages	**1,560 (83.5%)**	**310 (16.5%)**	**1,870**

While the proportion of non-disallowable instruments made by Commonwealth government departments and agencies is less than the equivalent in the UK, the concerns about non-disallowable regulations have been expressed more directly in Australia. A recent inquiry by the Senate Standing Committee for the Scrutiny of Delegated Legislation regarded the amount of non-disallowable instruments made per year as concerning. It referred to the amount of non-disallowable regulations potentially undermining Parliament's constitutional role in regard to legislating.[44] This report prompted a change to Senate Standing Orders to enable the Committee to consider non-disallowable instruments and to consider the appropriateness of exemptions applying to particular instruments.[45]

The greatest concern is when regulations not subject to parliamentary veto powers have broad social and economic significance. The most significant example of such non-disallowable regulations are the regulations made in periods of emergency. The provisions in the Biosecurity Act 2015 (Cth) that enable 'human biosecurity emergency' regulations were heavily relied on during the COVID-19 pandemic period.[46] They will be examined in chapter nine as they are expressly designed for emergencies. There are also regulations that are not subject to parliamentary veto and do not have emergency significance. A form of Commonwealth regulation referred to as 'Advances to the finance minister' is a good example of non-disallowable regulations. The Advances are regulations made under the annual Appropriation Acts to authorise expenditure where there is an urgent need, and the amounts were not included in the Appropriation Acts due to an error or due to the particular expenditure being previously 'unforeseen'.[47]

The non-disallowable nature of the Advances was criticised in the Senate Standing Committee for the Scrutiny of Delegated Legislation inquiry into exemptions

[44] ibid 99–100.
[45] ibid Recommendation 10 p 12. Senate Standing Order 23(4A).
[46] Biosecurity Act 2015 (Cth), ss 476 and 477.
[47] See, eg Appropriation Act (No 1) 2020–2021 (Cth), s 10(1). The Advances are legislative instruments not subject to disallowance: Appropriation Act (No 1) 2020–2021 (Cth), s 10(4).

from disallowance.[48] Particular uses of the power to make Advances have also been politically and legally controversial, which indicates that parliamentary review and veto powers are necessary and appropriate for them.

For example, the Commonwealth Government's use of these provisions for funding a postal survey on same-sex marriage in 2016 was particularly controversial. The Government's initial plan of having a formal plebiscite was abandoned due to the bill to authorise it being defeated in the Senate.[49] The Government's fall-back option was an informal postal survey funded by an Advance to the Finance Minister. The Advance for the postal survey was also controversial. Politically, it meant that the debate continued as to whether same-sex marriage reform should be dealt with through a form of public vote notwithstanding that Parliament had previously expressed its will by not supporting an equivalent plebiscite. And legally there were concerns that the Advance was not an authorised exercise of the enabling power in the Appropriation Act (No 1) 2017–2018 (Cth). A case was brought in the High Court challenging it, but was unsuccessful.[50] The same-sex marriage debate highlights that provisions that may initially seem to have primarily administrative significance, can become central to national political debates. The non-disallowable nature of the Advance enabled the Government of the time to achieve its objective of holding a form of public vote against the clear decision of the Parliament.

The concerns in the United Kingdom regarding giving guidance legal effect have also arisen in Australia. As in the UK, Australian government departments seek to give documents that are not legislative instruments legal status; however, the concerns are raised in regard to a different method, a technique referred to as 'incorporation by reference'. The reference to the guidance in the regulations gives the guidance legal status. This technique is examined in chapter seven.

Accordingly, similar dynamics can be seen in each country. Government agencies seek powers to make laws without parliamentary scrutiny. These similarities indicate that administrative officials are drawn to minimising scrutiny of their work. The differences relate to the mechanisms that are used. It is useful for administrative lawyers with interests in the accountability mechanisms applying to government officials to appreciate the techniques that administrators are drawn to achieve their goals.

III. Principles for Determining Exemptions from Parliamentary Scrutiny

In section II.A we saw that the House of Lords Delegated Powers and Regulatory Reform Committee has not elaborated general principles for identifying the

[48] Senate Standing Committee for the Scrutiny of Delegated Legislation (n 43) 58–61.
[49] Commonwealth, *Parliamentary Debates*, Senate, 7 November 2016, 2058.
[50] *Wilkie v Commonwealth* (2017) 263 CLR 487.

statutory instruments that may appropriately be exempted from parliamentary scrutiny. The Committee's general guidelines simply state that it must be justified. Other likely sources, such as the Parliamentary Counsel's Guide, also do not provide any particular principles. This is unfortunate because not subjecting regulations to parliamentary scrutiny and potential veto is, at least in a prima facie sense, a fundamental breach of the regulation-making norms developed in the 1930s debates and implemented through the twentieth century. The norm developed then was for systemic review to be provided by Parliament. The approach in Australia to relying on generally applicable, trans-substantive regulation-making legislation, has provided more scope for considering such principles. This section will focus on the principles developed for the Legislation Act 2003 (Cth).

The Legislation Act 2003 (Cth) provides for the general characteristics of regulations. These general characteristics help to indicate the category of administrative rules that generally should be subject to parliamentary review.[51] The inclusion of a provision ensuring that instruments that are 'legislative in character' are legislative instruments for the purposes of the Act was specifically recommended in the Administrative Review Council's report, *Rule Making by Commonwealth Agencies*, which prompted the making of the Act.[52] Part of the reason expressed there was to ensure that whether a regulation triggers the general regulation-making requirements (including parliamentary scrutiny) is not dependent on matters such as naming practices for regulations or on pressure by administrative agencies involved in preparing legislation.[53]

The Legislation Act includes a definition of legislative instruments as being instruments that 'determines the law or alters the content of the law, rather than determining particular cases or particular circumstances in which the law is to apply' and 'has the direct or indirect effect of affecting a privilege or interest, imposing an obligation, creating a right, or varying or removing an obligation or right'.[54] The definition is not exclusive; it is still possible for enabling provisions or regulations to state that particular regulations are not 'legislative instruments'.[55] However, it is still an important statement of principle. Regulations that determine the content of the law should have the status of legislative instrument and be subject to the provisions of the Act including parliamentary scrutiny.

There are benefits of having a general definition of legislative instruments. The first is it helps to distinguish between the kind of instruments, amongst the broad range that may be technically defined as regulations and included in

[51] Since the Legislation Act 2003 (Cth) was enacted, it has included provisions setting out the characteristics of a legislative instrument. Those characteristics were modified in 2015 to provide clarity: Acts and Instruments (Framework Reform) Act 2015 (Cth), item 12. See also A Blunn, I Govey and J McMillan, *2008 Review of the Legislative Instruments Act 2003* (Commonwealth of Australia, 2009) 13–16.

[52] Administrative Review Council (n 13) 19–20.

[53] ibid 19.

[54] Legislation Act 2003 (Cth), s 8(4).

[55] ibid s 8(6).

formal registers and databases of legislation, which have the accepted features of legislative laws. In other words, it helps to distinguish between legislative and administrative actions. While that distinction may seem outdated and unclear, in this context there is a particular need for a line to be drawn. Administrative actions with legislative characteristics (determining the content of generally applicable law and affects rights, interests and obligations) should generally be subject to parliamentary scrutiny and potential veto. On the other hand, there is no need for parliamentary review powers when those characteristics are not present. Parliament's role may no longer be the primary legislation-maker but its role has developed into it being a systemic reviewer of legislative action conducted by administrative officials. A general definition of legislative action accordingly helps to clarify executive–parliament relations.

The second benefit of including this principle in trans-substantive legislation is that exceptions stand out and can be exposed to criticism. The question then becomes what are the standards that enable exceptions to be made in a principled manner. The Senate Standing Committee on Delegated Legislation has recently reported on exemptions from disallowance and included general principles as to when exemptions should and should not be regarded as acceptable. Its two key principles are that 'exemptions from disallowance are not appropriate when an instrument affects the rights and interests of members of the public' and that 'an alternative form of accountability is required for particular exemptions'.[56] In particular the Committee stated numerous matters that should not be exempt such as the exercise of Henry VIII powers and regulations authorising government expenditure.[57] It also referred to justifications that are unlikely to be acceptable, such as that particular regulations deal with technical or scientific matters or that commercial certainty will be affected.[58]

These principles leave open types of instruments that appropriately may not be subject to disallowance. For example, instruments that provide only for commencement of Acts or regulations may not need to be subject to parliamentary processes. The primary Act or instrument will have already gone through that process. Instruments that deal only with administrative arrangements can be exempted if they do not have any direct or indirect effect on the content of the law or personal rights or interests. On the other hand, the urgency for new law to come into operation is not likely to be a good reason for exempting a regulation from parliamentary scrutiny. Urgency is not such a difficulty for instruments that come into effect when made or when registered and are subject to subsequent parliamentary scrutiny. Despite the urgency, the regulation is likely to determine the content of law and affect rights and interests, and therefore should be subject to parliamentary scrutiny. Such scrutiny would help to pick up drafting difficulties that can be pointed out by parliamentary committees and corrected. If there is

[56] Senate Standing Committee for the Scrutiny of Delegated Legislation (n 43) 115.
[57] ibid 115.
[58] ibid 116.

urgency that is explained in the explanatory materials, it would be highly unlikely that a house of Parliament would veto the regulation.

The Senate Standing Committee on Delegated Legislation's principles includes reference to alternative forms of accountability potentially justifying an exemption. However, it also stated that Parliament 'must remain capable of holding the executive to account for its exercise of delegated legislative powers'.[59] That suggests that alternative accountability mechanisms should involve other parliamentary mechanisms, such as scrutiny provided by a committee specialising in the particular area. That kind of alternative would most likely be regarded as justifying an exemption from the general parliamentary scrutiny systems.

Similarly, a mandatory requirement for public consultation would not be regarded as an alternative accountability mechanism. The Lords Delegated Powers and Regulatory Reform Committee has referred to consultation not supporting an exemption from parliamentary review.[60] Consultation is better understood as either a process enabling regulation-makers to be informed of issues or a democratic participation process, than as an accountability mechanism. Accountability suggests a process in which officials are questioned and required to provide a justification. The Lords Delegated Powers and Regulatory Reform Committee was therefore right to state that the inclusion of consultation is not suited as a justification for an exemption from parliamentary scrutiny. Consultation is better understood as contributing to administrative deliberation rather than an alternative to parliamentary scrutiny.

The Senate Standing Committee on Delegated Legislation referred in its report to exemptions for the parliamentary review being justified in 'exceptional circumstances' only.[61] That approach should be regarded as being consistent with the norms developed in the 1930s debates and implemented through the remainder of the twentieth century. One of the most important conclusions in those debates was that systemic review of regulations is necessary and that Parliament is the institution best suited to conducting such review. In that context, exemptions from Parliamentary scrutiny would be a very narrow range of regulations. Broadening of exempt regulations should expose governments to criticism on the basis of avoiding standard processes inherent in the UK and Australian parliamentary democracies.

IV. Conclusion

It is helpful to recognise that attempts to exclude parliamentary scrutiny and veto powers are a particular reflection of inevitable tensions between parliament and the executive. It is also important to recognise that administrative officials

[59] ibid 114.
[60] Delegated Powers and Regulatory Reform Committee (n 32) 5.
[61] Senate Standing Committee for the Scrutiny of Delegated Legislation (n 43) 115–16.

with powers to draft primary and secondary legislation have obvious incentives to structure such laws so that the exercise of regulation-making powers avoid parliamentary scrutiny. Lord Hewart recognised this dynamic in the late 1920s. The issues addressed in this chapter indicate that his concerns, expressed by Lord Hewart as a form of conspiracy, continue to cause tensions. The norm of parliamentary scrutiny for regulations with legislative characteristics remains effective. The challenge is to contain exemptions within principled limits.

In this chapter, I have highlighted principles expressed in relevant laws and parliamentary reports that should help to provide limits. I have not attempted to be comprehensive. My main purpose has been to identify the aspects of the regulation-making systems in the UK and Australia that are in tension with the norms developed in the 1930s and implemented throughout the twentieth century, examined in part one of the book. Pointing to principles that may help distinguish appropriate exemptions, it is intended as the starting point for a more developed analysis.

7

Incorporation by Reference of Guidance and Private Standards

As we saw in part one, the system of safeguards that was debated in the 1920s and 1930s, and subsequently implemented throughout the twentieth century, was developed in recognition that the technical detail of laws implementing welfare state policies is appropriately left to administrative officials rather than parliaments. What then of administrative officials using regulations to delegate the technical details of welfare laws to administrative officials to include in guidance or to private standard-setters and, most importantly, for the guidance and standards to be given legal effect?

I will argue that incorporation by reference of these documents into regulations can involve a departure from the system of safeguards in the UK and Australia. In particular, in some forms it can involve delegation of law-making power without parliamentary scrutiny and public consultation that generally apply to regulation-making.

It is helpful to start by explaining the different forms of incorporation by reference of documents and private standards, and in particular to distinguish between 'static' and 'dynamic' incorporation.[1] Each of these forms of incorporation can be understood in more depth by asking whether they involve forms of delegation of regulation-making authority. Dynamic incorporation occurs when regulations incorporate a document at a particular time and any changes that are subsequently made to the document. Dynamic incorporation can be regarded as a form of delegation because it enables the document-maker to control the content of the regulation into the future.[2] It is not an abdication of authority as administrative officials will remain in control over whether this form of incorporation is to continue. Officials can amend the regulation to incorporate a different document or a different version of the document. However, dynamic incorporation distances the document from regulation-making safeguards (in particular, parliamentary scrutiny and consultation) when changes are made to the incorporated

[1] The terminology of 'dynamic' and 'static' was to my knowledge initially adopted by M Dorf, 'Dynamic Incorporation of Foreign Law' (2008) 157 *University of Pennsylvania Law Review* 103, 104–105.

[2] D Pearce and S Argument, *Delegated Legislation in Australia*, 5th edn (LexisNexis Butterworths, 2017) 413.

document. Dynamic incorporation is likely to be convenient for administrative officials as they will not have to amend the regulation when the document or standard changes. The problem is that this can also be understood to be a form of unchecked delegation of regulation-making power, and therefore a form of executive aggrandisement.

Static incorporation involves incorporation of a version of a document at a particular time, so that any changes to it are not included in the incorporation. For static incorporation, changes to the document will require amendment of the regulation to incorporate the new version of the document. Static incorporation is less like delegation of law-making authority. It involves the regulation-maker selecting specific documents at the time the regulation is made or a designated time. It does not enable the document-maker to control the future content of the regulation. However, it can resemble delegation if administrative officials consistently amend the regulation to incorporate each update to the document. There may be incentives for agencies to amend regulations to incorporate updated documents. It may be because administrative officials recognise that the document-maker's expertise on the topic is more developed than the administrator's expertise, or there may be pressure from industry for the updated document to be incorporated.

There is also a third form on incorporation by reference that is usually associated with regulation in the European Union. I will refer to this as 'conformity-based incorporation'. A standard may be referred to in a regulation as an authorised means for determining whether a person or business has complied with generally stated principles included in the regulation, such as that consumer products must be safe. Conformity with the standard raises a presumption that the business or individual has also complied with the general requirements of the Act or regulation. This presumption of compliance necessarily creates an incentive, with a legal basis, on those businesses and individuals to comply with the requirements stated in the standard. Acting on the incentive necessarily means reliance on the incorporated standard and its updates in order to ensure compliance with the Act or regulation. Conformity-based incorporation usually involves static incorporation, as the incorporated standard will be clearly identified and already existing. This incorporation does not include changes and new versions of the document or standard. Nevertheless, there are problematic forms of delegation involved. As we will see in this chapter, the incorporation of a particular document or standard is usually an administrative decision without parliamentary scrutiny.

I will examine the issues raised by incorporation by reference in this chapter to develop an understanding of the extent of the inconsistency with the safeguards developed in the twentieth century and to make some suggestions for reform. Section I explains two current forms of incorporation by reference: the incentives for domestic administrative officials to adopt them; and the processes by which they are usually made. Section II examines the difficulties presented by incorporation by reference for parliamentary control. Section III examines the common lack of public access to standards that are incorporated by reference. Section IV involves suggestions for reform.

I. Documents Commonly Incorporated by Reference

A. Administrative Guidance

Incorporation by reference is a drafting technique in which a document that is not included in an Act or regulation is referred to as being part of the Act or regulation. The document becomes legally effective when it is incorporated by reference. There are no particular requirements as to the characteristics of the documents that are incorporated. However, there are documents that are commonly incorporated by reference. I will focus on two such documents: administrative guidance; and standards made by private, often international, standard-setting organisations such as the International Organization for Standardization (ISO).

It is worthwhile starting with some example regulations in the UK and Australia that incorporate by reference administrative guidance. The Food (Promotion and Placement) (England) Regulations 2021 provide an example of static incorporation.[3] Regulation 3 deals with food and drinks that are to be regarded as 'less healthy' by reference to a points system included in a document referred to as the 'Nutrient Profiling Technical Guidance'. Regulation 2 states that this Guidance was made on a certain date, and a footnote includes a hyperlink where the Guidance can be accessed. The inclusion of the date that the Guidance was made indicates that they are incorporated on a static basis and do not include subsequent changes made to it.

An example of dynamic incorporation by reference can be seen in the Australian Student Assistance Regulations 2021 (Cth).[4] These regulations were initially made with many provisions that incorporated by reference administrative guidance referred to as the 'ABSTUDY Policy Manual', which dealt with administration of benefits for Aboriginal and Torres Strait Islander people to support access to education and apprenticeships.[5] The Policy was incorporated by reference on a dynamic basis as it was defined as being a document that could be accessed on the Department of Social Services' website 'as existing from time to time'.[6] The explanatory statement for the regulation provided a hyperlink to the Policy Manual.

[3] The incorporation by reference provisions in this regulation were challenged in *Kellogg Marketing and Sales Company (UK) Limited v Secretary of State for Health and Social Care* [2022] EWHC 1710 (Admin).

[4] See also, Therapeutic Goods (Standards for Biologicals – General and Specific Requirements) (TGO 109) Order 2021 (Cth), s 4 definition of 'TGA Approach to TSE' and s 10(1)(e); Transport Safety Investigation Regulations 2021 (Cth), s 6 'Manual of Air Traffic Services' produced by Airservices Australia and the Department of Defence.

[5] Most of the provisions in the Student Assistance Regulations 2021 incorporating by reference the ABSTUDY Policy Manual in this regulation were amended to remove the incorporation following concerns being raised by the Senate Standing Committee for the Scrutiny of Delegated Legislation, 'Delegated Legislation Monitor, Monitor 10 of 2021', available at www.aph.gov.au/Parliamentary_Business/Committees/Senate/Scrutiny_of_Delegated_Legislation/Monitor/mon2021/index.

[6] Student Assistance Regulations 2021 (Cth), s 5.

These examples highlight that administrative guidance is one kind of document that are incorporated by reference into regulations. They highlight that incorporation by reference transforms documents that initially have purely administrative significance into having the status of law. Longstanding administrative law principles in each country recognise that administrative guidance may have the appearance of law, but they are not law, and administrators must remain open-minded about decisions made by reference to guidance and be willing to make exceptions.[7] Incorporation by reference of administrative guidance changes these principles by transforming guidance into law.

B. Private Standards

Private standards are standards made by standard-setting organisations such as the ISO and ASTM International, formerly named the American Society for Testing and Materials. They are often incorporated into regulations for technical matters that require regulation. For example, in the UK the Air Navigation (Carbon Offsetting and Reduction Scheme for International Aviation) Order 2021 includes ISO standards for verification of carbon dioxide emissions.[8] In Australia, the Consumer Goods (Quad Bikes) Safety Standard 2019 regulates four-wheeled, off-road vehicles often used in farming, by reference to standards made by the American National Standards Institute Inc and standards made by the European Committee for Standardization.

There are two general ways in which the incorporation of private standards into regulations clashes with the safeguards developed and implemented in the twentieth century. The first is that it can involve a form of delegation to a private organisation. As we saw in chapter two, the 1930s debates were based on the concern raised by Lord Hewart that departmental staff were drafting legislation that would delegate law-making authority to themselves. The concern with incorporation of private standards is that it can involve delegating law-making powers to private organisations; a step beyond what was raised by Lord Hewart and not contemplated by the contributors to the 1930s debates or considered in the Donoughmore Committee's report. The concern was however expressed in a general manner in the *Dignan* case by Evatt J. He referred to delegation of regulation-making powers as being acceptable when it is to an authority that is responsible to Parliament, but potentially raises constitutional questions 'The further removed the law-making authority is from continuous contact with Parliament'.[9] While this concern has not

[7] See, *British Oxygen Co. Ltd v Minister of Technology* [1971] AC 610; *Drake v Minister for Immigration and Ethnic Affairs* (1979) 24 ALR 577.

[8] eg Air Navigation (Carbon Offsetting and Reduction Scheme for International Aviation) Order 2021, regs 4, 34, 35.

[9] *Victorian Stevedoring and General Contracting Co Pty Ltd and Meakes v Dignan* (1931) 46 CLR 73, 120.

been raised in Australian cases, it nevertheless seems to arise for incorporation of private standards that can be regarded as a form of delegation.

The second way in which incorporation of private standards clashes with the safeguards developed in the twentieth century concerns access to private standards. As we saw in chapter four, consultation (either as required by law or non-mandatory means) and public access to regulations have been features of regulation-making laws and norms since the end of the nineteenth century and were confirmed in the Donoughmore Committee's report. Incorporation of private standards is in tension with these aspects of the safeguards. As I will explain further below, the forms of incorporation by reference that resemble delegation avoid the consultation processes that are usually employed when regulations are formally changed through amendment processes. In addition, private standards are not available in government-provided databases of Acts and regulations. Regulated parties, members of the public and researchers are expected to purchase them and otherwise will have difficulty accessing them.

There are numerous incentives for administrative officials to rely on private standards. The obvious general reason is that the standard-setter rather than the administrative institution bears the cost of their development.[10] Administrative officials may see private standards as being based on a superior level of expertise due to the technical knowledge of those who contribute to private standard setting.

There is also international law that requires domestic governments to adopt standards in their regulations. For example, Article 2.4 of the World Trade Organization's Technical Barriers to Trade Agreement ('TBT Agreement') provides that international standards shall be used for domestic technical regulations, except when they would be ineffective means for achieving regulatory objectives. The significance of adoption of such standards is that, according to Article 2.5 of the TBT agreement, the state is recognised as not creating an 'unnecessary obstacle to international trade' that would be in breach of the TBT agreement. In other words, incorporating these standards into regulations provide a 'regulatory safe harbour' for the purposes of the TBT Agreement.[11] Bilateral trade agreements commonly include similar incentives. When the UK was a member of the EU, it was subject to the EU's free trade agreements which often include incentives based on the WTO's TBT agreement to use international standards when making technical regulations. The free trade agreement between the UK and Australia implements the international standards provisions of the TBT Agreement.[12] Australia's other bilateral agreements also have such provisions.[13]

[10] Dorf (n 1) 133.

[11] See eg G Shaffer, 'How the WTO Shapes the Regulatory State' in F Bignami and D Zaring, *Comparative Law and Regulation: Understanding the Global Regulatory Process* (Edward Elgar, 2016) 455.

[12] Australia–United Kingdom Free Trade Agreement, Art 7.6 (adopted Adelaide, 17 December 2021 and London, 16 December 2021; entry into force 31 May 2023).

[13] See eg Australia–United States Free Trade Agreement, Art 8.2–8.5 (adopted 18 May 2004; entry into force 1 January 2005) ATS 2005 1.

The purpose of these aspects of international trade law is harmonisation of standards. The standards with which businesses have to comply are harmonised standards made by private standard-setters and then incorporated into domestic laws. The basic purpose is to simplify compliance with regulatory standards for globalised businesses. It facilitates export opportunities.[14] International and domestic standard-setters commonly justify their processes and standards as being for the purpose of harmonisation drawn from the WTO's TBT agreement.[15] Harmonisation is achieved through national standard-setters participating in international standard setting processes and making standards based on consensus processes.[16]

Private standards are also supported and encouraged by governments. Both the UK and Australia have memoranda of understanding with standards associations recognising them as national standard-setting organisations and providing for financial support.[17] Incorporation of private standards is encouraged in Australia through Commonwealth Government policy statements. The Commonwealth Government has published its policy on industry regulations that includes a principle that administrative agencies should accept international standards and not impose any additional requirements unless reasons can be provided for doing so.[18]

The UK and Australian Governments therefore support private standards. The questions for this chapter relate to the extent to which they affect the regulation-making safeguards. Is reliance on private standards a form of delegation of regulation-making authority to private organisations that excludes parliamentary supervision and public consultation? Additionally, to what extent is the limited public access to private standards a problem for the principles developed in the twentieth century for regulation-making?

There are additional questions about private standards and the safeguards of regulation-making. There are two that I do not address. First, do they restrict

[14] T Büthe and W Mattli, *The New Global Rulers: The Privatization of Regulation in the World Economy* (Princeton University Press, 2011) 6–8.

[15] International Organization for Standardisation and International Electrotechnical Commission, 'Guide 59: ISO and IEC Recommended Practices for Standardization by National Bodies' (2nd edn, 2019), Art 1; British Standards Institution, 'A Standard for Standards – Principles of Standardization' BS 0:2016 (2nd edn, 2016), Art 5.3; Standards Australia, 'Standardisation Guide 001: Preparing Standards' (Version 4.15, 2019), Art 8.1.

[16] For explanations of these processes see, H Schepel, *The Constitution of Private Governance: Product Standards in the Regulation of Integrating Markets* (Hart Publishing, 2005), 101–07; CN Murphy and J Yates, *The International Organization for Standardization (ISO): Global Governance through Voluntary Consensus* (Routledge, 2009) 26–32; and Büthe and Mattli (n 14) 138–46.

[17] Memorandum of Understanding Between the United Kingdom Government and the British Standards Institution in Respect of its Activities as the United Kingdom's National Standards Body, Arts 1.3 and 4.3(iv), available at www.gov.uk/government/publications/standardisation/standardisation; Memorandum of Understanding Between the Commonwealth Government and Standards Australia Ltd, Arts 7.1 and 9.1, available at www.industry.gov.au/trade/australias-standards-and-conformance-infrastructure.

[18] Department of Industry, Innovation and Science, 'Best Practice Guide to Using Standards and Risk Assessments in Policy and Regulation', available at www.industry.gov.au/trade/australias-standards-and-conformance-infrastructure.

access to the courts? Incorporation and adoption of private standards do not raise particular concerns about access to the courts. The usual judicial review principles are most likely to apply when such standards are converted into legal norms in regulations. Secondly, do private standard-setters use public participation processes when making their standards? This issue is often raised in the private standard-setting literature,[19] but is not directly relevant to the issues in this chapter. The issues that I address concern incorporation by reference of private standards into regulations. The question in that context relates to consideration of the standards when they are incorporated by reference into a regulation rather than the processes used by private standard-setters when making their standards.

II. Circumventing the Safeguards

In this section I address the concerns that arise when incorporation by reference involves a form of delegation. I will argue that not only is there a form of delegation, but that delegation is also likely to circumvent regulation-making safeguards in relation to parliamentary scrutiny and public consultation. We will also see that there are differences in the laws relating to incorporation by reference. In the UK the principles have been developed in case law, while in Australia they have developed through legislation.

A. United Kingdom

There are examples in UK regulations of incorporation by reference of administrative guidance and private standards. We will see that there is case law that draws on constitutional principles that relies on the static–dynamic distinction to determine when they are acceptable or not. There has also been criticism of incorporation by parliamentary scrutiny committees. The EU regulatory system and Brexit complicate matters. The EU has a more complex form of incorporation by reference, which I referred to in the introduction to this chapter as 'conformity-based incorporation'. The EU approach has recently been adopted in the UK during the Brexit process. This form of incorporation by reference also raises concerns about delegation of law-making power to private organisations and the circumvention of safeguards that would otherwise apply to regulations.

[19] See eg Productivity Commission, 'Standard Setting and Laboratory Accreditation' (Research Report, November 2006) ch 8; Büthe and Mattli (n 14) 222–26; S Wood 'Exploring the Relationship between Administrative Norms and Competence in Transnational Governance: ISO, ISEAL and Sustainability Standards' (2016) 21 *Tilburg Law Review* 193, 213–15.

Static incorporation, in which a particular version of a standard is incorporated by reference, has been utilised in UK regulations.[20] As explained in the introduction, static incorporation does not raise concerns about delegation without parliamentary supervision. Any changes to the standard require amendments to the regulation in order for the new version of the standard to be incorporated.[21] Parliamentary supervision and consultation processes will generally be available as a check on the amendment to the regulation.

However, there are also examples of dynamic incorporation in the UK that do raise concerns. Regulation 3 of the Furniture and Furnishings (Fire) (Safety) Regulations 1988[22] refers to particular British Standards and goes on to say 'subject to any amendments made thereto and approved by the Secretary of State'. This makes clear that the standards are adopted with subsequent amendments (that is, dynamically) and also that the Secretary of State has an approval role for amendments to the standard. The important point is that it is a governmental check on changes to the standard rather than a parliamentary check. There is of course the slight possibility that the minister could be questioned in Parliament about any approval that is given. However, it is clear that there is no additional parliamentary check; one of the key features of regulation-making safeguards. There is nothing stated in the regulation in regard to consultation for the approval.

The UK courts have developed principles influenced by the distinction between static and dynamic incorporation. The line of case law has developed in relation to incorporation by reference of administrative guidance into regulations. The first of these cases, *R v Secretary of State for Social Services, ex p Camden London Borough Council*,[23] recognised that static incorporation by reference is likely to be accepted as being authorised by the enabling provision in the relevant Act, but that is unlikely to be the case for dynamic incorporation. In the *Camden London Borough Council* case, it was relevant that incorporation by reference of a particular, existing document was potentially within Parliament's scrutiny.[24] The implication was that even if the incorporated document was not included with the regulation tabled in Parliament, it would be within Parliament's powers to request the document and include it in its scrutiny.

This point has been influential in subsequent cases; in particular that documents that do not exist at the time the regulation is made, or are existing but can be changed, are beyond the scope of Parliamentary scrutiny. Any changes to the incorporated document after the regulation is made will necessarily be beyond the scope of parliamentary scrutiny. This form of incorporation by reference is

[20] See eg Water Supply (Water Quality) Regulations 2016, SI 2016/614, reg 9(3) and fns 2–3; Natural Mineral Water, Spring Water and Bottled Drinking Water (England) Regulations 2007, SI 2007/2785, Sch 12, paras 15, 16; Building Regulations 2010, SI 2010/2214, reg 6(3).

[21] See egWater Industry Act 1991 (UK), s 213; Food Standards Act 1990 (UK), s 48(3); Building Act 1988 (UK), s 1(4).

[22] SI 1988/1324.

[23] *R v Secretary of State for Social Services, ex p Camden London Borough Council* [1987] 1 WLR 819.

[24] ibid 827–28.

unlikely to be authorised by the enabling Act.[25] In *R (Kellogg Marketing and Sales Company (UK) Limited) v Secretary of State for Health and Social Care*, this was referred to as a matter of constitutional principle relating to publicity of laws, parliamentary scrutiny and ministerial accountability.[26]

While the case law principles have been developed in the context of incorporation by reference of administrative guidance, there has also been incorporation by reference of private standards in the UK. As an EU Member State, it participated in the EU's approach to private standards in which goods and products' conformity with private standards raises a presumption of compliance with legal requirements.

The EU's system for incorporating by reference private standards into regulations is complex. It is referred to in the EU as the 'new approach', which was developed in a series of resolutions, directives and regulations starting in the 1980s. A European Council resolution made in 1985 set out the key features of the system.[27] EU Directives were to be limited to providing for 'essential safety requirements' to which products must conform if put on the market. Standards made by private standard-setters elaborate the essential safety requirements on request by the EU Commission[28] and these standards are then recognised by the Commission by publishing them in the EU Official Journal.[29] Conformity with the technical standards engages a presumption of compliance with the essential safety requirements of the directive.[30]

These aspects of the EU's new approach featured in UK regulations prior to Brexit. UK product safety laws provide a good example. The EU Directive 2001/95/EC on General Product Safety in December 2001 was transposed into UK law by the General Product Safety Regulations 2005 (UK). Regulation 5 sets out the 'essential requirements' establishing obligations on manufacturers and others in the supply chain to only place 'safe products' on the market. Regulation 6(2) establishes a 'presumption of conformity' by which a product will be presumed to be safe if it complies with a 'voluntary national standard of the United Kingdom giving effect to a European standard the reference of which has been published in the Official Journal of the European Union'. The EU standards that are transposed into UK standards were made available for purchase by the British Standards Institution.

[25] *Pankina v Secretary of State for the Home Department* [2010] EWCACiv 719, [2011] QB 376 [24], [29]; *R (Alvi) v Secretary of State for the Home Department* [2012] UKSC 33, [2012] 1 WLR 2208 [62].

[26] *R (Kellogg Marketing and Sales Company (UK) Limited) v Secretary of State for Health and Social Care* [2022] EWHC 1710 (Admin) [91], [94].

[27] Council Resolution 85/C of 7 May 1985, A New Approach to Technical Harmonization and Standards, Annex II 'Guidelines for a New Approach to Technical Harmonization and Standards' [1985] OJ C 136/01.

[28] Directive 98/34/EC of 22 June 1998, Procedure for the Provision of Information in the Field of Technical Standards and Regulations [1998] OJ L 204/37, Art 6. See also HCH Hofmann, GC Rowe and AH Türk, *Administrative Law and Policy of the European Union* (Oxford University Press, 2011) 596.

[29] ec.europa.eu/growth/single-market/european-standards/harmonised-standards_en.

[30] See eg Directive 2001/95/EC of 3 December 2001 on General Product Safety, Art 3(2).

The primary features of the EU's new approach to regulatory standards have been adapted by Brexit legislation for continued operation in the UK. In relation to product safety, to continue the example, this was implemented by amendments to regulation 6 the General Product Safety Regulations 2005 by the European Union (Future Relationship) Act 2020 and the Product Safety and Metrology Etc (Amendment Etc) (EU Exit) Regulations 2019.[31] The amendments simply removed the references to European standards and the Official Journal of the European Union, and replaced them with UK national standards and international standards, stating that the Secretary of State would identify the standards that are accepted. Publishing the list of recognised standards is not by a statutory instrument but 'in a manner the Secretary of State considers appropriate'.[32] They are, at the time of writing, published by the Department for Business, Energy and Industrial Strategy as a 'notice of publication' on the GOV.UK website.[33] The post-Brexit approach to product standards in the UK is therefore equivalent to the EU approach but with the UK standards association and officials having the primary roles within it rather than EU officials.

The conformity-based incorporation that applies in the UK raises concerns regarding delegation of law-making power to private officials. It is helpful to start by explaining the criticisms that have been made by administrative lawyers of the EU new approach. Herwig Hofmann, Gerard Rowe and Alexander Türk refer to it as a form of 'co-regulation'.[34] While compliance with the technical standards may seem voluntary, there is a strong incentive to comply with the private standards that have been adopted as they provide the only express, legally recognised means for achieving compliance with mandated essential requirements. Harm Schepel explains that the reason for insisting that compliance with standards is voluntary is to support the claim that there is no delegation to a private body that would raise constitutional difficulties.[35]

However, scholars have raised doubts about whether this can be justified. One concern, expressed by Carlo Colombo and Mariolina Eliantanio, is that it will be difficult for businesses to comply with their obligations under the essential requirements of a directive without also relying on the associated private standard.[36] Hofmann, Rowe and Türk add that the private standards incorporated into the EU new approach are controlled by EU laws and compliance with them has legal

[31] European Union (Future Relationship) Act 2020, s 19 and Sch 4; Product Safety and Metrology Etc (Amendment Etc) (EU Exit) Regulations 2019, s 12 and Sch 9.

[32] General Product Safety Regulations 2005, reg 6(2A)(b).

[33] Office for Product Safety and Standards, 'Guidance – Standards: General Product Safety' (26 October 2022), available at www.gov.uk/government/publications/standards-general-product-safety.

[34] Hofmann, Rowe and Türk (n 28) 588.

[35] H Schepel, 'The New Approach to the New Approach: The Juridification of Harmonized Standards in EU Law' (2013) 20 *Maastricht Journal of European and Comparative Law* 521, 523–24.

[36] C Colombo and M Eliantonio, 'Harmonized Technical Standards as Part of EU Law: Juridification with a Number of Unresolved Legitimacy Concerns?' (2017) 24 *Maastricht Journal of European and Comparative Law* 323, 335.

significance.[37] And Schepel has questioned the distinction that is inherent in the new approach between the essential requirements being legal standards based on policy and the associated private standards being a matter of purely technical detail. He argues that private standards often involve policy judgments.[38]

How then can we understand the reliance on technical standards in the conformity-based form of incorporation by reference according to the safeguards on regulation-making? It is clear that those norms emphasise parliamentary supervision of the exercise of delegated powers. Even in the 1920s and 1930s, the primary period of debate, it was clear that the content of regulations often related to technical detail. Conformity-based incorporation by reference involves private organisations conducting that work. The EU's approach to conformity-based incorporation includes checks on the standards that are associated with an EU directive. It provides a process for Member States to make objections to technical standards recognised by the EU.[39] However, the UK's post-Brexit conformity-based approach to product standards does not include an equivalent check. The Secretary of States' recognition of particular private standards according to regulation 6 of the General Product Safety Regulations 2005 is not a statutory instrument subject to parliamentary scrutiny. There is also no reference to public consultation for the Secretary of State's decision. Yet, the recognised product standards will have legal significance.

Accordingly, there are three different ways in which private standards can be adopted in the UK: static; dynamic; and conformity-based incorporation. Of these three different forms of relying on private standards only static incorporation enables operation of regulation-making safeguards.

B. Australia

Australia's approach to incorporation by reference is also structured by the distinction between static and dynamic incorporation. However, the distinction has not developed as a matter of case law but of statutory law. Section 14 of the Legislation Act 2003 generally authorises static incorporation by reference. Dynamic incorporation, sometimes referred to as 'time-to-time' incorporation in Australia, requires express authority to be provided by the Act that empowers administrative officials to make regulations. Section 14(2) of the Legislation Act 2003 implements this by prohibiting the incorporation of non-statutory materials in regulations on a time-to-time basis 'unless the contrary intention appears'. The relevant contrary intention can be supplied by a provision of an empowering Act that expressly provides for time-to-time incorporation.

[37] Hofmann, Rowe and Türk (n 28) 598–99.

[38] Schepel (n 16) 255–56.

[39] Regulation (EU) No 1025/2012 of 25 October 2012 on European Standardisation [2012] OJ L 316/12, Art 11.

The Legislation Act 2003 also includes a rule for enabling access to documents incorporated by reference. Section 15J provides that the explanatory statement for regulations that include documents incorporated by reference must 'contain a description of the incorporated documents and indicate how they may be obtained'.[40] That suggests that private standards incorporated by reference have to be accessible to members of the public who need to comply with them and those with other interests. However, the Act does not require them to be freely available or for them to be included with other legislative instruments in the Federal Register of Legislation website. We will see below that the Senate Committee on Delegated Legislation has its own requirement for access to private standards incorporated by reference.

It is worthwhile briefly examining the development of these provisions of the Legislation Act 2003 (Cth), prior to analysing their tension with regulation-making safeguards. The provisions have their initial source in amendments to the Acts Interpretation Act 1901 (Cth) in 1964,[41] which were in very similar terms to the current provision, section 14 of the Legislation Act 2003 (Cth). The purpose of the provision was explained by the Attorney-General in Parliament as being essentially for convenience.[42] The particular problem that prompted the reform was that there was a desire for courts and tribunals to use the High Court's scale of witness expenses. The Attorney-General stated that it would be convenient for any change made by the High Court to the scale to automatically apply in the other courts and tribunals. The only concern about such incorporation related to parliamentary control and this turned out to not be a concern for the Attorney-General because he thought that dynamic incorporation was limited to incorporation of Acts, regulations and rules made under Acts. That is, the laws that would be incorporated were already subject to parliamentary scrutiny.

However, the Attorney-General's explanation of parliamentary control missed an important aspect of the new provisions that had great significance for parliamentary supervision. It overlooked the fact that the provision also enabled incorporation of non-statutory documents to be incorporated in a dynamic manner. These non-statutory documents would not be subject to parliamentary scrutiny or the usual forms of public consultation. The Attorney-General's explanation in Parliament accordingly raises the question regarding the operation of regulation-making safeguards for documents incorporated by reference in a dynamic manner, but provides a misleading answer. It also provides no answer to the question of parliamentary supervision of incorporation of private standards – which are by their nature, non-statutory documents. That suggests that the question of incorporation of private standards was not considered at the time of the

[40] Legislation Act 2003 (Cth), s 15J(2)c).
[41] Acts Interpretation Act 1964 (Cth), s 5.
[42] Commonwealth, *Parliamentary Debates*, House of Representatives, 13 May 1964, 1857 (Mr Snedden).

1964 amendments that first inserted an incorporation by reference provision into Commonwealth legislation.

The concern about parliamentary scrutiny of incorporated documents was addressed by the Administrative Review Council in its 1992 Rulemaking report.[43] The Council confirmed that Parliament does not review non-statutory documents incorporated by reference.[44] Its main concern related to the drafting of such documents, understood generally rather than as private standards, and that they are more susceptible to lack of clarity and ambiguity due to not being prepared by legislative drafters.[45] The Council recommended that any documents incorporated by reference should be tabled in Parliament with the regulation. This recommendation was partly adopted in the Legislation Act 2003 (Cth). Section 41 of that Act enables the houses of Parliament to require any document that is incorporated by reference to be tabled in the house when a regulation is subject to disallowance.[46] However, that power seems not to have been used. My search of the Commonwealth Parliament database indicates that section 41 has not been used to require documents incorporated by reference in regulations to be made available for inspection by either of the houses of Parliament.

The result is that while parliamentary scrutiny of incorporated documents has been recognised as a potential problem at different stages of the development of legislation regarding incorporation by reference, no effective solution has been considered, let alone implemented. The current operation of the Legislation Act 2003 enables parliamentary scrutiny to be avoided through dynamic incorporation by reference. Dynamic incorporation can be recognised not only as a delegation of law-making power but also one that cannot be supervised by Parliament. As we have seen, subsequent changes to an incorporated document automatically have legal effect without any need to amend the incorporating regulation. This may not raise a large concern if provisions enabling dynamic incorporation are exceptional or rare. However, they are now common. At the time of writing, there are 96 current Commonwealth Acts that include such provisions.[47]

It is apparent therefore that the approaches to incorporation by reference in Australia leave ample space for avoiding parliamentary scrutiny of the documents incorporated. Dynamic incorporation by reference is inconsistent with the regulation-making safeguards developed in the twentieth century, and in particular with parliamentary scrutiny. In section IV below, I make suggestions that would bring incorporation by reference into line with the safeguards.

[43] Administrative Review Council, 'Rule Making by Commonwealth Agencies' (Report No. 35, 1992) paras 6.40–6.56.

[44] ibid para 6.53.

[45] ibid para 6.54.

[46] A period of 15 sitting days: Legislation Act 2003 (Cth), s 42.

[47] Federal Register of Legislation (www.legislation.gov.au), search term 'despite subsection 14(2) of the Legislation Act 2003'. See eg Therapeutic Goods Act 1989 (Cth), s 10(4); Industrial Chemicals Act 2019 (Cth), s 180(3); Health Insurance Act 1973 (Cth), s 124ZT(7).

III. Free Public Access

We saw in chapter four that the regulation-making safeguards historically included a requirement that regulations are printed, published and made available to the public. In the late twentieth century and the early years of the twenty-first this was extended to government-provided databases that publish legislative law freely on the internet. This form of access to law is now so common in the UK and Australia, that arguably a principle, or at least a reasonable expectation, of simple and free access to law has been established. These systems of course provide for access to regulations made by ministers, government departments and agencies.

However, documents and standards that are incorporated by reference into regulations are not made available in these government-provided databases. There is a simple reason that this is the case, in regard to private standards. The sale of the standards is an important aspect of the standard-setters' business model;[48] it is necessary to recover their costs. The standard-setters' interest is therefore not to make their standards available generally, for example freely through the internet, but to make the standards available for a cost. However, that is not the case for all standards. Some are available at no cost,[49] but that is only to say that this problem does not arise for those particular standards. The concern for the regulation-making principles is that others are available for a price.

In any case, the problem for free public access to private standards is more critical when such standards are incorporated by reference into regulations. Incorporation of a private standard converts a standard that would otherwise be voluntary into being part of the legal system. However, incorporation by reference does not include the text of the incorporated standard in the regulation. The standard is converted into law without the actual text being included in government-provided databases, the modern form of providing access to law.

Access to documents that are incorporated by reference has been raised in the UK by the Joint Committee on Statutory Instruments and it has commonly made clear that details regarding access should be provided.[50] In Australia, the provisions of the Legislation Act 2003 impose some access obligations, but they are minimal and vague. Concerns were raised about it by the Administrative Review Council in its 1992 report that started the reform process leading to the Legislation Act 2003. The Council was concerned about access to incorporated material generally (not only private standards) and it recommended that incorporated documents should be included in the proposed public register of legislation as should any changes to

[48] Murphy and Yates (n 16) 43.

[49] See eg ES Bremer, 'On the Cost of Private Standards in Public Law' (2015) 63 *University of Kansas Law Review* 279, 315–16.

[50] Joint Committee on Statutory Instruments, *Transparency and Accountability in Subordinate Legislation* (2017–19, HL 151, HC 1158) 14.

the incorporated document. The Council also recommended that incorporation of documents should not come into effect until registered.[51]

This recommendation was not implemented in the Legislation Act 2003. Instead, the provisions for access to incorporated documents is included in the provision requiring the regulation-maker to prepare an explanatory statement to be tabled in Parliament and lodged for inclusion on the Federal Register.[52] This requirement is minimal, especially when compared with the Administrative Review Council's recommendation. It does not require inclusion of the incorporated document on the register or that there is general public access to it. Its main purpose is to provide a person affected by the incorporated standard with sufficient information to access it.

The reports leading to the Legislation Act 2003 indicate that there was no particular reference to the incorporation of private standards. This is likely to be due to the debates occurring primarily in the 1990s at the beginning of the period of increased reliance on private standards in regulation-making that was encouraged by the WTO Technical Barriers to Trade Agreement and by domestic governments.

There are other norms that seek to ensure adequate public access to incorporated materials. The Senate Committee on Delegated Legislation has developed its scrutiny practices to require that public access is to be provided. Until the end of 2019, it provided Guidelines setting out its expectation that incorporated documents be available on the internet, in public libraries and Department or agency offices. The Committee raised concerns with regulation-makers when these forms of access are not provided.[53] In 2019 the Senate Standing Orders were amended to enable the Committee to scrutinise regulations for whether 'any document it incorporates, may be freely accessed and used'.[54] The provision was recommended in the Committee's 2019 report preceding the changes to the Standing Orders on the basis that the Committee's scrutiny functions include ensuring 'that all persons subject to or interested in the law may readily and freely access its terms'.[55]

These changes are consistent with other recommendations made in governmental reports since the Legislation Act 2003 came into effect. In these reports, incorporation of private standards has come to the foreground. The Productivity Commission stated in 2006 that in principle incorporated standards should be made freely available or at low cost and recommended that government provide funding for access to Australian Standards that become mandatory due to being incorporated into regulations.[56] Similarly, a review of the Legislation Act in 2008

[51] Administrative Review Council (n 43) para 8.34.

[52] Legislation Act 2003 (Cth), ss 15G(4), 15J.

[53] See eg Senate Standing Committee on Regulations and Ordinances, *Delegated Legislation Monitor 1 of 2019*, (13 February 2019) 54–56.

[54] Senate Standing Order 23(3)(f).

[55] Senate Standing Committee on Regulations and Ordinances, *Parliamentary Scrutiny of Delegated Legislation*, (3 June 2019), para 3.73.

[56] Productivity Commission (n 19) 127, 130.

stated that more needs to be done to improve public access to standards that are incorporated by reference. The report recommended that documents that cannot be accessed should not be incorporated, that standards that are incorporated should be provided for free or at low cost, and that agencies should ensure printed copies of incorporated standards are available in major libraries.[57] These concerns have therefore been expressed but without change to the legislative provisions.

Before concluding this section, it should be pointed out that Standards Australia, the primary standard-setting organisation in Australia, has developed a distribution policy for its standards that addressed public access. It states that Standards Australia is committed to 'broadening access' to its standards and that access has been made through public libraries.[58] Beyond that, it stated that it was committed to providing online access for personal use of their standards within the parameters of its own financial sustainability and that this would occur by December 2023.[59] In this way, Standards Australia explained the tension between the pressure for public access to standards and standard-setters' financial constraints but without committing to a method that strikes a balance between the two.

As we have seen, the discussion in official reports in Australia of incorporation by reference has shifted from general references to technical documents in the early 1990s to the more recent analysis that focuses primarily on private standards. That makes sense given the incentives on agencies to incorporate private standards that have developed in that time. There is however a real tension between the standard-setters' interest in providing standards at a cost and the public interest in free access to law. Access to law was a value that was recognised in the Donoughmore Report, but not as a concern requiring consideration.[60] The Committee was likely to have regarded it as being resolved by the Rules Publication Act 1893 (UK). However, the modern reliance on private standards brings that problem back into focus. The Australian developments highlight that as yet there is no legal solution that satisfies regulation-making safeguards.

IV. Safeguard Reform

As we have seen in this chapter, incorporation by reference can involve delegation of regulation-making power in a manner that circumvents the usual safeguards. This is particularly concerning when the documents incorporated in this way are private standards. As we saw in chapter two, the increased reliance on regulations

[57] Legislative Instruments Act Review Committee, *2008 Review of the Legislative Instruments Act 2003* (2009), 29–30.

[58] Standards Australia, 'Distribution and Licensing Policy Framework' (November 2019) 8, available at www.standards.org.au/getmedia/14df8731-a25b-4343-b007-b6eef039dea9/Standards-Australia-Distribution-and-Licensing-Policy.aspx.

[59] ibid 9.

[60] Committee on Ministers' Powers, Report (London, 1932) ('Donoughmore Committee Report') 47.

in the late nineteenth century and early twentieth century was a response by parliaments to deal with the technical detail of modern legislative laws. A similar dynamic applies in the current regulatory period. Administrators have incentives to delegate the development of the technical details of regulatory laws to experts who are better placed to make them. Additionally, as with the debates about regulation-making more generally in the 1920s and 1930s, there are concerns about how such delegation affects regulation-making safeguards. This time the primary concern is that sub-delegating the technical detail to non-government, private organisations breaks the supervisory connections between standard-setters and Parliament.

For the purposes of this book, it is worth taking a pragmatic approach to incorporation of private standards, similar to that of the functionalists and the Donoughmore Committee itself in the 1920s and 1930s debates, and accept that reliance on private standard setting is inevitable particularly due to their role in harmonising regulatory standards for the purposes of globalisation. The question then shifts to the one raised by the functionalists and the Donoughmore Committee: how can incorporation of private standards into regulations be subject to parliamentary supervision? To answer that question, the particular institutional competences of the standard-setters should be considered. Supervisory mechanisms should be designed to enable review of policy issues without interference with the positive features that standard-setters bring to their role.

If private standards are understood to be purely technical there may not be such a need for parliamentary scrutiny. However, standards often deal with regulation of consumer protection, public health and environmental impacts – subject areas that involve restricting business practices and commercial products to minimise public harms. Laws that affect the balance between these interests have long been recognised as having policy significance.

Additionally, private standard-setting processes have often been criticised for being a closed form of decision-making; one that is dominated by industry and insufficiently factoring in non-government organisations' and consumers' views.[61] These concerns suggest that these processes risk industry interests being preferred over restricting the harms caused by those industries. The question, then, is whether incorporation processes can involve broader input into, and potentially public debate about, the content of standards that are incorporated into, or given legal significance by, regulations. There are numerous reforms that could be adopted to enable this to occur.

One potential reform is to limit incorporation to static forms. Static incorporation lessens concern about delegation that arises in both dynamic incorporation and the UK's conformity-based incorporation. The concerns about delegation are reduced for static incorporation because the standard-setter has no ongoing control over the content of the regulation that incorporates the standard.

[61] Productivity Commission (n 19) ch 8; Büthe and Mattli (n 14) 220–26; Wood (n 19) 214.

A particular version of the standard is adopted. Administrative officials choose a standard as it is at a particular time. Parliament can scrutinise the initial incorporation of the standard and when the standard-setter makes changes to the standard that prompt amendments to the regulation, parliament will be able to scrutinise the amendments made to the regulation.

Accordingly, static incorporation enables ongoing parliamentary supervision. It enables dialogue between parliament and administrators regarding their choice of standards at the time a regulation is made and when regulations are amended that update a particular standard. While it is less convenient for administrators as they will need to amend regulations, it generally facilitates escalation of issues with standards to parliaments that have a veto power. Of course. implementing such a restriction would not be straightforward. It would require amending incorporation by reference provisions in legislation (such as section 14 of the Legislation Act) to limit incorporation by reference of documents and standards to static forms. This change to the Legislation Act 2003 would not however be a complete prevention of dynamic incorporation by reference. It would not prevent subsequent, sector-specific, legislation from enabling regulations to incorporate standards in a dynamic manner. The risk of such provisions being added into sector-specific legislation would need to be managed by adding to the scrutiny criteria for the committees in the UK and Australia that review bills.

The second reform would be to enact mandatory public consultation processes for the regulation providing for incorporation of administrative guidance or private standards. The rationale for such provisions would be that while the guidance or standard will have been made by administrative internal processes or the standard setters' consensus process, the conversion of the standard into law through incorporation by reference is a public process. Stakeholders who may not have had a fair opportunity to participate in the administrators' or standard-setters' processes will have the opportunity to make submissions to administrators and escalate their concerns to Parliament.

New Zealand law imposes such requirements. Schedule 2 of the Legislation Act 2019 (NZ) requires administrative officials to:

- give public notice of the proposal to incorporate material;
- ensure that copies of the incorporated material are publicly available;
- provide an opportunity for members of the public to make a comment; and
- determine that it is appropriate to incorporate the particular material.

This provision enables input into the decision to adopt a particular standard by persons who may not have participated in the making of the initial document or standard. It should be noted that Schedule 2 includes a no-invalidity clause stating that failure to comply with these processes will not invalidate any regulation that incorporates material. This provision removes any incentive to bring judicial review proceedings to enforce the requirements, but it does not necessarily mean that the consultation requirements are unsupervised. The Regulations Review Committee's scrutiny role remains operative.

The important point is that there are potential reforms that would mitigate concerns about incorporation by reference of documents and standards. Legal provisions limiting such adoption to static forms and imposing public consultation requirements enable parliamentary scrutiny and processes that allow for debate in the public sphere when documents and standards are incorporated into law by regulations. Those debates would otherwise occur only within administrative processes internal to departments and agencies or privately in standard-setters' processes.

V. Conclusion

It is helpful to recognise the particular problem that arises with incorporation by reference as being an incremental change to more general incorporation by reference laws and practices. The focus in the past was on incorporation of technical government documents more generally. It was not until the 2000s that the discussion shifted to incorporation of private standards. That is appropriate given the new reliance in the 1980s and 1990s on private standards, when the WTO and EU laws focused on harmonisation as a means to improve globalisation. This helps us to appreciate that this new role for private standards was not made with an equal focus on how it can be reconciled with parliamentary democracy and in particular the regulation-making safeguards.

In this chapter I have sought to explain the conflict with regulation-making safeguards presented by giving legal effect to administrative guidance and private standards. However, there is scope for changes to be made that would ensure that the existing safeguards play a role in relation to incorporation by reference of administrative guidance and private standards. The potential reforms that I have set out in section IV would be important steps in resolving the conflict. There may be other concerns about incorporation by reference that are worthy of investigation. However, for the issues examined in this book the incremental nature of the solutions to the problems raised seem manageable. They are traditional solutions to a new problem.

8

Henry VIII Clauses

Henry VIII clauses are common in both Australia and the UK. They are controversial because they upend the accepted relationship between Parliament's role in making and amending Acts, and the executive's role in implementing and administering Acts. Henry VIII clauses are included in primary legislation to authorise administrative officials to make regulations that amend or modify primary legislation. They minimise, rather than exclude, parliamentary scrutiny because they enable the primarily administrative, regulation-making process to be used to amend Acts.

This chapter explains what was said in the 1930s debates about Henry VIII clauses and examines their modern uses. Both countries have seen a resurgence of inclusion of Henry VIII powers in Acts far beyond the limits expressed in the 1930s debates. In the UK this is particularly apparent in generally applicable legislation that commonly has constitutional significance. In Australia they are common in economic legislation. In both countries Henry VIII clauses have been heavily relied on in emergency legislation. As additional norms apply for emergency legislation, Henry VIII powers in that context will be examined separately in chapter nine.

Before turning to the concerns about Henry VIII clauses in detail, it is worth explaining their name: King Henry VIII was popularly regarded as personifying autocratic executive government.[1] They are also referred to in this way to reflect the Act of Proclamations 1539, which gave the King broad powers to legislate.[2] The name has stuck for these colloquial reasons rather than any precise correspondence between the powers included in the Act of Proclamations and modern Henry VIII clauses. Many commentators have emphasised the differences between the Act of Proclamations and modern Henry VIII clauses, in particular the Donoughmore Committee, which referred to the historical reference as 'far-fetched'. Nevertheless, the Donoughmore Committee continued to use the term,

[1] Committee on Ministers' Powers, Report (London, 1932) ('Donoughmore Committee Report') 36; NW Barber and AL Young, 'The Rise of Prospective Henry VIII Clauses and their Implications for Sovereignty' [2003] *Public Law* 111, 112.

[2] Donoughmore Committee Report (n 1) 36; JWF Allison, 'The Westminster Parliament's Formal Sovereignty in Britain and Europe from a Historical Perspective' (2017) 34 *Giornale Di Storma Costituzionale* 57, 62–63.

often prefaced by 'so called' and including scare quotes. The Committee referred to it as a 'nickname'.[3] Even if it is not historically accurate, it should now be regarded as a widely used shorthand for a kind of statutory provision. The shorthand also helpfully supports criticisms that these statutory provisions undermine the role of Parliament in parliamentary democracies. The term is a good reminder of the need to check on this form of executive aggrandisement.

The name came into modern use starting in debates in 1929 just prior to the establishment of the Donoughmore Committee. The first reference to it seems to have been in Parliamentary debates in 1929 on the Local Government Bill and a provision enabling modification of the Act.[4] This was picked up by an article in *The Times* and by Lord Hewart, who clearly agreed with the *Times* article. The article stated that the precedent for the provision in the Local Government Bill was 'the dispensing powers under the Stuarts and the statute … which declared that anything enacted by King Henry VIII or by Order in Council should have the force of law'.[5]

Henry VIII powers are often referred to as raising constitutional concerns. They have been referred to as a 'constitutional outrage' when used outside of narrow circumstances and emergencies.[6] Such language is substantiated by recognising that Henry VIII powers turn the accepted relationship between parliament and the executive on its head by enabling legislation made by the executive to amend or modify primary statutes made by parliament. In doing so they circumvent the parliamentary debate by elected representatives that provides the legitimating feature for primary legislation in parliamentary democracies. The constitutional concerns are therefore grounded on a functional understanding of parliaments as providing for transparency and debate. However, Henry VIII clauses are not so problematic when parliamentary supremacy is understood formally,[7] as parliaments retain power to repeal them.

While all Henry VIII provisions are potentially controversial, they come in forms which can be more or less problematic. They can be drafted narrowly to apply in a small range of circumstances that are focused on the specific subject matter of the enabling legislation, or a part of the legislation, in a limited timeframe. Or they can be applied broadly to enable changes to be made to a range of legislation. The breadth of the potential changes will inevitably affect the degree of concerns raised: narrow Henry VIII powers can be criticised but may be tolerated

[3] Donoughmore Committee Report (n 1) 36. See also Cecil Carr, *Delegated Legislation* (Cambridge University Press, 1921), 50–52; Lord Judge, 'Ceding Power to the Executive; the Resurrection of Henry VIII' (King's College London, 12 April 2016) 4–6, available at www.kcl.ac.uk/archive/news/law/newsrecords/2015-16/Ceding-Power-to-the-Executive.

[4] HC Debates vol 224, col 974 (30 January 1929) (Sir Henry Slessor).

[5] *The Times*, 16 February 1929 quoted in Lord Hewart of Bury, *The New Despotism* (Ernest Benn Ltd, 1929) 57.

[6] Lord Rippon, 'Henry VIII Clauses' (1989) 10 *Statute Law Review* 205, 207.

[7] Allison (n 2) 62–63.

and very wide Henry VIII clauses are likely to raise substantial concerns about circumventing Parliament.

As will be explained in the next section, the Donoughmore Committee criticised Henry VIII clauses and accepted them within narrow limits. The Committee's analysis established the primary norm by which commentators have assessed Henry VIII clauses since.[8] Commentators have accepted that they were largely not used in the decades following the Donoughmore Committee's report.[9] The same commentators, and others,[10] also emphasise that this is no longer the case and that there has been a resurgence of Henry VIII powers in legislation in the UK since the 1980s. The concerns are also raised in Australia but not to the same extent. The concern is not so much with their widespread use in Commonwealth legislation, but in their systemic use in economic legislation; in particular, the Corporations Act 2001 (Cth).[11]

Henry VIII clauses played a large role in the 1930s debates and were accepted there within very narrow limits. The continuing tension with Henry VIII clauses arises because recent parliaments have pushed far beyond those limits. They are now enacted in broad forms to deal with systemic issues. This chapter examines how Henry VIII clauses were understood in the 1930s debates and the subsequent developments. It then elaborates principles for scrutinising, interpreting and criticising Henry VIII provisions in modern political and public law contexts drawing on the primary concern of the Donoughmore Committee, limiting their breadth.

I. Henry VIII Powers in the 1930s Debates

A. United Kingdom

As has been explained, Henry VIII powers were heavily criticised by Lord Hewart and the Donoughmore Committee. We will see that John Willis recognised such criticism and only accepted them due to their use in practice for narrow and technical purposes. These debates were based on the inclusion of Henry VIII powers in the decades prior to the 1930s debates. The Donoughmore Committee set out nine Acts that included Henry VIII clauses from 1888 to the time of its report.[12] These

[8] See, eg, Rippon (n 6) 205–06; Barber and Young (n 1) 113; G Marshall, 'Metric Measures and Martyrdom by Henry VIII Clause' (2002) 118 *Law Quarterly Review* 493, 496–97.

[9] See, eg, CK Allen, *Law and Orders* (Stevens and Sons, 1945) 102; Rippon (n 6) 205–06; Barber and Young (n 1) 119.

[10] See eg Marshall (n 8) 497; Lord Judge (n 3) 10.

[11] See, eg, S Bottomley 'The Notional Legislator: The Australian Securities and Investments Commission's Role as A Law-Maker' (2011) 39 *Federal Law Review* 1; T Van Geelen, 'Delegated Legislation in Financial Services Law: Implications for Regulatory Complexity and the Rule of Law' (2021) 38 *Company and Securities Law Journal* 296.

[12] Donoughmore Committee Report (n 1) Annex 2.

clauses were commonly referred to in their Acts as, 'power to remove defects' or 'power to remove difficulties'.

The political background to the 1930s debate included a debate in the House of Commons in 1929 regarding the Local Government Bill.[13] The debate on the Henry VIII clause started with the observation by Gerald Hurst that the provision raised 'a really important constitutional issue', which was explained in the following manner:

> [T]his bill in its current form seeks to give effect to a power of suspension and dispensation which has been illegal in this country since the Bill of Rights, and which it seems unnecessary to re-enact in these days for the benefit of a Government department. A great many critics much more competent than I have spoken in a hostile spirit upon this growing tendency of Parliament largely to extend the powers of Government departments, but this is the largest of all executive powers. It is a power to legislate, in fact, because it is a power to override the provisions of an Act of Parliament.[14]

The Minister for Health who proposed the Bill dismissed the concern. He referred to the numerous Henry VIII clauses that had already been made and claimed there was no evidence that they have been abused.[15]

This parliamentary debate set the framework for the subsequent debate involving Lord Hewart, John Willis and the Donoughmore Committee. Lord Hewart introduced his topic with a Henry VIII clause as the primary example of the problem he would address in the book.[16] These clauses fueled his concern about the bureaucratic conspiracy upending the parliament–executive relationship.[17] The chapter on 'administrative lawlessness' included a long passage dealing with the Local Government Bill, the parliamentary debates, and the Minister's minimal amendments in response to the concerns raised.[18] Lord Hewart's proposed solution was more blunt than the solutions put forward by other contributors to the debates: they should be abolished.[19] So for Lord Hewart, Henry VIII clauses were one of a number of problems with modern legislation that can be regarded as raising concerns of 'systematic' attempts to empower executive officials at the expense of parliaments and courts.[20]

The significance of Henry VIII clauses to the 1930s debates is not only reflected in Lord Hewart's introduction of the main problem he sought to address. It is also indicated in John Willis dedicating a whole chapter of his book to Henry VIII clauses. The first sentence of that chapter was directed to Lord Hewart: that while Henry VIII powers had been criticised in the early decades

[13] HC Debates Vol 224, col 970–1001 (30 January 1929).
[14] ibid cols 970–71.
[15] ibid col 976 (Minister of Health - Mr Chamberlain).
[16] Hewart (n 5) 3–4.
[17] ibid 8.
[18] ibid 53–57.
[19] ibid 155.
[20] ibid 159.

of the twentieth century, none were 'so furious or so one-sided as that launched by Lord Hewart'.[21]

The general point of Willis's argument was that while it is understandable that lawyers and laypersons would be, in his word, 'aghast' at such clauses, the important point is how they are used.[22] This highlights that Willis's analysis of them would draw on his realist methodology; the application of Henry VIII clauses in practice was of most importance. When he analysed the uses of Henry VIII clauses from 1925 to 1930, he found that they were all of minor, 'trifling', importance.[23] Willis was not alone in this view. Cecil Carr stated in 1941 that regulations made under these powers are usually 'surprisingly innocuous' and 'innocent enough'.[24] Willis drew on this assessment of the uses of Henry VIII clauses to argue that they appropriately redirect minor matters to government departments rather than Parliament. Accordingly he regarded such powers as being appropriate, particularly when limited to enabling administrators to adjust older legislation to reconcile them to a new Act and to deal with 'unusual or trivial' matters that are likely to arise and that Parliament is not likely to deal with itself.[25] He also indicated that the strict time limits included in Henry VIII clauses of the time mitigated the concerns.[26]

The Donoughmore Committee's report can be regarded as a synthesis of Lord Hewart's critique and John Willis's counterargument. Without naming Lord Hewart, the report expressly rejected the bureaucrat's conspiracy claim,[27] but accepted that they are generally problematic, and that ministers have an important role in justifying them to Parliament.[28] On the other hand, the main point of the Report's analysis was similar to Willis's argument; Henry VIII clauses are acceptable within limits. The Donoughmore Committee classified regulations made under Henry VIII provisions in its category of 'exceptional type of delegated legislation' in contrast to 'normal type'.[29] The Donoughmore Report stated that they

> cannot but be regarded as inconsistent with the principles of Parliamentary government that the subordinate law-making authority should be given by the superior lawmaking authority power to amend a statute which has been passed by the superior authority.[30]

This view led the Committee to regard the then current explanations for them as unpersuasive and that they were only acceptable when limited to minor matters and the responsible minister provides a clear justification. This meant that they

[21] J Willis, *The Parliamentary Powers of English Government Departments* (Harvard University Press, 1933) 146.
[22] ibid 151–52.
[23] ibid 164.
[24] C Carr, *Concerning English Administrative Law* (Columbia University Press, 1941) 44.
[25] Willis (n 21) 149.
[26] ibid 152.
[27] Donoughmore Committee Report (n 1) 59.
[28] ibid 59, 64.
[29] ibid 30–31.
[30] ibid 59.

should be limited to bringing an Act into operation and have a one-year maximum time limit.[31]

The most interesting aspect of the UK 1930s debates is that there seems to be no substantive disagreement with Lord Hewart's concern that Henry VIII clauses are generally problematic. Willis seemed to treat that concern as at least understandable as did the Donoughmore Committee, even though both distanced themselves from Lord Hewart's argument. The substantive differences were in the solutions. For Lord Hewart, Henry VIII clauses should be abolished but the other contributors accepted that they should be permissible within very limited circumstances.

B. Australia

Henry VIII clauses have attracted much less attention in Australian debates. On the one hand the Henry VIII terminology that was developed in the UK 1930s debates has become part of Australian public law terminology and there are numerous reports that have criticised them. For example, the Administrative Review Council's report in 1992 into regulation-making referred to 'it is clearly inappropriate for a body subordinate to Parliament to amend or alter an Act made by Parliament'.[32] However, it is fair to say that these provisions have not prompted the kind of outrage they have received in the UK. This is particularly the case in the Australian 1930s debates. The result is that the norms regarding the use of Henry VIII clauses did not take root in the same way as in the UK as a result of the Australian 1930s debates.

In fact, the Senate Committee's 1930 report did not expressly address Henry VIII clauses at all. Its characterisation of enabling provisions related to regulations being made consistently with the enabling Act,[33] without any reference to provisions enabling amendment or modification of that, or any other, Act. The closest it came to addressing Henry VIII clauses was in its recommendation for a committee to scrutinise bills to determine whether 'the clause of each bill conferring a regulation-making power does not confer a legislative power which ought to be exercised by Parliament itself'.[34]

The lack of direct analysis or concern regarding Henry VIII provisions by the 1930 Senate Committee is interesting because it is very likely that it was aware of Henry VIII provisions. The Committee referred to Lord Hewart's book being recently published and that it was referred to in numerous submissions.[35] As we

[31] ibid 61, 65.

[32] Administrative Review Council, *Rule Making by Commonwealth Agencies* (Report No 35, 1992) para 2.33.

[33] Senate, *Report from the Senate Select Committee Advising on Establishing Standing Committees*, Parliament of Australia (Report April 1930) para 13.

[34] ibid para 23.

[35] ibid para 16.

have just seen, Lord Hewart's criticism of Henry VIII clauses was prominent at the outset of his book.

The 1930 Senate Committee's lack of analysis of Henry VIII clauses is also surprising due to the prominent Henry VIII provision in the Transport Workers Act 1928 that had recently been enacted and was criticised in Senate debates. Section 3 of that Act authorised the Governor-General to make regulations that would have the force of law 'notwithstanding anything in any other Act but subject to the Acts Interpretation Act 1901–1918 and the Acts Interpretation Act 1904–1916'. In the Senate debates for this Act, Senator Needham argued that s 3 meant that

> absolute power is given to the Government, irrespective of any act on the statute book. Thus, the Government is to receive a blank cheque. This means legislation by the Governor-General instead of legislation by Parliament.[36]

So although there was awareness of and concerns about Henry VIII powers at the time of the 1930 Senate Committee's inquiry, these provisions were not expressly addressed. That prevented norms from being established that they are generally not appropriate but accepted within tight parameters, as understood by the Donoughmore Committee.

The Henry VIII provision in the Transport Workers Act 1928 was subject to a constitutional challenge in the *Dignan* case, examined in section II of chapter two. The High Court in *Dignan* accepted that section 3 did not breach the separation of powers principles in the Commonwealth Constitution and was valid. Surprisingly, the fact that it was a Henry VIII clause rather than the more usual form of enabling provision was not given any particular or separate analysis in the High Court's decision in *Dignan* even though the Henry VIII characteristics were at the forefront of the applicant's argument. The first paragraph of the applicant's argument, as set out in the authorised report of the case,[37] emphasised that the enabling provision in the Act was ultra vires because it gave the force of law to regulations 'notwithstanding anything in any other Act', which they rightly understood to include the otherwise most relevant Act, the Commonwealth Conciliation and Arbitration Act 1904, and other Commonwealth Acts. The argument continued by stating that 'Regulations so made cannot override the laws of the sovereign body'.[38] However, the fact that section 3 was a Henry VIII clause did not draw any particular comment or, as might now be expected, criticism. As we saw in chapter two, the High Court focused on Parliament's ability to repeal or amend the enabling provision, and the limits being provided by the Commonwealth Parliament's powers under section 51 of the Commonwealth Constitution and Parliament not abdicating its function.

[36] Commonwealth, *Parliamentary Debates*, Senate, 22 September 1928, 7200.

[37] *Victorian Stevedoring and General Contracting Co Pty Ltd and Meakes v Dignan* (1931) 46 CLR 73, 77.

[38] ibid.

While a Henry VIII power was the primary provision of legislation that prompted much debate in the 1930s in Australia, its significance as such a provision was not examined in the 1930 Senate Committee report and the High Court's judgment in *Dignan*. This makes the Australian 1930s debates an exception to my general point that the norms for regulation-making were established in the 1930s. With regard to Henry VIII clauses, norms were established at that time in the UK by the Donoughmore Committee, but for Australia the opportunity to develop equivalent norms was not taken up. That is partly due to the particular approach taken by the High Court in *Dignan* and possibly because the main conflict regarding the exercise of the Henry VIII clause in the Transport Workers Act 1928 occurred after the 1930 Senate Committee's report was published.

II. Current Uses of Henry VIII Powers

A. United Kingdom

As explained in the introduction to this chapter, academics, politicians and lawyers have raised concerns about a resurgence of Henry VIII clauses since the 1980s in UK legislation and that such clauses have broadened in scope. The norm established by the Donoughmore Committee, that I referred to as a kind of synthesis of the arguments made by Lord Hewart and John Willis was that Henry VIII clauses are generally inappropriate and the scope of the exemptions should be limited to transitional arrangements for implementing new legislation. We will see in this section that the resurgence of Henry VIII clauses is not only significant for its quantity, but also for the inclusion of Henry VIII clauses that go beyond the limits expressed by the Donoughmore Committee.

The following analysis is not intended to be comprehensive. It focuses on the breadth of Henry VIII provisions and criticisms of them. Accordingly, I start with some examples of broad Henry VIII provisions in order to identify the problem and then examine the criticisms of them by academics, practitioners, courts and parliamentary committees. This criticism indicates that the norms established in the 1930s remain a common reference point for criticism of Henry VIII clauses.

The point I want to make is that the resurgence of the use of Henry VIII powers and the criticism that it receives confirms the ongoing relevance of the Donoughmore Committee's synthesis of the issues. While the norms in relation to Henry VIII clauses may no longer influence administrative officials in the drafting process and have weak influence in parliaments, they are commonly drawn on by critics. Critics can use the Donoughmore Committee's norms to argue that the inclusion of broad Henry VIII provisions upends accepted executive–parliament relations inherent in parliamentary democracies.

i. Resurgence

The more recent criticisms of Henry VIII clauses started in the late 1980s in a series of publications by Lord Rippon.[39] I will start with the examples of Henry VIII provisions that he criticised and then move on to such provisions in subsequent legislation that were even broader. These subsequent Acts include Henry VIII clauses that have additional significance due to being included in highly important, constitutional statutes. Legislation applied in the COVID-19 pandemic also included Henry VIII provisions, but I have not included them in this section; they are examined in chapter nine.

Some of the Henry VIII clauses referred to by Lord Rippon were powers to deal with transitional arrangements. They authorised amendments to past Acts and Acts made in the particular session of Parliament for the purpose of implementing the new legislation. For example, section 194 of the Local Government and Housing Act 1989 provided:

> The Secretary of State may by order made by statutory instrument make provision … amending, repealing or revoking (with or without savings) any provision of an Act passed before or in the same session as this Act.

This provision seems to be within the transitional purpose of the norms established by the Donoughmore Committee, but was drafted in broader form than the Committee's recommendations. The provision enabled implementing steps to be taken and were time-limited, not by one year as stated by the Committee, but a relatively short period. They also authorised changes to a potentially broad range of legislation.

However, other provisions that Lord Rippon referred to from that period were broader and more problematic. These provisions, at least on their face, authorised amendments to 'any Act' related to their particular subject matter. For example, the Children Act 1989, Sch 11, para 5(a) provided that:

> An order under this Schedule may–(a) make such consequential, incidental or transitional provision as the Lord Chancellor considers expedient, including provision amending any other enactment so far as it concerns the jurisdiction of any court or justice of the peace.

The Courts and Legal Services Act 1990, s 3(4)(d) provided that:

> Regulations under subsection (3) … may make provision amending or repealing any provision made by or under any enactment, so far as may be necessary or expedient in consequence of the regulations.

These provisions are not limited to transitional arrangements or Acts passed in the current session. Nor are they limited to a particular time, such as one year as

[39] Rippon (n 6); Lord Rippon, 'Constitutional Anarchy' (1990) 11 *Statute Law Review* 184; Lord Rippon, *Making the Law* (Hansard Society, 1993) paras 268–70.

recommended by the Donoughmore Committee, which makes it clear that they were drafted far more broadly than the Donoughmore Committee's limits.

These kinds of broad Henry VIII clauses have continued to be included in ordinary Acts and Acts with constitutional significance, and have continued to be criticised. For example, barristers Isabel McArdle and Sarabjit Singh QC criticised section 4(2) of the Childcare Act 2016 as an example of a recent ordinary Act with a broad Henry VIII clause.[40] That section authorises regulations to be made that, 'amend, repeal or revoke any provision made by or under an Act (whenever passed or made)'. This Henry VIII clause is limited by subject matter – childcare – and includes an affirmative resolution procedure.[41] However, it is unlimited in relation to the Acts it can amend, on its face extending to prospective Acts, and in regard to the period in which it operates. This is a more recent example of a Henry VIII clause with some limits, but it still operates far beyond the Donoughmore Committee's norms.

The Delegated Powers and Regulatory Reform Committee criticised the delegations of power provided in the initial version of the bill.[42] These criticisms prompted some amendments and the Committee reported again on it.[43] The Committee's criticism of the provisions of the bill in these two reports were more general than may be expected. The Committee criticised the breadth of the delegation of power and the parliamentary scrutiny procedures provided, but did not expressly criticise the inclusion and characteristics of the Henry VIII power included in it. It is hard to know why there was no express criticism, but it may have been due to the Henry VIII clause being explained in a departmental briefing to the Committee and it being subject to an affirmative resolution parliamentary scrutiny procedure.[44]

While it is important to recognise the use of broad Henry VIII powers in recent ordinary Acts, there is an additional development that marks out recent decades as having particular importance for the use of Henry VIII powers in the UK. This is their inclusion in Acts that have constitutional significance.[45] The prominent examples that have included Henry VIII provisions are the European Communities Act 1972, s 2(2) and (4),[46] and the Human Rights Act 1998, s 10(2) and (3).[47]

[40] R English interview with I McArdle and S Singh QC, 'Henry VIII Powers undermining parliamentary supremacy' (Law Pod UK, 5 May 2021), available at ukhumanrightsblog.com/2021/05/04/law-pod-uk-new-episode-henry-viii-powers-undermining-parliamentary-supremacy.

[41] Childcare Act 2016, ss 4(4), (5)(d).

[42] Delegated Powers and Regulatory Reform Committee, *Childcare Bill* (HL 2015–16, 12) paras 7–13.

[43] Delegated Powers and Regulatory Reform Committee, *Childcare Bill – Government Amendments* (HL 2015–16, 37).

[44] Department of Education, 'Delegated Powers Memorandum – Childcare Bill 2015', paras 26–27, available at www.parliament.uk/globalassets/documents/DPRR/2015-16/Bills/Childcare/11-Childcare-DP-Memo.pdf.

[45] See *Thoburn v Sunderland Council* [2002] EWHC 195 (Admin), [2003] QB 151, [62]; *R (Miller) v Secretary of State for Exiting the European Union* [2017] UKSC 5, [2018] AC 61, [67], [81].

[46] *Thoburn* (n 45) [27], [41], [62].

[47] See Barber and Young (n 1) 121–22.

Brexit legislation provides recent important examples of constitutional statutes with broad Henry VIII clauses. The European Union (Withdrawal) Act 2018, section 8 was enacted for particular, unusual purposes, including the purpose of correcting problems in statutory law arising from withdrawal from the EU. The Act provides for these corrections to be made by way of regulations. Other broad Henry VIII powers in Brexit-related legislation are the Taxation (Cross-Border Trade) Act 2018, section 51(3) and the European Union (Future Relationship) Act 2020, section 31(2). These Acts are similar to emergency legislation due to their unusual and urgent nature but are worth referring to in this chapter due to their constitutional significance. In particular, the main Henry VIII clause in the European Union (Withdrawal) Bill and the subsequent Act was criticised for its breadth and parliamentary scrutiny procedures. The criticism came from parliamentary committees (including the Delegated Powers and Regulatory Reform Committee[48] and the Lords Constitution Committee[49]), scholars,[50] members of the legal profession[51] and public interest groups.[52]

The resurgence of Henry VIII clauses in UK legislation has a number of important aspects. The first is that there is general recognition that they are more commonly included in legislation than in the past. Secondly, it is generally recognised that Henry VIII clauses in current legislation are far broader than the Donoughmore Committee's recommendations. This remains controversial and is criticised. Thirdly, Henry VIII clauses are now included in Acts with constitutional significance – a development that would be very surprising to all contributors in the UK 1930s debates. And fourthly, Henry VIII provisions are now commonly scrutinised by parliamentary committees. The focus is not only on their breadth (which was the focus in the 1930s debates), but also on the parliamentary scrutiny procedure.

ii. Criticisms

As we have seen, the resurgence of Henry VIII provisions in the UK has been subjected to criticism. It is worth analysing these criticisms to understand the

[48] Delegated Powers and Regulatory Reform Committee, *European Union (Withdrawal) Bill* (HL 2017–19, 22) paras 14–31, 107; Delegated Powers and Regulatory Reform Committee, *European Union (Withdrawal) Bill* (HL 2017–19, 73) paras 6–12, 50–58; Delegated Powers and Regulatory Reform Committee, *European Union (Withdrawal) Bill: Government Amendments* (HL 2017–19, 124) paras 4–10; Delegated Powers and Regulatory Reform Committee, *European Union (Withdrawal) Bill: Further Government Amendments* (HL 2017–19, 128).

[49] Select Committee on the Constitution, *European Union (Withdrawal) Bill: interim report* (HL 2017–19, 19) paras 48, 56; Select Committee on the Constitution, *European Union (Withdrawal) Bill* (HL 2017–19, 69) paras 185–88, 214–22.

[50] See, eg, M Elliott and S Tierney, 'Political Pragmatism and Constitutional Principle: the European Union (Withdrawal) Act 2018' [2019] *Public Law* 37, 48–52.

[51] I McArdle interview with English (n 40).

[52] A Sinclair and J Tomlinson, 'Plus ça change? Brexit and the Flaws of the Delegated Legislation System' (Public Law Project, 13 October 2020), 17–19, available at publiclawproject.org.uk/resources/plus-ca-change-brexit-and-the-flaws-of-the-delegated-legislation-system.

relevance of the Donoughmore Committee's analysis to modern concerns with Henry VIII clauses. I have sought to argue throughout that the 1930s debates set initial standards for the delegation of regulation-making powers. Those debates and the Donoughmore Committee's analysis of Henry VIII clauses have influenced parliamentary committees, courts, academics and practitioners. The Donoughmore Committee's analysis and recommendations continue to be referred to it in reports and literature often expressly and, if not referred to expressly, modern criticisms commonly align with it. However, the minimalist approach expressed in the Donoughmore Committee's report is not accepted by government and the administrative officials involved in drafting legislation. This is the only conclusion that can be drawn from the common inclusion of broad Henry VIII provisions in bills and in the Government's explanation for the practice.

Prompted by growing concerns about decreasing accountability of governments to Parliament, the Delegated Powers and Regulatory Reform Committee ('Delegated Powers Committee') published a report in 2021 into the relationship between the executive and Parliament.[53] The section on Henry VIII powers quoted the Donoughmore Committee that the responsible minister must justify a Henry VIII power in a bill 'to the hilt' and that such clauses 'should be avoided unless demonstrably essential'.[54] These references were added to highlight the longstanding controversial nature of Henry VIII powers. Yet, the Delegated Powers Committee's approach to Henry VIII powers is not as stringent as the Donoughmore Committee's narrow limitations. The Delegated Powers Committee regards them as requiring particular justification and be subject to affirmative resolution parliamentary scrutiny procedures.[55] This tends to show that while the concerns and criticism of Henry VIII powers continues in the Delegated Powers Committee's scrutiny of bills, it has resisted imposing the more specific and narrower limits that were included in the Donoughmore Committee's report.

The UK courts have expressed principles for interpreting Henry VIII clauses that align with the Donoughmore Committee's recommendation without referring to the Committee directly. In *R (Public Law Project) v Lord Chancellor*[56] the UK Supreme Court quoted with approval previous cases and statutory interpretation texts to make clear that constitutional considerations regarding the relationship between the executive and Parliament require Henry VIII clauses to be interpreted narrowly.[57]

The joint judgment's approach in *Public Law Project* was expressly based on the line of case law developed by the UK courts in the resurgence period. This line of

[53] Delegated Powers and Regulatory Reform Committee, *Democracy Denied? The Urgent Need to Rebalance Power between Parliament and the Executive* (HL 2021–22 106).

[54] ibid para 76.

[55] ibid para 77; D Vangimalla, 'Compendium of Legislative Standards for Delegating Powers in Primary Legislation' (Hansard Society, 25 April 2022) [3.4]–[3.9], available at www.hansardsociety.org.uk/publications/reports/compendium-of-legislative-standards-for-delegating-powers-in-primary.

[56] *R (Public Law Project) v Lord Chancellor* [2016] UKSC 39, [2016] AC 1531.

[57] ibid [26] quoting D Greenberg (ed), *Craies on Legislation*, 10th edn (2015) para 1.3.11.

case law starts with an influential statement by Lord Donaldson in *McKiernon v Secretary of State for Social Security* who stated that neither negative or affirmative resolution procedures are equivalent to parliamentary scrutiny of Acts because the scrutiny is 'subject to much briefer, if any, examination by Parliament and cannot be amended'. He then went on to say:

> The duty of the courts being to give effect to the will of Parliament, it is, in my judgment, legitimate to take account of the fact that a delegation to the Executive of power to modify primary legislation must be an exceptional course and that, if there is any doubt about the scope of the power conferred upon the Executive or upon whether it has been exercised, it should be resolved by a restrictive approach.[58]

The Supreme Court's reference to these sources for guidance on interpreting Henry VIII clauses is highly significant. It recognises the resurgence of wide Henry VIII provisions, criticises them on constitutional grounds, and expresses an interpretive methodology for them. In this way, it can be understood to align closely with the Donoughmore Committee's analysis. Courts can legitimately draw on constitutional principles regarding executive–parliament relationships to read down Henry VIII clauses where there is uncertainty regarding their scope.

As we saw in the explanation of the resurgence of Henry VIII clauses, there has been a steady stream of recent criticism of Henry VIII clauses by scholars and commentators. Their criticism is commonly on the grounds of the increase of inclusion of Henry VIII clauses, their breadth and the view that parliamentary scrutiny procedures for regulations do not match parliamentary scrutiny for Acts. The 1930s debates and the Donoughmore Committee's recommendation for their narrow use are commonly the starting point for this kind of analysis.[59]

The resurgence of use of Henry VIII clauses and nature of the criticism of them provides evidence that the Donoughmore Committee's analysis has not affected legislative practices but has continued to influence criticisms. The Donoughmore Committee's report on this issue provides a starting point for analysis and criticism: a norm that acts as a constitutional convention for Henry VIII clauses in the UK. Breach of that norm attracts criticism of government for including them in bills and to Parliament for accepting them.

There is also a fairly clear indication of government officials not accepting the Donoughmore Committee's approach to Henry VIII clauses due to the fact of the wide inclusion of them in Acts since the start of the resurgence in the 1980s. Evidence provided by the First Parliamentary Counsel to the Delegated Powers

[58] *McKiernon v Secretary of State for Social Security* (1989–90) 2 *Administrative Law Review* 133, 140. Cited by Lord Keith of Kinkel in *R v Secretary of State for Social Security, ex p Britnell* [1991] 1 WLR 198, 204 and Lord Bingham in *R v Secretary of State for the Environment, Transport and the Regions, ex p Spath Holme Ltd* [2001] 2 AC 349, 382.

[59] Marshall (n 8) 496–97; Barber and Young (n 1) 113; Lord Judge (n 3) 9; A Tucker, 'Parliamentary Scrutiny of Delegated Legislation' in A Horne and G Drewry (eds) *Parliament and the Law* (Hart Publishing, 2018) 347, 359; J King, 'The Province of Delegated Legislation' in E Fisher, J King and AL Young, *The Foundations and Future of Public Law* (Oxford University Press, 2020) 145, 150–51.

Committee highlights aspects of the drafting process when Henry VIII clauses are initially proposed. She stated that their inclusion can be due to time constraints on government, leading to drafters focusing on implementing the desired policy into the bill and including Henry VIII provisions to enable amendments to other Acts necessary to implement the new Act to be dealt with later.[60] It can also be due to departments initially adding a general Henry VIII power in a bill that later in the drafting process turns out to be necessary only for a particular part of the bill.[61] These explanations indicate the continuing tensions with Henry VIII clauses. Departmental officials see them as convenient for their purposes and their starting point is often to draft them broadly. On the other hand, parliamentary committees, courts, scholars and practitioners see them as inverting norms for law-making in parliamentary democracies. Accordingly, the problems identified in the 1930s debate continue to raise concerns.

B. Australia

As explained in section I.B of this chapter, there was no real criticism of Henry VIII clauses in the 1930s debates in Australia. That should be regarded as surprising given that the High Court was required to examine one in the primary Australian case on delegation of regulation-making power and that the provision that was examined by the High Court had been criticised in the Senate shortly before the Senate Committee's inquiry into establishing scrutiny committees. In recent decades, there has been a resurgence of Henry VIII provisions in Australia, which is particularly apparent in economic legislation. There has been some criticism of their use in that context and also more general criticism from a constitutional perspective. However, it is fair to say that the criticism has lacked the outraged tone of some of the UK criticism and is not as widespread.

The Australian resurgence is most clearly seen in Commonwealth economic legislation. The most well-known example is the Corporations Act 2001, which at the time of writing includes 19 exemption and modification provisions. Exemptions and modifications provisions in similar form are included in other Acts.[62] They authorise exemptions for individuals and classes of individuals from provisions of the Act and they authorise modifications of the Act by regulatory

[60] Delegated Powers and Regulatory Reform Committee, *Democracy Denied? The Urgent Need to Rebalance Power between Parliament and the Executive* (HL 2021–22, 106) para 81.

[61] E Gardiner, First Parliamentary Counsel, 'House of Lords Delegated Powers and Regulatory Reform Committee, Corrected oral evidence: The Delegation of Legislative Power' (26 May 2021) answer to question 7, available at committees.parliament.uk/oralevidence/2269/html.

[62] See, eg, National Consumer Credit Protection Act 2009 (Cth), ss 107–110, 161–164; Superannuation Industry (Supervision) Act 1993 (Cth), ss 326–336; Retirement Savings Accounts Act 1997 (Cth), ss 172–180; Competition and Consumer Act 2010 (Cth), s 56GE.

agencies and ministers. This makes them different to Henry VIII clauses as usually understood. Rather than authorising *amendments* to be made to the enabling Act or other Acts, these Henry VIII provisions authorise *exemptions and modifications* from parts of the Act. The interesting and unusual feature of the exercise of these powers is the exemptions and modifications are operative but are not expressed in the Act. The provisions of the Act that are exempted or modified remain in place, on their face unaffected by the exemption or modification but nevertheless changed as a matter of law.[63]

Professor Stephen Bottomley has tracked the emergence of these provisions to the 1970s and the development of companies legislation.[64] They were prompted by a desire for flexibility, which led to the inclusion of provisions enabling exemptions for particular persons from some of the provisions of that legislation. This was gradually expanded in the 1980s to exemptions for classes of securities and classes of persons.[65] This history of gradual expansion can also be seen in the Corporations Act 2001. When the Act commenced it had four sets of exemption and modifications provisions[66] and, as we have just seen, more than 20 years later, the Corporations Act currently has 19 sets of such provisions.

In this way, Commonwealth economic legislation has gradually developed a particular form of Henry VIII clause. We can now turn to the criticisms of these provisions and in particular the kinds of criticism that are influenced by concerns about their effect on parliamentary democracy. It should be noted that Professor Bottomley, writing in 2011, noted that there had at that time been no criticism of these provisions most likely due to the pragmatism of those who practice in this area of law.[67] Still, Professor Bottomley himself was critical of them and others have since joined him.

The Commonwealth Government initiated an inquiry in 2020 by the Australian Law Reform Commission (ALRC) into the Corporations Act 2001 (Cth) as a response to criticisms of its complexity by the Royal Commission into Misconduct in the Banking, Superannuation and Financial Services Industry that reported in 2019.[68] The Royal Commission referred to concerns being raised in its inquiry by numerous stakeholders about the complexity of financial legislation due to the increase in exceptions and recommended that they be eliminated as far as possible.[69] The ALRC is currently inquiring into how such simplification of the

[63] Bottomley (n 11) 24; Van Geelen (n 11) 306.
[64] Bottomley (n 11)12.
[65] ibid 13–14.
[66] Corporations Act 2001 (Cth), ss 111AR–111AX, 340–343, 601QA–601QB and 1113.
[67] Bottomley (n 11) 17, 28.
[68] Royal Commission into Misconduct in the Banking, Superannuation and Financial Services Industry, 'Final Report' (2019).
[69] ibid 494–96.

Corporations Act can be carried out. The terms of reference require the ALRC to inquire into 'how delegated powers should be expressed in legislation, consistent with maintaining an appropriate delegation of legislative authority'.[70]

The ALRC's first report confirms that the exemptions and modifications provisions have been a 'driver of legislative complexity' of the Corporations Act.[71] The report emphasises the difficulty of 'navigating' the legislation, that the statutory scheme is 'opaque', and lacks 'coherence'.[72] This is particularly due to modifications powers resulting in the text of the Act not being authoritative, as the provisions of the modification instrument prevail over the text of the Act.[73] The ALRC also raised concerns in its interim report about the effect of exemptions and modifications provisions on the relationship between the executive and Parliament in a parliamentary democracy.[74] It stated that its proposed recommendations for the Corporations Act would make the modifications powers redundant.[75]

There has also been criticism of these provisions in the academic literature. Professor Bottomley examined the exemptions and modification provisions of the Corporations Act in detail and criticised them on numerous grounds including that the laws are poorly designed for regulatory purposes, have rule of law and separation of powers difficulties, and are not subject to a mandatory consultation process.[76] His suggested reform proposals focused on providing a more effective role for Parliament.[77] More recently, Tess Van Geelen has made similar criticisms to those made in the ALRC interim report. Her additional insight is that exemptions and modification provisions make legal change so convenient for agency officials that it creates a disincentive for the Government to seek formal statutory changes to the Corporations Act through parliamentary processes.[78]

As this makes clear, Commonwealth economic legislation has been the focus of recent debates about Henry VIII clauses in Australian legislation. More general concerns have also been raised about Henry VIII clauses. For example, the Senate Scrutiny of Bills Committee scrutinises bills for the inclusion of Henry VIII clauses and regularly raises concerns about them in its reports. The Committee scrutinises them for being prima facie within its scrutiny criterion 'inappropriate delegation of legislative powers' and requires explanation of their appropriateness

[70] Australian Law Reform Commission, *Interim Report A: Financial Services Legislation* (ALRC Report 137, 2021) 5.
[71] ibid para 10.14.
[72] ibid para 10.3.
[73] ibid paras 10.60–10.63.
[74] ibid paras 10.16, 10.60.
[75] ibid paras 10.37, 10.83.
[76] Bottomley (n 11) 17–28.
[77] ibid 28–30.
[78] Van Geelen (n 11) 309.

and the safeguards that will ensure their appropriateness.[79] Its annual reports regularly note that such provisions are drawn to the attention of the Senate.[80]

The High Court has criticised Henry VIII clauses and drawn on the UK case law to enable a narrow interpretation and application of them. The starting point for the analysis is commonly that while there is no formal constitutional concern with them, they are nevertheless criticised.[81] While these criticisms are not elaborated, they are taken to be self-evident, and they have led courts to interpret them narrowly, often citing the UK courts' interpretive approach in the cases explained in section II.A.ii of this chapter in support.[82]

While Australian courts have not accepted the potential constitutional difficulties with Henry VIII clauses due to their enabling the executive to amend and modify statutory provisions made by Parliament, public law scholars have argued that constitutional law should be developed to enable such provisions to be limited. The concerns are commonly tied to criticism on constitutional grounds of broad delegations of regulation-making power to administrative officials, the High Court's tolerance of them that is reflected in the *Dignan* case examined in chapter two, and the potential options for limiting that tolerance. Henry VIII clauses are regarded in this scholarship as a primary example of these problems.[83] The significance of these articles for my purposes is that they are evidence of constitutional concerns with Henry VIII clauses in Australia. While the arguments tend to focus on the High Court's reasoning in *Dignan* rather than general principles of parliamentary democracy as in the UK academic literature, the criticisms are driven by the same concerns.

In summary, we can see that effectively the same concerns have been expressed by similar institutions in Australia as in the UK. The recent use of Henry VIII clauses has not extended to Acts with constitutional status as has occurred in the UK, but their use can be regarded as widespread, particularly in Commonwealth economic legislation. It is fair to say that in that context their use is systemic rather

[79] Senate Standing Committee for the Scrutiny of Bills, *Consolidated Guidelines*, 2nd edn (2022) 18.

[80] Senate Standing Committee for the Scrutiny of Bills, *Annual Report 2018* (2019) 33–34; Senate Standing Committee for the Scrutiny of Bills, *Annual Report 2019* (2020) 28; Senate Standing Committee for the Scrutiny of Bills, *Annual Report 2020* (2021) 29.

[81] *Public Service Association and Professional Officers' Association Amalgamated (NSW) v Director of Public Employment* [2012] HCA 58, (2012) 250 CLR 343, [18] (French CJ); *ADCO Constructions Pty Ltd v Goudappel* [2014] HCA 18; (2014) 254 CLR 1, [31] (French CJ, Crennan, Kiefel and Keane JJ).

[82] *Public Service Association and Professional Officers' Association Amalgamated Union of New South Wales v New South Wales* [2014] NSWCA 116, (2014) 242 IR 338 [103]–[105] (Basten JA); *Maritime Union of Australia v Minister for Immigration and Border Protection* [2016] HCA 34, (2016) 259 CLR 431, [30] and fn 33.

[83] See, eg, D Meyerson, 'Rethinking the Constitutionality of Delegated Legislation' (2003) 11 *Australian Journal of Administrative Law* 45, 52; GA Moens and J Trone, 'The Validity of Henry VIII Clauses in Australian Federal Legislation' (2012) 24 *Giornale Di Storia Costituzionale* 133, 134; G Appleby, 'Challenging the Orthodoxy: Giving the Court a Role in Scrutiny of Delegated Legislation' (2016) 69 *Parliamentary Affairs* 269, 276, 281–82.

than constitutional. And similarly to the situation in the UK, bills continue to be drafted including Henry VIII clauses and they also continue to be criticised by parliamentary committees and interpreted narrowly by courts.

III. Scrutinising, Interpreting and Criticising Henry VIII Clauses

As we saw in section II of this chapter, there has been a resurgence of Henry VIII clauses in both countries in recent decades, and the Donoughmore Committee's restrictive approach to them has been broadly accepted by parliamentary committees, courts and public law scholars, but not by governments and parliaments, as evidenced by their frequent resort to them. The situation may be recognised as a stalemate or continuing tension that is unlikely to be resolved. It is also clear that the current context is different to that of the 1930s. There are now parliamentary committees that scrutinise bills on grounds that include whether Henry VIII clauses have been added.

In this context, it would seem to be helpful to develop more detailed principles by which Henry VIII clauses can be criticised. This would enable parliamentary committees, courts and stakeholder groups to sharpen their scrutiny, interpretation and critiques of particular Henry VIII clauses. The review of the historical arguments and developments in this chapter provides a perspective from which some general principles can be developed. It is apparent that the general guidance provided by parliamentary committees and the principles developed by courts for Henry VIII clauses are under-developed. While scrutiny of bills committees were thought to be suited to drawing attention to such provisions of bills and helping to curtail them,[84] they have not apparently prevented or limited their use. The resurgence has largely occurred in the period since scrutiny of bills committees were established in each country.[85] Their guidelines suggest that these committees focus on requiring a justification and providing for parliamentary scrutiny procedures,[86] rather than detailed principles for analysing their potential breadth. The concern is, as Lord Judge has stated, that governments can easily offer some justification.[87] Courts have developed their interpretive approach to them, but there is little in the way of principles to guide that interpretation.

In this context, it is helpful to develop some modern norms for scrutinising, interpreting and criticising Henry VIII clauses and the justifications that

[84] See, eg Rippon (n 6).

[85] See ch 2, section III.

[86] Delegated Powers and Regulatory Reform Committee, *Democracy Denied? The Urgent Need to Rebalance Power between Parliament and the Executive* (HL 2021–22 106) paras 77 and 84; Senate Standing Committee for the Scrutiny of Bills, *Consolidated Guidelines*, 2nd edn (2022) 18.

[87] Lord Judge (n 3) 12–13.

are provided by governments for them in order to determine whether they are acceptable, borderline or clearly problematic. Professors Barber and Young have provided a framework for analysing the breadth of Henry VIII clauses by examining the conditions and considerations that may provide substantive qualifications, the range of Acts that can potentially be amended or modified, and time limits on the exercise of the Henry VIII power.[88] It is necessary to add to this framework the parliamentary scrutiny procedures provided for the exercise of a Henry VIII clause as being relevant to any assessment of them.

Conditions and considerations: Henry VIII clauses are often criticised due to the lack of, or vagueness of, the conditions and considerations included with the Henry VIII clause. For example, Isabel McArdle criticised the Henry VIII powers in section 51 of the Taxation Cross-Border Trade Act 2018 due to it being conditioned on a ministerial assessment of whether it is 'appropriate'.[89] Similarly, Tess Van Geelen criticised the delegation of power by a Henry VIII clause to the Australian Securities and Investment Commission which 'effectively grants ASIC an unfettered power to delve into matters of policy as it sees fit'.[90]

The inclusion of clearer and more detailed substantive conditions and considerations in Henry VIII clauses ensures that Parliaments consider the scope and purpose of the Henry VIII power when enacting it and enables courts and scrutiny of regulations committees to ensure that the exercise of Henry VIII powers are within the scope of the statutory power. More generally it helps to ensure that each branch performs their general constitutional function: parliaments enacting provisions that reflect policy decisions, administrative officials implementing those policies, and courts ensuring that administrators implement the powers within the parameters set by parliaments.

Scope of Acts that can be amended or modified: Henry VIII clauses can be drafted in a way that enables either a broad range of Acts to be amended or modified or a very limited range. The narrowest Henry VIII clauses apply to past Acts in a narrow field. They can also be drafted to gradually expand to authorise amendments and modifications to Acts made in the same session of Parliament, to past Acts in a very wide range of sectors, to the enabling Act for current and future provisions, and to any future Acts. The Donoughmore Committee's narrow approach to Henry VIII clauses accepted that they were permissible for what can be regarded as transitional purposes, 'for the limited purpose of bringing an Act into operation'.[91] We saw in section II.A.ii of this chapter that administrative officials may seek to justify the inclusion of Henry VIII clauses on this basis. Beyond limited transitional purposes, Henry VIII clauses should be exposed to criticism as risking Ministers and agencies overriding the decisions of parliaments.

[88] Barber and Young (n 1) 113.
[89] Interview with English (n 40).
[90] Bottomley (n 11) 8; Van Geelen (n 11) 305, 309.
[91] Donoughmore Committee Report (n 1) 61.

The UK experience with the scope of Acts that can be amended or modified is particularly instructive due to prominent Acts, such as the European Community Act 1972, including prospective Henry VIII clauses. Professors Barber and Young have highlighted that prospective Henry VIII clauses raise additional concerns relating to parliamentary sovereignty, and in particular the principle that parliaments cannot restrict, or fetter, a subsequent parliament's law-making powers.[92] The exercise of a prospective Henry VIII power to change an Act that was made after the Henry VIII clause was enacted raises concerns that the earlier Act has fettered the powers of the later Parliament. An exercise of the Henry VIII power in the earlier Act can override the later Parliament's exercise of power. Parliament's deliberation and decision in relation to the later Act will be nullified by executive action authorised by the previously made Henry VIII power. This is far beyond the Donoughmore Committee's limits on Henry VIII clauses and should be exposed to serious criticism.

Time limits on the exercise of the Henry VIII power: The Donoughmore Committee referred to Henry VIII clauses as being acceptable when they are limited to one year of operation.[93] There are examples of such provisions being included in recent, prominent legislation: section 8(8) of the European Union (Withdrawal) Act 2018 and sections 475 and 477 of the Biosecurity Act 2015 (Cth), which authorised much of the Commonwealth's COVID-19 pandemic regulations. While time limits can provide a safeguard on the exercise of Henry VIII clauses, it is also necessary to assess whether they can be extended and the safeguards on the powers to extend.

Parliamentary scrutiny procedures: Henry VIII clauses should also provide for the highest level of parliamentary scrutiny available for the exercise of the power. This is referred to in the guidelines provided by the parliamentary committees for scrutinising bills in each country.[94] Commentators have also suggested that parliamentary procedures could be extended to require ministers or senior departmental staff to give a 'public explanation' in Parliament, presumably verbally.[95] The important point is that the inclusion of Henry VIII provisions in bills and exercise of them should be subjected to additional, heightened parliamentary scrutiny. The lack of provision for such scrutiny should be subject to criticism.

It is worth considering in this context Lord Hewart's concern that Members of Parliament insufficiently engage with the problems arising due to delegation of law-making power. He argued that public criticism was necessary and

[92] Barber and Young (n 1) 114–15. See also Marshall (n 8) 498–99.

[93] Donoughmore Committee Report (n 1) 65.

[94] *Democracy Denied? The Urgent Need to Rebalance Power between Parliament and the Executive* (HL 2021–22 106) paras 77 and 84; Senate Standing Committee for the Scrutiny of Bills, *Consolidated Guidelines*, 2nd edn (2022) 18.

[95] Lord Judge (n 3) 13.

recommended that the media should give them more attention and for the development of committees to inform Parliament.[96] Of course, these committees are well-established now but have not been able to stem the flow of Henry VIII clauses enacted in each country.

IV. Conclusion

In this chapter we have seen that Henry VIII clauses were a primary focus of the 1930s debates. The difference between the primary parties to that debate were not as large in substance as they seem on the surface. While the Donoughmore Committee rejected Lord Hewart's hyperbole and did not accept his solution, it is clear it agreed that Henry VIII clauses raise fundamental concerns for parliamentary democracies. The norm established in that period – that they are acceptable only within very narrow limits – remains largely accepted by all but those administrative officials who draft primary legislation and the parliaments that approve them.

Lord Hewart's general solution seems right – more needs to be done in parliamentary and public debate to make clear the problems with over-reliance on Henry VIII clauses. It is clearly a continuing tension. With the establishment of parliamentary committees for scrutinising bills, the institutional structure is in place to raise concerns, and potentially prevent or minimise such provisions being enacted. However, the committees are not as effective in this function as may be expected. This suggests that resistance to, and debate about, Henry VIII clauses is not as prominent as is necessary to minimise them. In this context, I have sought in this chapter to draw from commentary from a range of sources, some guidelines for scrutinising, interpreting, and most importantly, criticising Henry VIII clauses.

[96] Hewart (n 5) 153–54.

9

Emergency Regulations

One of the primary themes of emergency law scholarship and practice is whether there should be checks on the executive in these periods. The idea is usually associated with Carl Schmitt's view that executive power is, and should be, effectively unconstrained in emergency periods.[1] In the UK and Australia since World War I that becomes largely a question of the checks on regulation-making, as it is now well recognised that that war marked a shift from law-making in war-time being made according to prerogative powers to being made under statutory provisions delegating powers to the executive.[2] This reliance on regulation-making in wars and other emergencies has continued since then.[3] The questions regarding checks on the executive during emergency periods concern the extent to which safeguards on regulation-making are operative. I will highlight in this chapter that the uses of regulations in emergency periods have commonly raised concerns about executive aggrandisement.

This chapter focuses on regulation-making in the UK and Australia during the COVID-19 emergency in 2020–21. It examines the ways in which COVID-19 regulation-making matched the dynamics of law-making that are recognised to apply in emergency periods: the expansion of executive power and contraction of parliamentary scrutiny and public consultation, and the use of deferential approaches to judicial review. It then focuses on reports by parliamentary committees examining the minimisation of parliamentary scrutiny in the UK and exemption of many COVID-19 regulations from parliamentary scrutiny in Australia.

[1] See eg T Ginsburg and M Versteeg, 'The Bound Executive: Emergency Powers during the Pandemic' (2021) 19 *I•CON* 1498, 1502–03.

[2] C Bond, *Law in War: Freedom and Restriction in Australia During the Great War* (New South Wales Press, 2020) 16–17; P Seaward, 'Emergency Powers in Parliament: A Short History' in P Evans, C Salmon Percival, P Silk and H White (eds), *Parliaments and the Pandemic* (Study of Parliaments Group, 2021) 195.

[3] For WW II, see R Else Mitchell, 'Delegated and Sub-Delegated Legislation' (1943) 17 *Australian Law Journal* 75; CK Allen, *Law and Orders* (Steven and Sons, 1945) ch 5; J Eaves, *Emergency Powers and the Parliamentary Watchdog: Parliament and the Executive in Great Britain*, 1939–1951 (Hansard Society for Parliamentary Government, 1957). For the global financial crisis, see M Aronson, 'The Great Depression, This Depression, and Administrative Law' (2009) 37 *Federal Law Review* 165; S Bottomley 'The Notional Legislator: The Australian Securities and Investments Commission's Role as A Law-Maker' (2011) 39 *Federal Law Review* 1, 3–4; R Fox and J Blackwell, *The Devil is in the Detail: Parliament and Delegated Legislation* (Hansard Society, 2014) ch 10; A Tucker, 'Parliamentary Scrutiny of Delegated Legislation' in A Horne and G Drewry (eds), *Parliament and the Law* (Hart Publishing 2018) 353–55.

The starting point for this chapter is that regulations are relied on for most of the legal work in emergency periods primarily because they facilitate urgent, executive law-making. They also often come with attempts to exclude and minimise safeguards, in particular parliamentary scrutiny and public consultation. One of the most significant points to come out of the COVID-19 period is the recognition in parliamentary inquiries that the contraction of parliamentary scrutiny was not simply an exception to the general norms for regulation-making in each country but a step in a pre-existing trend to resistance to, and reduction of, parliamentary scrutiny.

I. Emergency Law in the 1930s Debates

The heavy reliance on regulations in WWI influenced the 1930s debates. Paul Seaward, a historian of the UK Parliament, has noted that the delegation of regulation-making powers in WWI was the key starting point for the 1930s debates and the Donoughmore Committee's inquiry.[4] However, regulation-making in emergency periods was not the focus of the debates or the reports. The focus was on general norms rather than norms to be used in emergency periods. Accordingly, the Donoughmore Committee's report and the Senate Committee's 1930 report did not yield norms for regulation-making in emergency periods. Emergency periods were regarded as exceptions to the general norms without any attempt the define or clarify the safeguards that were appropriate in those times.

Lord Hewart regarded expansion of the executive as having been 'bequeathed and encouraged' during WWI.[5] He was not critical of the expansion in that period, but he stated that he hoped that 'the flood of restrictions and regulations with the force of law that overspread the country during the war opened the eyes of the public to the extent to which liberty may be imperiled by such a system'.[6] The problem for Lord Hewart was that the heavy reliance on regulations continued after the war.[7]

As we saw in chapter two, John Willis's response to Hewart took a much longer view of the development of regulation-making and so for Willis, WWI was a stage in the increased reliance on regulations rather than the primary starting point. Willis still regarded it as a very important stage. For him, as also for Hewart, it was in that period that regulations came to prominence for ordinary people.[8] Willis referred to war-time legislation, the Defence of the Realm Act 1914, prompting members

[4] Seaward (n 2) 196.
[5] Lord Hewart of Bury, *The New Despotism* (Ernest Benn Ltd, 1929) 15.
[6] ibid 101.
[7] ibid 99–100.
[8] J Willis, *The Parliamentary Powers of English Government Departments* (Harvard University Press, 1933) 53.

of the public to question the authority of overbearing officials.[9] Consistently with this view, Willis regarded the reliance on regulation-making during WWI as a form of authoritarianism. He stated that during the four years of the war, 'and for those years only, the nation lived under what was in effect a central despotism'.[10] Willis's use of the terminology of despotism, the famous title of Lord Hewart's book, implies that Willis conceded that despotism may be acceptable in emergency periods such as WWI, but not otherwise. In this way, the WWI experience was important for Willis as a stage in the reliance on regulations as the principal form of legislative law. However, the focus of his book, as for Lord Hewart, was not on the checks and safeguards that may be appropriate in emergency periods but on the significance of delegation of law-making powers in ordinary times. It is worth noting that the more pragmatic contributor to the 1930s debates, Cecil Carr, made clear in his book that reliance on regulations had for centuries been essential for emergency periods relating to wars and epidemics.[11]

The Donoughmore Committee report was in a similar vein to Hewart and Willis's analyses. Heavy reliance on regulation-making during emergencies was referred to in the Donoughmore Committee's report, but its analysis did not extend to emergency regulations and the principles to be applied then. The Committee recognised that one of the accepted reasons for delegating regulation-making powers, such as pressure on parliamentary time and the technical content of law, is to make emergency laws.[12] The Committee regarded emergency regulations as an 'exceptional type' due to their inclusion of matters that in normal periods would only be dealt with by primary legislation.[13] It stated that it could only provide what we would now regard as a proportionality principle: 'It is of the essence of constitutional Government that the normal control of Parliament should not be suspended either to a greater degree, or for a longer time, than the exigency demands'.[14] Beyond this general principle, it stated that each emergency should be dealt with separately and that it is not possible to set more particular norms for delegating powers to be used in emergency periods.[15]

In Australia, the 1930s Senate Committee did not address WWI and its aftermath. Its focus was instead on increasing the capacity of the Senate to conduct its scrutiny functions. Accordingly its report did not contribute to regulation-making in emergency periods.

All contributors to the 1930s debates in the UK therefore recognised that the use of regulations in emergency periods was to be expected and was acceptable. The focus of the debates was the democratic legitimacy of delegations of

[9] ibid 53.
[10] ibid 27.
[11] CT Carr, *Delegated Legislation* (Cambridge University Press, 1921) 22–26.
[12] Committee on Ministers' Powers, Report (London, 1932) ('Donoughmore Committee report') 52.
[13] ibid 31–33.
[14] ibid 52.
[15] ibid 52–53.

regulation-making power in ordinary times and the safeguards that should be applied in that context.

There was more direct analysis of regulation-making in emergency periods in World War II. That was particularly due to Lord Atkin's famous judgment in *Liversidge v Anderson* and his statement: 'In this country, amid the clash of arms, the laws are not silent. They may be changed, but they speak the same language in war as in peace'.[16] Cecil Carr also made an important contribution to developing norms for emergency regulations in WWII focusing on the continued role of Parliament and the need for time limits.[17] In Australia, Rae Else-Mitchell published an important criticism of Australia's WWII regulations focusing on the lack of, and weakening, of parliamentary scrutiny, public consultation and judicial review.[18] The contributions in WWII suggest that the concerns had shifted from acceptance of emergency powers without norms to be applied in such periods, to the safeguards that should be operative and effective during emergency periods.

II. Law-Making During the COVID-19 Pandemic

We can now turn to a case study of the reliance on regulations and the institutional arrangements during the COVID-19 emergency period. The above analysis, as well as the debates that occurred during the COVID-19 period in the UK and Australia, suggest that rather than asking whether safeguards are appropriate or not in an emergency period, it is more helpful to examine the appropriateness of particular checks and how effective are those that are operational. Academic literature on emergency law highlights that it is inevitable that the role of the executive expands and that the roles of parliaments and the courts contract.[19] The important questions are:

- What should the alternative checks in emergency periods be?
- How much of an expansion of the executive is appropriate?
- How should parliaments' and courts' roles adjust and adapt to the crisis?

The comparative legal and political scholarship on the COVID-19 period helps us to see these questions and how they have been answered in different countries.[20]

[16] *Liversidge v Anderson* [1942] AC 206 (HL), 244.

[17] C Carr, *Concerning English Administrative Law* (Columbia University Press, 1941) 69–70.

[18] Else-Mitchell (n 3) 75–76, 78–79.

[19] See eg R Gordon and N Cheesman, 'Legislative leadership in the time of COVID-19' (Developmental Leadership Program, 2021) 6–8, available at apo.org.au/node/311944; Ginsburg and Versteeg (n 1) 1505.

[20] J Grogan, 'States of Emergency: Analysing Global Use of Emergency Powers in Response to COVID-19' (2020) 22 *European Journal of Law Reform* 338; R Cormacain, 'Keeping Covid-19 Emergency Legislation Socially Distant from Ordinary Legislation: Principles for the Structure of Emergency Legislation' (2020) 8 *The Theory and Practice of Legislation* 245.

This scholarship helpfully raises some analytical frameworks for studying emergency laws.

The first point concerns the types of emergency laws. Scholars often refer to emergency laws being either constitutional, legislation that pre-exists the particular emergency, or legislation made for the particular emergency.[21] These categories are obviously incomplete, at least for the countries relevant to this book, the UK and Australia. The experience in these countries in the COVID-19 period is that the most common form of legislative law is regulations. Yet the point remains important because it highlights that constitutions and legislation may anticipate and prepare for emergencies in advance or legislation and regulations may be made at the time of the emergency. But whether the legislation pre-exists the emergency or not, government officials are likely to be delegated powers to make regulations that manage the social and economic issues arising during emergency periods.

The second point is the types of emergencies. It is important to treat differently wars and national security emergencies, public health, financial emergencies and natural disasters. For example, secrecy is likely to be very important in a national security emergency, but not in a public health emergency or a financial crisis.[22] Tom Ginsburg and Mila Versteeg also argue that while there may be good reasons for the executive branch to have few restrictions in a national security emergency due to the concentration in that branch of secret information, that does not necessarily mean it will be the case in a public health emergency or financial crisis.[23]

The scholarship on the COVID-19 emergency has also helpfully restated principles for emergency-focused legislation. Cormacain expressed the following principles for emergency legislation as being that such legislation is necessary, proportionate, connected to the emergency and time-limited.[24] These principles assume that the protections on rights and liberties that ordinarily apply are affected in a manner that is proportionate to the kind of emergency that is occurring. Other scholars add principles regarding institutional arrangements and, in particular, the checks that should apply to emergency laws: the safeguards on law-making provided by the legislature and judiciary should remain in place even if they contract to some extent.[25]

There are three points to draw from the comparative scholarship on the COVID-19 pandemic. The first is that it is important to understand the type of emergency, in this case a public health and economic emergency. Focusing on the type of emergency helps to recognise that a particular case study will necessarily be limited and also to distinguish it from other types of emergency that will have different characteristics. Secondly, in both the UK and Australia the regulations

[21] Ginsburg and Versteeg (n 1) 1506–9; Gordon and Cheesman (n 19) 23.

[22] Ginsburg and Versteeg (n 1) 1509–13; Gordon and Cheesman (n 19) 8–9.

[23] Ginsburg and Versteeg (n 1) 1510–11.

[24] Cormacain (n 20) 245, 246–51; Grogan (n 20) 353.

[25] Grogan (n 20) 349–54.; Ginsburg and Versteeg (n 1) 1532–33; Gordon and Cheesman (n 19) 24–25.

that did much of the legal work were made under existing public health-focused legislation that included emergency powers. And thirdly, the comparative scholarship indicates that the legal responses to the COVID-19 emergency were multi-dimensional, but my focus is on the safeguards on the exercise of regulation-making powers; the important public law issue that is relevant to the themes of this book.

The purpose of this section of the chapter is to identify the techniques used in the UK and Australia for social and economic regulation to manage the COVID-19 pandemic. It is a case study of techniques employed in each country. Most of the techniques will be familiar from earlier chapters in this part of the book; however, they can be regarded as more extreme examples. The most important reason for studying the COVID-19 laws is to examine criticisms by parliamentary committees in that period of the sidelining of parliaments in regulation-making. In the next section I will examine these criticisms directly.

A. United Kingdom

The UK's COVID-19 response involved making new emergency-specific legislation, reliance on existing public health legislation, and substantial use of regulations under these statutory frameworks. The relevant primary legislation included broad enabling provisions for making regulations. It is helpful to start by recognising that COVID-19 affected the operation of Parliament, but it was not closed down. The House of Commons was subject to a series of changes from March 2020 which included at different times hybrid procedure involving some members attending in person and others remotely and voting by proxy. The Commons select committees operated by electronic means from mid-March 2020.[26] The House of Lords moved to electronic proceedings in April 2020 and then to hybrid proceedings in June 2020 whereby a limited number of peers could attend in person and the remainder attended remotely.[27]

COVID-19 specific legislation was fast-tracked through Parliament from 23 to 25 March 2020. The Contingencies Fund Act 2020 modified the available contingencies amount from two per cent of the authorised supply expenditure for the previous year to 50 per cent. This was a vast increase to support businesses

[26] D Natzler, 'How the House of Commons has Adapted to the Pandemic' in P Evans, C Salmon Percival, P Silk and H White (eds), *Parliaments and the Pandemic* (Study of Parliaments Group, 2021) 8–9; C Lee, C Brown and M Hamlyn, 'The Impact in the Commons Chamber' in P Evans, C Salmon Percival, P Silk and H White (eds), *Parliaments and the Pandemic* (Study of Parliaments Group, 2021) 19, 23–24; S Priddy, 'Coronavirus timeline: End of Hybrid Proceedings in the House of Commons' (House of Commons Library, 8 September 2022).

[27] E Scott, 'House of Lords: Remote Participation and Hybrid Proceedings' (House of Lords Library, 8 July 2021) 1–2; D Beamish, 'How the House of Lords has Adapted to the Pandemic' in P Evans, C Salmon Percival, P Silk and H White (eds), *Parliaments and the Pandemic* (Study of Parliaments Group, 2021) 12–14.

and provide for job retention to manage the economic aspects of the crisis. The Coronavirus Act 2020 Bill dealt with other social and economic aspects of the emergency. It passed all stages in the House of Commons on 23 March 2020, the House of Lords on 24–5 March 2020 and received Royal Assent on 25 March.[28] The Act amended existing Acts and introduced new statutory powers to mitigate the impacts of the COVID-19 emergency.[29] The statutory powers included Henry VIII clauses with limited parliamentary procedure provisions.[30] The temporary nature of the Act was developed as a safeguard highlighting its emergency purpose. The Act provided for a parliamentary review date of six months from when the Act passed and an expiry date of two years.[31]

These two Acts passed at the beginning of the legal response to the COVID-19 crisis can be regarded as familiar techniques for a public health and economic emergency due to their authorisation of increased government spending, broad delegations of powers with reduced parliamentary scrutiny, and the temporary nature of the provisions as an emergency specific safeguard.

The UK Government also relied on existing legislation, the Public Health (Control of Disease) Act 1984, and in particular its powers to make regulations for international and domestic purposes.[32] The lockdown regulations for England and Wales that applied during the COVID-19 period were made under this Act. The parliamentary scrutiny provisions for these powers are complex and relatively weak. Generally, a negative resolution procedure applies,[33] but for regulations made under section 45C to prevent the spread of infection or contamination an affirmative resolution procedure would apply.[34] However, an exception to the exception for infections and contaminations applied for emergency regulations. Emergency regulations could be made without a draft being approved by Parliament. Instead, a regulation would need to be made and laid in each House of Parliament and then a 28-day period applied in which the regulation must be approved by Parliament or cease to have effect.[35] This emergency procedure was applied for the lockdown regulations.[36] The parliamentary procedure provisions were therefore complicated, but in the end the emergency power alleviated the otherwise strong parliamentary scrutiny provision that was expressly stated to

[28] Natzler (n 26) 5–7.

[29] Explanatory Notes to the Coronavirus Act 2020, para 1.

[30] See, eg, Coronavirus Act 2020, ss 22(4) and (9), 34, 88. See also Delegated Powers and Regulatory Reform Committee, *Coronavirus Bill* (HL 2019–21, 9).

[31] Coronavirus Act 2020, ss 89, 90, 98. For a more detailed examination of this Act, see P Grez Hidalgo, F de Londras and D Lock, 'Parliament, the Pandemic, and Constitutional Principle in the United Kingdom: A Study of the Coronavirus Act 2020' (2022) 85 *Modern Law Review* 1463.

[32] Public Health (Control of Disease) Act 1984, ss 45B–45F.

[33] ibid, s 45Q(1).

[34] ibid, s 45Q(4).

[35] ibid, s 45R(2)–(4).

[36] T Hickman, 'Abracadabra Law-making and Accountability to Parliament for the Coronavirus Regulation' in P Evans, C Salmon Percival, P Silk and H White (eds), *Parliaments and the Pandemic* (Study of Parliaments Group, 2021) 43.

apply to special restrictions and restrictions that would have a significant effect on personal rights.[37]

The most well-known and controversial regulations were the lockdown laws made under the provisions of the Public Health (Control of Disease) Act 1984 referred to in the previous paragraph. I will focus on the lockdown regulations applying in England. The initial regulation applying in England – the Health Protection (Coronavirus, Restrictions) (England) Regulations 2020 – was made on 26 March 2020 and continued until July 2021.[38] It included provisions defining the emergency period and providing for regular reviews, required some businesses to close, imposed restrictions on others, and imposed restrictions on movement and gatherings.[39] The substance of the initial and subsequent lockdown regulations were criticised on the ground that the enforcement provisions were drafted in broad and subjective terms and were granted to too broad a range of persons.[40] They were similarly criticised on the basis that they were not sufficiently certain.[41]

The English lockdown regulations were subject to parliamentary scrutiny but the practices involved in that scrutiny were criticised by interest groups, academics and practitioners. The most common criticisms were that the Government falsely made announcements that they were in force prior to the actual regulation being made, some regulations became operative hours after being made, regulations were often in force for weeks before they were debated in Parliament, some regulations were changed or revoked by the time Parliament had the opportunity to consider them, and emergency procedures were used when there was no emergency for the particular regulation.[42]

We will see for Australia at the Commonwealth level that regulations with similar characteristics and restrictions were completely exempt from parliamentary scrutiny. The UK lockdown regulations were subject to parliamentary scrutiny but that did not prevent concerns being raised by numerous interested persons and organisations. The concerns were appropriately summed up by Tom Hickman as being that the parliamentary scrutiny that occurred was a matter of form with very little substance.[43] I will come back to this in section III below.

[37] Public Health (Control of Disease) Act 1984, s 45Q(4).

[38] See J Brown and E Kirk-Wade, 'Coronavirus: A History of English Lockdown Laws' (House of Commons Library, 22 December 2021) 26–43; S Barber, J Brown and D Ferguson, 'Coronavirus: Lockdown Laws' (House of Commons Library, 14 July 2022) 4.

[39] Health Protection (Coronavirus, Restrictions) (England) Regulations 2020, ss 3–7 and Sch 2.

[40] T Hickman, 'Eight Ways to Reinforce and Revise the Lockdown Law' (UK Constitutional Law Blog, 15 April 2020), available at ukconstitutionallaw.org/2020/04/16/tom-hickman-eight-ways-to-reinforce-and-revise-the-lockdown-law.

[41] R Cormacain, 'Can I go to the Park Please Dad? Everyday Lessons in Legal Certainty in the English Coronavirus Regulations' (UK Constitutional Law Blog, 15 May 2020), available at ukconstitutionallaw.org/2020/05/15/ronan-cormacain-can-i-go-to-the-park-please-dad-everyday-lessons-in-legal-certainty-in-the-english-coronavirus-regulations.

[42] See Hickman (n 36) 45–50; R Fox, M Russell, J Tomlinson and R Cormacain, 'The Marginalisation of the House of Commons under Covid' (Hansard Society, 29 April 2021), available at www.hansardsociety.org.uk/publications/briefings/the-marginalisation-of-the-house-of-commons-under-covid-has-been-shocking-a.

[43] Hickman (n 36) 48.

Of the three safeguards on regulation-making, public consultation is likely to be the first to be discarded in an emergency period. Governments rely on regulations in emergency periods as they can be made quickly, and public consultation can be a time-consuming exercise. So, as would be expected, there was no public consultation conducted for the main English lockdown regulations. The explanatory memorandum for the initial lockdown regulation stated that there was no public consultation for it.[44] The same was said for subsequent replacement regulations.[45] While this was commonly the case for lockdown laws, it was not necessarily the case for all COVID-19 regulations. For example, stakeholder, rather than public, consultation was held for the Adoption and Children (Coronavirus) (Amendment) Regulations 2020.[46] The COVID-19 period highlights that regulation-making is likely to be made quickly, particularly in the initial response. In the following weeks and months, the regulations can be amended and adjusted in the context of, and in response to, changes in circumstances, and public discussion and debate.

As famously occurred in historical emergency periods for regulations affecting liberties,[47] the lockdown regulations and decisions made under those regulations were challenged in judicial review proceedings. There was discussion soon after the lockdown regulations were made as to whether those regulations were invalid[48] or not.[49] They were subsequently determined to be valid. The most significant case was *R (Dolan) v Secretary of State for Health and Social Care*.[50] *Dolan* involved a challenge to the lockdown regulations initially made in March 2020. The Court emphasised that Parliament intentionally provided for broad powers due to the emergency nature of the purpose.[51] The Court also emphasised that it should provide a wide margin of appreciation on the basis of institutional competence, democratic accountability and expert advice.[52] This reasoning is consistent with the research that courts are generally deferential in emergency periods.[53] On the

[44] Explanatory memorandum for the Health Protection (Coronavirus, Restrictions) (England) Regulations 2020, para 10.

[45] See explanatory memoranda para 10 for the following regulations: Health Protection (Coronavirus, Restrictions) (No 2) (England) Regulations 2020; Health Protection (Coronavirus, Local COVID-19 Alert Level) (Medium) (England) Regulations 2020; Health Protection (Coronavirus, Restrictions) (England) (No 4) Regulations 2020.

[46] Explanatory memorandum for the Adoption and Children (Coronavirus) (Amendment) Regulations 2020 paras 7.2 and 10. But note that the consultation was determined to not have been conducted properly and was declared invalid: *R (Article 39) v Secretary of State for Education* [2020] EWCA Civ 1577.

[47] See eg, *R v Halliday* [1917] AC 260; *Liversidge v Anderson* [1942] AC 206.

[48] R Craig, 'A Response to Professor King' (UK Human Rights Blog, 6 April 2020), available at ukhumanrightsblog.com/2020/04/06/lockdown-a-response-to-professor-king-robert-craig.

[49] J King, 'The Lockdown is Lawful' (UK Constitutional Law Blog, 1 April 2020), available at ukconstitutionallaw.org/2020/04/01/jeff-king-the-lockdown-is-lawful.

[50] [2020] EWCA Civ 1605, [2021] 1 WLR 2326.

[51] [2020] EWCA Civ 1605, [2021] 1 WLR 2326 [59], [65], [71].

[52] [2020] EWCA Civ 1605, [2021] 1 WLR 2326 [97].

[53] See eg, Ginsburg and Versteeg (n 1) 1518.

other hand, a challenge to decisions made under the lockdown regulations was successful.[54]

While historical and comparative analyses indicate that courts are very likely to be deferential to challenges to regulations during emergency periods, there has nevertheless been criticisms of the UK courts, in particular in relation to *Dolan*.[55] Richard McKenzie-Gray Scott adds the important point that deferential judicial review is particularly problematic when it is applied to regulations that have been subject to minimal or weak parliamentary scrutiny, as we have seen was the case for the lockdown laws, referring to it as facilitating 'executive abuse'.[56] The safeguards that would usually apply to regulations, can be seen to have been arguably ineffective or, at least in regard to public consultation, non-existent. This is of course particularly concerning given the substantial impact on individuals, community, and economic life.

B. Australia

My analysis of the Australian experience with the COVID-19 emergency period has an important difference to my examination of the UK experience as it does not focus on lockdown laws. The lockdown laws in Australia were made by states and territory governments rather than the Commonwealth Government. The equivalent Commonwealth regulations, and the most controversial, related to a ban on international travel.

The most relevant general feature of the Commonwealth's response to the COVID-19 emergency was that Parliament was adjourned initially for five months. The legislation that was most heavily relied on for managing the COVID-19 period included, as would be expected, delegation of powers to deal with social and economic matters and broad Henry VIII clauses. However, it also included a particularly controversial feature; the statutory provisions delegating powers to make highly important regulations stated that those regulations were not disallowable by Parliament. We will see in section III.B below that this aspect of the statutory framework for the COVID-19 response prompted parliamentary inquiries and some reform.

Before examining the regulations that were made during the COVID-19 period it is relevant to recognise that the Commonwealth Parliament was adjourned

[54] *Leigh v Commissioner of Police of the Metropolis* [2022] EWHC 527 (Admin) [86].

[55] See eg Lord Sumption, 'COVID-19 and the Courts – Expediency or Law?' (2021) 137 *Law Quarterly Review* 355; D McGrogan, '"It is Unarguable that what happened under these Regulations Amounted to a Deprivation of Liberty": Dolan v Secretary of State for Health and Social Care' [2021] *Public Law* 671.

[56] R McKenzie-Gray Scott, 'Rebalancing Upstream and Downstream Scrutiny of Government during National Emergencies' (UK Constitutional Law Blog, 21 September 2021), available at ukconstitutionallaw.org/2021/09/21/richard-mackenzie-gray-scott-rebalancing-upstream-and-downstream-scrutiny-of-government-during-national-emergencies.

apparently on an indefinite basis[57] from 23 March 2020, but it was made clear in the Senate that it was intended to be until 11 August, a period of five months.[58] In the end, the adjournment was not a complete closure until 11 August as there were reduced sitting periods in April and May and one sitting week in June. The adjournment and reduced sitting periods during the early, critical stage of the emergency period was significant for regulation-making. In Australia, the general position is for parliamentary scrutiny to occur after regulations have commenced. The adjournment prevented disallowance motions being made in the months in which Parliament was not sitting and when the Government was making many, far-reaching COVID-related regulations. The adjournment was criticised at the time on the basis that Parliament could potentially have been held in an online format[59] and that Parliament's functions (representation, authorising legislation, holding the executive accountable and deliberation) were all particularly necessary in the emergency.[60]

There were two primary legislative frameworks for managing the COVID-19 emergency. New legislation was made for economic management and new omnibus legislation amended numerous Acts. The Government also relied on existing legislation that had been designed for human biosecurity emergencies. Both the new and existing legislation had familiar characteristics: they enabled management of major social and economic matters, included Henry VIII clauses, and as mentioned earlier, the public health legislation included exemptions from disallowance.

The new Acts authorised and managed emergency funding for COVID-19 specific programmes. The parliamentary process for both of these Acts was brief. The relevant bills were introduced into Parliament and passed each house in one day. They were then granted assent and commenced very soon after. These Acts were passed on sitting days that were exceptions to the adjournment and when a small number of Members of Parliament and senators were in attendance.[61]

The Coronavirus Economic Response Package (Payments and Benefits) Act 2020 (Cth) provided for government provision of financial support.[62] This Act was only 21 sections long and was expressly designed to provide the Treasurer with

[57] Commonwealth, *Parliamentary Debates*, House of Representatives, 23 April 2020, 2903.

[58] Commonwealth, *Parliamentary Debates*, Senate, 23 April 2020, 1862.

[59] A Twomey, 'A Virtual Australian Parliament is Possible – and may be Needed – During the Coronavirus Pandemic' (The Conversation, 25 March 2020), available at theconversation.com/a-virtual-australian-parliament-is-possible-and-may-be-needed-during-the-coronavirus-pandemic-134540.

[60] S Mills, '"Where no Counsel is, the People Fall": Why Parliaments Should Keep Functioning During the Coronavirus Crisis' (The Conversation, 27 March 2020), available at theconversation.com/where-no-counsel-is-the-people-fall-why-parliaments-should-keep-functioning-during-the-coronavirus-crisis-134772.

[61] See S Mills, 'Parliament in a Time of Virus: Representative Democracy as a "Non-Essential Service"' (2020) 34 *Australasian Parliamentary Review* 7, 13–17.

[62] Coronavirus Economic Response Package (Payments and Benefits) Act 2020 (Cth), s 3.

power to make rules that would be administered by the Tax Commissioner.[63] The Payments and Benefits Act was expressly designed as a framework Act delegating power to make regulations for financial support during the emergency period. It clearly had a crucial role in preventing or minimising economic problems that were foreseeable for the emergency period. In particular it provided authority for the Jobkeeper payment made according to regulations under the Act.[64] The Australian National Audit Office reported that the Commonwealth Government made payments of $88 billion under this regulation which were received by 3.6 million people in its initial six-month period and 1.8 million people when it was extended by six months.[65] This was clearly a highly important scheme for managing the economy during the COVID-19 emergency.

The other new legislation were much longer omnibus Acts[66] amending a range of Acts relating to matters such as employment, tax, social security and war veterans' benefits, and child support. The Parliament also enacted legislation authorising government funding.[67] These Acts included an expansion of the Finance Minister's powers to provide by regulations for expenditure where there is an urgent need that is not foreseeable.[68] This added $800 million to the amounts of $295 million and $380 million included in the annual appropriation Acts.[69] These Acts included common features of emergency legislation. They included Henry VIII clauses, for example, to provide for modifications of, and exemptions from, the Corporations Act 2001 (Cth).[70] The sections providing for advances to the Finance Minister minimised parliamentary scrutiny by enabling them to be made by non-disallowable regulations.[71] The important point is that these amending Acts were made to prepare for an emergency period by providing additional powers to governments with the exercise of some powers being beyond the scope for parliamentary scrutiny.

There was also existing public health legislation designed to deal with emergencies that was relied on in the COVID-19 period. The most prominent of these was the Biosecurity Act 2015 (Cth). This Act includes a very broad enabling

[63] Explanatory Memorandum, Coronavirus Economic Response Package (Payments and Benefits) Bill 2020 (Cth), s 4.

[64] Coronavirus Economic Response Package (Payments and Benefits) Rules 2020 (Cth).

[65] Australian National Audit Office, *Administration of the JobKeeper Scheme* (Auditor-General Report No 22 2021–22, 4 April 2022) paras 1.7 and 1.10.

[66] Coronavirus Economic Response Package Omnibus Act 2020 (Cth) and Coronavirus Economic Response Package Omnibus (Measures No. 2) Act 2020 (Cth).

[67] Appropriation (Coronavirus Economic Response Package) Act (No 1) 2019–2020 (Cth) and Appropriation (Coronavirus Economic Response Package) Act (No 2) 2019–2020 (Cth).

[68] Appropriation (Coronavirus Response) Act (No 1) 2021–2022 (Cth), s 10(2) and Appropriation (Coronavirus Response) Act (No 2) 2021–2022 (Cth), s 12(2).

[69] Explanatory Memorandum, Appropriation (Coronavirus Economic Response Package) Bill (No. 2) 2019–2020 para 21.31–21.35.

[70] Coronavirus Economic Response Package Omnibus Act 2020 (Cth), Sch 8.

[71] Appropriation (Coronavirus Economic Response Package) Act (No 1) 2019–2020 (Cth), s 10(4) and Appropriation (Coronavirus Economic Response Package) Act (No 2) 2019-2020 (Cth), s 12(4).

provision which was used in important ways during the COVID-19 emergency. Section 477 of this Act provides for the Minister for Health to make regulations during a biosecurity emergency period to prevent or control the spread of disease. It includes some important features for our purposes. It includes a form of Henry VIII clause (regulations made under it are to apply 'despite any provision of any other Australian law' during the emergency period),[72] and an exemption from disallowance removing the general form of parliamentary scrutiny.[73] The provisions of the Act are also significant for providing high penalties, including imprisonment, for non-compliance with the regulations made under section 477.[74] These powers were subjected to criticism. They were criticised at the time they were made by the Scrutiny of Bills Committee[75] and subsequently by the Senate Delegated Legislation Committee in its report on the use of delegated powers during the COVID-19 period.[76]

Section 477 authorised one of the most well-known regulations made in the early period of the COVID-19 emergency, the Biosecurity (Human Biosecurity Emergency) (Human Coronavirus with Pandemic Potential) (Overseas Travel Ban Emergency Requirements) Determination 2020 (Cth). This regulation operated as one of the initial measures for dealing with COVID-19 in March 2020 until 17 April 2022. As its title indicates, it provided for a ban on overseas travel. It was subject to exemptions for defined persons, such as a 'member of the crew of an aircraft or vessel'[77] and persons granted an exemption due to their 'exceptional circumstances'.[78] This design, a broad ban plus a very broad exemption provision, was criticised for not providing criteria or considerations for the decisions to provide an exemption and the lack of provision for merits review.[79] Administration of the overseas travel ban regulation was criticised by the Australian National Audit Office for the inconsistency of decisions in regard to exemptions.[80] While the design difficulties would most likely have been questioned if this regulation was subject to disallowance, the fact that it was exempt from disallowance procedures meant that it was not subject to the committee scrutiny that would usually apply to regulations.

[72] Biosecurity Act 2015 (Cth), s 477(5).

[73] ibid s 477(2).

[74] Biosecurity Act 2015 (Cth), s 479.

[75] Senate Standing Committee for the Scrutiny of Bills, *Alert Digest* (Digest No 2 of 2015, 4 March 2015) 11–12, 23–24.

[76] Senate Standing Committee for the Scrutiny of Delegated Legislation, *Inquiry into the Exemption of Delegated Legislation from Parliamentary Oversight: Interim Report* (2 December 2020) 33–34.

[77] Biosecurity (Human Biosecurity Emergency) (Human Coronavirus with Pandemic Potential) (Overseas Travel Ban Emergency Requirements) Determination 2020 (Cth), s 6(b).

[78] Biosecurity (Human Biosecurity Emergency) (Human Coronavirus with Pandemic Potential) (Overseas Travel Ban Emergency Requirements) Determination 2020 (Cth), s 7.

[79] A Edgar, 'Law-making in a Crisis: Commonwealth and NSW Coronavirus Regulations', AUSPUBLAW (30 March 2020), available at www.auspublaw.org/blog/2020/03/law-making-in-a-crisis-commonwealth-and-nsw-coronavirus-regulations.

[80] Australian National Audit Office, 'Management of International Travel Restrictions during COVID-19' (Auditor-General Report No 12 2021–22, 8 December 2021) paras 4.77–4.84.

The focus so far has been on Parliament and its various roles in relation to the COVID-19 emergency, but of course other safeguards are potentially operative with a reduced role due to the emergency conditions. In regards to consultation, the explanatory statements for the overseas travel ban regulation and subsequent amendments, either state that the consultation that occurred was internal to government and make no reference to any form of public consultation[81] or make a vague, general statement that emergency protocols were used that included 'appropriate consultation'.[82] The lack of public consultation may seem necessary in an emergency period when laws need to be made urgently in response to changing conditions, but the point should also be made that the exclusion of parliamentary scrutiny and its democracy-enhancing function, was not balanced out by additional public consultation. While there was no formal public consultation there was media attention regarding the overseas travel ban from the time it was announced[83] and subsequently reporting on the difficulties it created for individuals.[84]

The overseas travel ban regulation was unsuccessfully challenged in the courts[85] and so was administration of it.[86] In these cases the emergency nature of the regulation was expressly factored into the courts' analysis. In particular, it influenced the courts' interpretation of the Biosecurity Act 2015 (Cth)[87] and how the grounds of review raised by the applicants were understood in the context of the legislative scheme.[88]

[81] Explanatory Statement, *Biosecurity (Human Biosecurity Emergency) (Human Coronavirus with Pandemic Potential) (Overseas Travel Ban Emergency Requirements) Determination* 2020; Explanatory Statement, *Biosecurity (Human Coronavirus with Pandemic Potential) Amendment (No 1) Determination* 2021; Explanatory Statement, *Biosecurity (Human Coronavirus with Pandemic Potential) Amendment (No 2) Determination* 2021; Explanatory Statement, *Biosecurity Legislation Amendment (Emergency and Entry Requirements) Determination* 2022.

[82] Explanatory Statement, *Biosecurity (Human Biosecurity Emergency) (Human Coronavirus with Pandemic Potential) (Overseas Travel Ban Emergency Requirements) Amendment (No 1) Determination* 2020; Explanatory Statement, *Biosecurity (Human Biosecurity Emergency) (Human Coronavirus with Pandemic Potential) (Overseas Travel Ban Emergency Requirements) Amendment (No 1) Determination* 2021; Explanatory Statement, *Biosecurity Legislation (Human Coronavirus with Pandemic Potential) Amendment (No 1) Determination* 2021.

[83] N Hayder, 'Scott Morrison Extends Coronavirus Restrictions with New Limits on Weddings and Funerals, More Business Closures' ABC News (24 March 2020), available at www.abc.net.au/news/2020-03-24/scott-morrison-announces-new-measures-to-slow-coronavirus-spread/12086206.

[84] See eg, N Salim, Tracey Shelton and Jason Fang, 'Migrant Workers and International Students Stuck in Australia due to Coronavirus Travel Bans' ABC News (8 April 2020), available at www.abc.net.au/news/2020-04-08/asia-pacific-students-migrant-workers-travel-stuck-coronavirus/12105458; R Shine, '"Red tape" Forcing Families to wait for Compassionate Exemption to Coronavirus Travel Ban, Grieving Son Says' ABC News (25 June 2020), available at www.abc.net.au/news/2020-06-25/coronavirus-travel-ban-exemption-red-tape-criticised/12388946.

[85] *LibertyWorks Inc v Commonwealth* (2021) 286 FCR 131. See also *Newman v Minister for Health and Aged Care* [2021] FCA 517.

[86] *Baker v Commissioner of the Australian Border Force* [2020] FCA 836.

[87] *LibertyWorks Inc v Commonwealth* (2021) 286 FCR 131, 144–45 [58]–[63].

[88] *Baker v Commissioner of the Australian Border Force* [2020] FCA 836, [60]–[64].

The High Court has emphasised that the executive is the appropriate branch for handling emergencies.[89] That is, of course, stating the obvious. However, it also implies that courts will give leeway to the executive in regard to interpreting and applying emergency-focused laws and reviewing decisions made under those laws. The Australian COVID-19 cases indicate that this is especially the case when Parliament has provided broad powers to the executive. This was particularly clear in the Federal Court's analysis of section 477 of the Biosecurity Act 2015 (Cth), the provision authorising the overseas travel ban regulations. It is also worth noting that the Federal Court did not consider the exemption from disallowance and parliamentary scrutiny, and the poor design of the instrument. This highlights the courts are likely to be reluctant to engage with relevant aspects that may otherwise influence courts in judicial review proceedings.

The overseas travel ban regulation clearly affected a large sector of the public. There were over 350,000 applications for exemptions up to June 2021.[90] The regulation was very poorly designed and, as we have seen, the Auditor-General's review showed that the administration of that regulation was inconsistent. Some inconsistency may be expected in the administration of a discretionary power but the Auditor-General found serious problems including opposite results for applications involving very similar facts.[91] The lack of exposure to parliamentary scrutiny meant that the poor design was not questioned by the Senate Delegated Legislation Committee.

III. Review, Criticism and Reform in the COVID-19 Period

In other chapters I have focused on principles and considerations for managing the exemptions and minimising of regulation-making safeguards. For this chapter I will focus instead on recent, parliamentary reports into the legal response to the COVID-19 emergency. These reports in both countries were made following inquiries with input by government officials, parliamentarians and scholars. The reports provide important guidance on the controls on regulation-making in managing future emergencies. In particular, they highlight problem areas and provide recommendations primarily as to what is unacceptable in parliamentary democracies. As we saw in section I of this chapter, the 1930s debates and reports did not provide guidance on emergency periods. The focus at that time was on general norms rather than norms for emergency periods. Focusing on the parliamentary reports regarding the COVID-19 emergency is also consistent with

[89] *Pape v Federal Commissioner of Taxation* (2009) 238 CLR 1, 89 [233] (Gummow, Crennan and Bell JJ); *Palmer v Western Australia* (2021) 272 CLR 505 [155] (Gageler J).

[90] Australian National Audit Office (n 80) para 4.67.

[91] ibid paras 4.82–4.84.

the methodology of this book, drawing on parliamentary debates and committee reports as much as possible.

Accordingly, the contributions of scholars and legal practitioners will be a secondary focus in this part of the chapter. It is, however, worthwhile briefly recognising that they have been highly critical. Keith Ewing argued in an article published in April 2020 that necessarily focused on the very early months of the COVID-19 emergency, that the UK's response involved 'the abdication of legislative authority, financial scrutiny, and ministerial accountability'.[92] These views were repeated in subsequent analysis in 2020[93] and since then.[94] Similar views have been expressed regarding Australia. In their analysis of Australia's response to the COVID-19 emergency in a comparative law collection, Rizzi and Tulloch argued that the response was relatively successful at managing COVID-19; however, they concluded that the means employed to do this included sidelining parliamentary scrutiny and restricting freedoms with 'little independent oversight'.[95] This conclusion was drawn after considering many different aspects of the Commonwealth and state governments' measures for responding to the COVID-19 emergency. I generally agree with these conclusions, but will focus on regulation-making powers and the regulations made according to those powers.

The rest of this section will focus on parliamentary reports and the guidance they can provide about emergency laws. There are generally expressed principles in international and human rights laws for legal and governmental responses to emergencies,[96] and the parliamentary reports into the legal and governmental responses to COVID-19 supplement these principles particularly in relation to regulation-making.

A. United Kingdom

Widespread concerns with the UK Government's regulation-making during the COVID-19 emergency prompted parliamentary committees to hold inquiries and publish reports in 2021 and 2022. Some of these reports dealt directly with the Government's handling of the COVID-19 emergency. Other reports

[92] KD Ewing, 'Covid-19: Government by Decree' (2020) 31 *King's Law Journal* 1, 2.

[93] M Russell and L James, 'MPs are right. Parliament has been sidelined' (*Constitution Unit*, 28 Sept 2020), available at constitution-unit.com/2020/09/28/mps-are-right-parliament-has-been-sidelined; J Sumption, 'Government by Decree: Covid-19 and the Constitution' (Cambridge Freshfields Annual Law Lecture, 27 October 2020), available at resources.law.cam.ac.uk/privatelaw/Freshfields_Lecture_2020_Government_by_Decree.pdf.

[94] Hickman (n 36) 47; J Grogan, '(Un)governing: The COVID-19 Response in the UK' in J Grogan and A Donald (eds), *Routledge Handbook of Law and the Covid-19 Pandemic* (Routledge, 2022) 64–66.

[95] M Rizzi and T Tullich, 'All Bets on the Executive(S)! The Australian Response to Covid-19' in J Grogan and A Donald (eds), *Routledge Handbook of Law and the Covid-19 Pandemic* (Routledge, 2022) 457; See also EL Windholz, 'Governing in a Pandemic: from Parliamentary Sovereignty to Autocratic Technocracy' (2020) 8 *Theory and Practice of Legislation* 93.

[96] See Cormacain (n 20) 249–52.

were prompted by the COVID-19 emergency and Brexit as both were seen as examples of broader problems with the relationship between the executive and Parliament that were part of a trend towards minimising the role of Parliament in regulation-making. In this section I will examine the reports published by the committees focusing on the COVID-19 emergency and in section C below I will come back to the reports focusing on the broader trends towards reduced parliamentary scrutiny.

Some of the criticisms made by scholars and practitioners in the very early stage of the emergency period regarding the content of the lockdown laws in the UK were repeated in the parliamentary committee reports. In particular, the concerns about the breadth and uncertainty of some of the lockdown and other emergency restrictions provisions were repeated. The Joint Committee on Statutory Instruments' report stated that unclear criminal offence provisions were not acceptable and that some provisions lacked rationality due to there being no apparent underlying purpose.[97] The Committee also criticised the sub-delegation of powers to ministers to provide for temporary measures and switch on and off lockdown regulations.[98] It stated that flexibility should be achieved by means other than sub-delegating powers.[99]

Other concerns expressed in these reports were focused more directly on minimising parliamentary scrutiny. This concern included the inappropriate use of guidance by the UK Government.[100] The House of Lords Secondary Legislation Scrutiny Committee stated that the Government had blurred the line between regulations and guidance.[101] The Joint Committee on Statutory Instruments added that guidance cannot be used as a 'back-door form of legislating' or to add to laws or to fix problems with laws.[102] The House of Lords Constitution Committee emphasised that guidance cannot conflict with the regulation for which it is designed to provide guidance.[103] The use of guidance in these ways misleads members of the public as to the content of the law. It presents guidance as if it is law even though it is not authorised as a regulation and does not go through formal regulation-making processes.

The committee reports also highlighted concerns regarding the temporary operation of COVID-19 regulations due to the inclusion of sunsetting provisions.

[97] Joint Committee on Statutory Instruments, *Rule of Law Themes from COVID-19 Regulations* (2021–22, HL 57, HC 600) paras 29–38.

[98] ibid paras 11–28.

[99] ibid para 25.

[100] See also T Hickman, 'The Use and Misuse of Guidance during the UK's Coronavirus Lockdown' (15 June 2020), available at papers.ssrn.com/sol3/papers.cfm?abstract_id=3686857; N Finch, S Halliday, J Tomlinson, J Meers and M Wilberforce, 'Undermining Loyalty to Legality? An Empirical Analysis of Perceptions of "Lockdown" Law and Guidance during COVID-19' (2022) 85 *Modern Law Review* 1419.

[101] Secondary Legislation Scrutiny Committee, *Interim report on the Work of the Committee in Session 2019–21* (2019–21 HL Paper 200) paras 20–21.

[102] Joint Committee on Statutory Instruments, *Rule of Law* (n 97) paras 47, 55–56.

[103] Select Committee on the Constitution, *COVID-19 and the Use and Scrutiny of Emergency Powers* (2021–22, HL Paper 15) paras 127–56.

While the House of Lords Constitution Committee recognised this as being an important measure that is appropriate in an emergency period,[104] the Joint Committee on Statutory Instruments stated that it does not justify poor drafting.[105]

Other difficulties relating to the timing of regulations were criticised in these reports: lack of notice of commencement of regulations;[106] short notice for non-urgent regulations;[107] and that some regulations commenced before being laid in Parliament.[108] The latter concern was also expressed by the House of Commons Speaker in September 2020.[109] The Government responded by stating that Parliament will vote on 'significant national measures with effect in the whole of England or UK-wide' before such regulations come into force. However, the Commons library reported that this occurred for only four regulations.[110]

It is therefore very clear that serious concerns were raised into many different aspects of the COVID-19 emergency regulations. The concerns can be understood in terms of the rule of law and parliamentary scrutiny. The rule of law concerns related to unclear drafting of offences, presenting guidance as if it is law, and giving insufficient notice of restrictive laws. These concerns make it difficult for members of the public to gain knowledge of the law in order to comply with it. The parliamentary scrutiny concerns relate to regulations being made with insufficient parliamentary scrutiny. The two problems should be recognised as being related. Better parliamentary scrutiny enables rule of law problems to be identified, questioned and potentially corrected.

B. Australia

At the beginning of the COVID-19 emergency in March and April 2020 the Senate Delegated Legislation Committee recognised that some important regulations made by government to deal with the COVID-19 emergency were exempt from parliamentary scrutiny. That not only meant that Parliament could not disallow these regulations, but that the Senate Delegated Legislation Committee had no scrutiny function in relation to them. This was due to the Senate Standing Orders limiting the Committee's scrutiny to regulations 'subject to disallowance, disapproval or affirmative resolution by the Senate and which are of a legislative character'.[111]

[104] ibid para 65–68.

[105] Joint Committee on Statutory Instruments, *Rule of Law* (n 97) paras 84–89. See also Secondary Legislation Scrutiny Committee, *What Next? The Growing Imbalance between Parliament and the Executive: End of Session Report 2021–22* (2021–22 HL Paper 200) paras 13–15.

[106] Joint Committee on Statutory Instruments, *Rule of Law* (n 97) paras 62–66.

[107] Select Committee on the Constitution, *COVID-19* (n 103) para 169–78.

[108] Joint Committee on Statutory Instruments, *Rule of Law* (n 97) paras 67–73; Secondary Legislation Scrutiny Committee, *What Next? The Growing Imbalance between Parliament and the Executive: End of Session Report 2021–22* (2021–22 HL Paper 200) paras 8–12.

[109] HC Deb Vol 681, col 331 (30 September 2020).

[110] Barber, Brown and Ferguson (n 38) 9.

[111] Senate Standing Order 23(2).

The lack of authority to scrutinise COVID-19 regulations prompted the Committee to initiate an inquiry into exemptions from parliamentary oversight. The Committee held the inquiry and published an Interim Report in December 2020 focusing on the COVID-19 period and a Final Report in March 2021 dealing with exemptions from parliamentary scrutiny more generally. The reason for holding the inquiry not only for the emergency period but also more generally was expressed in the Interim Report. The Chair and Deputy Chair of the Delegated Legislation Committee referred in their introduction to Parliament and governments establishing practices that diminish Parliament's supervision of regulation-making. They referred to the regulations made during the COVID-19 emergency as being an example of a broader issue.[112]

The Committee's Interim Report emphasised that it is generally presumed that regulations are subject to disallowance procedures. It went on to say that it is particularly inappropriate to exempt regulations from disallowance when the regulation is made under a Henry VIII power and operates to modify or override primary legislation, provides for offences or the content of an offence that is potentially subject to custodial penalties, or provides for allocation of public funds above the limits set in Appropriation Acts.[113] It referred to disallowance generally not preventing urgent action as regulations in Australia generally commence on registration and operate prior to any scrutiny occurring. It also made clear that regulations affecting personal rights and liberties are particularly prominent in emergency periods and require parliamentary scrutiny in the same way they do in ordinary times.[114]

The Committee's interim report into the COVID-19 period also addressed the time limits on regulations dealing with emergency measures. In Australia, there is a general sunsetting period for regulations of 10 years,[115] but, as we have seen in regard to the UK COVID-19 regulations, it is appropriate to have a much shorter operating period for emergency regulations. The interim report found there was a great deal of variation in how this was managed for particular regulations.[116] It pointed out that the variation and the failure to specify a particular repeal date can enable emergency regulations made with limited parliamentary scrutiny to have continued effect. Lack of a particular repeal date can operate to minimise parliamentary scrutiny of laws as the regulation may have not been subject to parliamentary scrutiny when made or scrutinised on the basis that it is an emergency measure. Such concerns led the Committee to recommend that regulations made in emergency periods operate for three months.[117]

[112] Senate Standing Committee for the Scrutiny of Delegated Legislation, *Inquiry into the Exemption of Delegated Legislation from Parliamentary Oversight: Interim Report* (2 December 2020) xv.
[113] ibid para 4.55.
[114] ibid paras 4.46–4.55.
[115] Legislation Act 2003 (Cth), s 50.
[116] Senate Standing Committee for the Scrutiny of Delegated Legislation *Interim Report* (n 76) paras 6.41–6.43.
[117] ibid para 6.43.

Some government agencies claimed during the Committee's inquiry that making regulations non-disallowable is appropriate when regulations are based on scientific or technical expertise and that such laws were particularly prominent in the COVID-19 period. The interim report examined this claim and agreed with it to a very limited extent. The Committee stated that regulations that simply list a human disease as raising biosecurity risks can be regarded as being solely based on technical or scientific evidence which can justify regulations being exempt from parliamentary scrutiny.[118] However, regulations that are based on such expertise and impose restrictions on peoples' rights and interests should be understood to be political decisions and not suitable for an exemption. This distinction provides a helpful guideline for future emergencies when government agencies over-reach in their claims for exemptions from regulation-making safeguards. Scientific and technical expertise may justify an exemption from parliamentary veto powers, but it has limits and the limits are engaged when the law regulates individuals and organisations.

The Committee's interim report dealing with emergency periods also examined constraints on its scrutiny function during the first year of the COVID-19 pandemic. This involved the need for using teleconferences for committee meetings,[119] the likelihood of increased regulation-making during emergencies which can strain the resources of the Committee,[120] and the need to establish policy-focused scrutiny committees due to the high policy nature of regulations made in the emergency periods.[121] These can all be understood to be matters that ensure that forms of parliamentary scrutiny of regulations remain in place and can operate effectively within emergency periods. This is particularly important due to regulations shifting from being a high-volume form of law-making that occasionally involves broad and significant matters, to regulations being high-volume and commonly involving broad social and economic matters that are highly relevant to members of the public.

The Committee's two reports included many recommendations. Some recommendations were addressed to governments to propose amendments to primary legislation, in particular, the Biosecurity Act 2015 that was used heavily in the COVID-19 crisis.[122] Other recommendations were to the Senate to amend its standing orders to better facilitate scrutiny of regulations in emergency periods.[123] The Government dismissed each of the recommendations to change the Biosecurity Act 2015 (Cth),[124] but the recommendations directed to the Senate

[118] para 4.58.
[119] ibid para 7.25.
[120] ibid paras 7.61–7.63.
[121] ibid paras 7.64–7.67.
[122] ibid recommendations 5–9.
[123] ibid recommendation 16.
[124] *Australian Government Response to the Standing Committee for the Scrutiny of Delegated Legislation: Inquiry into the Exemption of Delegated Legislation from Parliamentary Oversight: Interim report*, available at www.aph.gov.au/Parliamentary_Business/Committees/Senate/Scrutiny_of_Delegated_Legislation/Exemptfromoversight/Additional_Documents?docType=Government%20Response.

were all accepted without disagreement or debate.[125] This included acceptance of the recommendation to expand the Committee's role to include scrutiny of non-disallowable regulations.[126]

C. Exposing Broader Concerns

In each country, the concerns expressed by parliamentary committees regarding regulation-making in the emergency period prompted further inquiries into parliamentary scrutiny of regulations and regulation-making powers outside of emergency periods. The concerns regarding the details of the regulation-making systems were different in each country, but the overall issues were the same: that the emergency period was a relatively extreme example of a trend in which parliamentary scrutiny was being minimised, resulting in the relationship between the executive and parliament becoming imbalanced in favour of the executive. These themes were developed by parliamentary committees in each country in reports published in 2021 and 2022.

In the UK a joint inquiry was held by two House of Lords committees, the Delegated Powers and Regulatory Reform Committee and the Secondary Legislation Scrutiny Committee. The titles of the Committees' reports make very clear their concerns: the Delegated Powers and Regulatory Reform Committee report was titled 'Democracy Denied? The Urgent Need to Rebalance Power between Parliament and the Executive'; and the Secondary Legislation Scrutiny Committee's report was titled 'Government by Diktat: A Call to Return Power to Parliament'.[127] The Secondary Legislation Scrutiny Committee followed up this inquiry with an additional report in 2022 that included a title developing the theme: 'What Next? The Growing Imbalance between Parliament and the Executive: End of Session Report 2021–22'.[128] These reports share the theme that steps to minimise parliamentary scrutiny of regulations that had developed in the past were scaled up to deal with Brexit and the COVID-19 emergency. Brexit and COVID-19 were therefore understood to represent steps in a pre-existing trend rather than exceptions to regulation-making norms.

In Australia, Senate committees with similar functions to the House of Lords committees also held inquiries and published reports into parliamentary scrutiny

[125] Commonwealth, *Parliamentary Debates*, Senate, 16 June 2021, 3055.

[126] Senate Standing Committee for the Scrutiny of Delegated Legislation, *Inquiry into the Exemption of Delegated Legislation from Parliamentary Oversight: Final Report* (16 March 2021) recommendation 10.

[127] Delegated Powers and Regulatory Reform Committee, *Democracy Denied? The Urgent Need to Rebalance power between Parliament and the Executive* (HL 2021–22, 106) paras 2–6; Secondary Legislation Scrutiny Committee, *Government by Diktat: A Call to Return Power to Parliament* (HL 2021–22, 105) para 1.

[128] Secondary Legislation Scrutiny Committee, 'What Next? The Growing Imbalance between Parliament and the Executive: End of Session Report 2021–22' (HL 2021–22, 200).

that were prompted by the COVID-19 emergency, but raised broader concerns about delegation of regulation-making powers that also provide exemptions from disallowance.[129] These reports emphasised the importance of parliamentary scrutiny to the role of Parliament in Australia's democratic system and the general inappropriateness of regulation-making powers in Acts providing exemptions from disallowance.

The difference between the UK reports and the Australian reports is that the UK reports focus on practices that have developed that minimise parliamentary scrutiny while the Australian reports deal with attempts simply to exclude it. At a higher level of generality, however, the themes are strikingly similar. The members of the House of Lords and Senate committees expressed their concerns in plain terms as to Parliament's role in regulation-making. The COVID-19 emergency, combined in the UK with Brexit regulation-making processes, raised concerns about law-making in emergency periods, but on a deeper level the concerns turned out to be long-term trends rather than discrete emergency responses that can be regarded as exceptional. The common theme was that the relationship between the executive and Parliament needs to be reset to correct the imbalance.

IV. Conclusion

In this chapter we have seen the ways in which the safeguards on regulation-making in the most recent emergency period, the COVID-19 pandemic, contracted. That is likely to be regarded as appropriate for judicial review, which is recognised to be conducted in a deferential manner in emergency periods, and public consultation which is likely to be excluded due to the urgent need for special laws. Parliamentary scrutiny may also be contracted as there is likely to be a great need for regulations to come into operation very urgently. However, we have also seen that minimising parliamentary scrutiny to token forms or excluding it completely is not appropriate and is open to criticism. In the COVID-19 period it prompted criticism from a range of places, and most importantly from parliaments themselves.

The experience of regulation-making during the COVID-19 crisis highlights another context in which tensions arise. It is the most recent example of a flare-up in executive–parliament relations in regard to regulation-making.

[129] Senate Standing Committee for the Scrutiny of Bills, *Second Report: Review of Exemption from Disallowance Provisions in the Biosecurity Act 2015* (Digest No 1 of 2022, 4 February 2022) paras 4.4.–4.6; Senate Standing Committee for the Scrutiny of Delegated Legislation, *Inquiry into the Exemption of Delegated Legislation from Parliamentary Oversight: Final Report* (16 March 2021).

10

Executive Aggrandisement, Parliamentary Democracy and Bicameralism

This book has examined the system of safeguards on regulation-making in two parliamentary democracies, the UK and Australia. In each country, the system consists of three safeguards: parliamentary scrutiny of bills and regulations; consultation; and judicial review of regulations. The general point I have sought to make clear is that the democratic legitimacy of regulations in these countries is dependent on this system of safeguards with three main elements. While all three safeguards have important functions in the regulation-making systems in both countries, I have argued that parliamentary scrutiny is the safeguard that has the primary role of providing democratic legitimacy for regulations in both countries.

In this final chapter, I apply the comparative law methodology to separate the conclusions regarding similarities between the two countries that suggest general features of regulation-making systems in parliamentary democracies and conclusions about the differences. The similarities between the UK and Australia in this aspect of law-making do not rise to the level of general conclusions regarding regulation-making in parliamentary democracies; research of other parliamentary democracies would be required for that. The differences between them are also highly important. They make clear that the safeguards operate differently in the two countries.

I will examine the similarities by focusing on the significance of executive aggrandisement in the two countries. The comparison between the UK and Australia suggests some primary characteristics of regulation-making in parliamentary democracies. This is due to longstanding similarities in the general characteristics of regulation-making in the two countries and developments that occurred in the twentieth century. The primary features of the debates in each country in the 1920s and 1930s, the development of parliamentary scrutiny committees, and the repeal of enforceable public consultation statutory provisions, are strikingly similar. The similarities in the exceptions to parliamentary scrutiny and the attempts to minimise it that were examined in part two of the book are also important. Recognising these developments in each country supports the conclusion that the three safeguards and their implementation in laws and institutions have important similarities in each country. In particular, the development of parliamentary scrutiny committees highlights that these additional controls on regulation-making were added as safeguards in face of the opposition and resistance of governments.

I will then examine the primary difference by focusing on the forms of bicameralism in the two countries and their significance for parliamentary scrutiny of regulations. The different forms of bicameralism are due to the elected basis for the Australian Senate in contrast with the appointed House of Lords. This difference is important for the primary issues addressed in the book; parliamentary scrutiny and executive–parliament relations. Other differences are no doubt important but are not as closely related to the main themes of the book. These differences relate to judicial approaches to consultation for regulations, and the role of judicially enforceable human rights legislation in the UK to judicial review of regulations where there is no equivalent in Australia at the Commonwealth level.

I. Executive Aggrandisement

A. Modern Public Law Theory

The development of norms for regulation-making in the 1930s, which included a primary role for parliamentary scrutiny of regulations and the subsequent implementation of those norms in the twentieth century, indicates that the executive does not have absolute control of parliaments in the UK and Australia, as Rose-Ackerman argued in her comparative administrative law scholarship.[1] The debates regarding the establishment of parliamentary committees to scrutinise bills and regulations in both countries indicates that this occurred despite government resistance to them. These committees and the parliamentary powers to veto regulations, provide the primary democratic control on regulation-making in the two countries. These forms of control on regulation-making should not be surprising in parliamentary democracies, given the role of parliaments in such constitutional systems for the macro-political function of legislation-making and supervising the executive; most relevantly here, in regard to regulation-making.

These developments highlight that the executive's relationship to the parliaments in both countries in regard to regulation-making does not involve complete control. In practice, this enables the parliaments in both countries to check regulations with the support of scrutiny committees. More generally, parliament's function of checking regulations enables regulations to be recognised as having a degree of democratic legitimacy. However, part two of the book highlights

[1] S Rose-Ackerman, 'Policy-Making Accountability: Parliamentary versus Presidential Systems' in D Levi-Faur (ed), *Handbook on the Politics of Regulation* (Edward Elgar, 2011) 176–77. See also S Rose-Ackerman S, *Democracy and Executive Power: Policymaking Accountability in the US, the UK, Germany, and France* (Yale University Press, 2021) 35, 53.

measures that have developed to avoid and minimise these parliamentary checks. These developments, some new and some expansions of well-known practices, can be regarded as forms of executive aggrandisement. From the perspective of those who regard executive control of parliaments being the hallmark of parliamentary systems, these practices would be regarded as expected. However, when regulation-making is understood as being legitimate within parliamentary democracies so long as safeguards are in place, including parliamentary scrutiny, the analysis must change to questioning the balance in the relationship between parliaments and the executive.

Recent scholarship examining executive aggrandisement can help understanding of these developments. Tarunabh Khaitan has provided a helpful definition and explanation of its operation in modern liberal democracies. He refers to it as involving incremental dismantling of the mechanisms that provide for the accountability of the executive.[2] Khaitan elaborates by referring to it as involving 'rollbacks' and 'weakening' of these accountability mechanisms that restrict opposition to the executive government's preferences, that are deliberately developed and implemented by the executive.[3] Drawing on studies of anti-democratic developments in numerous countries, he identifies the current forms of executive aggrandisement as typically being conducted incrementally, including through legislative means, rather than through formal constitutional change.[4]

While Khaitan does not focus on executive aggrandisement in relation to regulation-making processes, his analysis helps understanding of the developments in both countries to minimise and avoid parliamentary scrutiny for regulation-making that were analysed in part two of this book. It provides a better framework for analysing regulation-making processes and safeguards in parliamentary democracies than Rose-Ackerman's understanding of executive control. Khaitan assumes that democratic checks have been established and that executives have implemented measures to weaken them. I will elaborate in more detail later in this chapter how the developments examined in part two can be understood to be forms of executive aggrandisement.

Margit Cohn's recent work on the executive branch also examines executive aggrandisement.[5] She expressly rejects understanding the relationship between the executive and parliament as being the former controlling the latter, and instead regards it as a matter of tension between the branches.[6] The tension includes the executive branch's historical tendency for aggrandisement.[7] She refers to the tension as involving granting power to the executive to conduct essential functions

[2] T Khaitan, 'Executive Aggrandisement in Established Democracies: A Crisis of Liberal Democratic Constitutionalism' (2019) *17 I•CON* 342, 343.
[3] ibid 347, 351.
[4] ibid 352.
[5] M Cohn, *A Theory of the Executive Branch: Tension and Legality* (Oxford University Press, 2021).
[6] ibid 2, 25–27.
[7] ibid 2, 49–52.

in modern society with constraints provided by law on that power.[8] The difficulty in modern society is that the tendency to aggrandisement operates through those powers being granted, but with the checks on the exercise of the power being minimised.[9] Cohn develops this idea through her concept of 'fuzzy law', which comes in many different forms including, most relevantly here, statutes with open-ended provisions, that delegate regulation-making powers, and provide broad discretionary powers.[10] Cohn regards fuzzy laws such as these as providing a façade of legality.[11]

Cohn's analysis of executive aggrandisement supports the analysis in this book. Rather than recognising executive dominance of other branches such as the legislature, she sees relationships that involves tension. While Cohn's analysis of executive aggrandisement has a similar conceptual framework to the analysis of regulation-making powers in this book, it is important to recognise the primary difference. The constraints on executive powers that Cohn analyses are the substantive conditions, qualifications on the administrative powers provided by laws that enable executive actions and decisions. These are constraints on executive power that are different to those examined in this book. The constraints I have examined are institutional and procedural checks, and most importantly for part two, parliamentary scrutiny of the exercise of regulation-making powers.

Khaitan and Cohn offer analytical frameworks for understanding the functions and practices of the executive in modern democracies and the operation and techniques of executive aggrandisement. Rather than understanding the executive as simply controlling the parliament, the primary democratic institution in parliamentary democracies, they recognise practices by which executive governments seek to minimise constraints on their powers and avoid democratic accountability. Importantly, both recognise that the techniques employed for executive aggrandisement are commonly established by legislation. Parliaments can have a role in enabling executive aggrandisement. That should not lessen the concern. It suggests that it is likely to be the institution to go to in order to correct the developments and techniques examined in part two.

B. Twentieth-Century Reforms

To gauge whether executive aggrandisement is occurring and, if so, how it is occurring in regard to constitutional arrangements, it is helpful to have a reference point. In both the UK and Australia, the normative standards for regulation-making developed in debates between public lawyers about the role of regulation-making

[8] ibid 55.
[9] ibid 59, 69.
[10] ibid 59, 79–85.
[11] ibid 59–60.

in the two parliamentary democracies. As I highlighted in part one, there was agreement regarding safeguards on regulation-making being the obvious solution to the problems raised. The inquiries in both countries relied heavily on parliamentary scrutiny committees being the safeguard that was underdeveloped in the UK and missing in Australia. And as we saw in part one, the committees' recommendations were implemented during the twentieth century. In this way, the debates in the 1930s provided the normative framework underpinning regulation-making in both countries. The fact that the inquiries' solutions were implemented confirms their status as providing standards for democratically legitimate regulation-making in both countries.

Lord Hewart's criticism of regulation-making can be understood to be based on forms of executive aggrandisement. As we saw in chapters two and three, his criticism prompted the Donoughmore Committee inquiry and had an influence on the Australian Senate's inquiry in 1930. Lord Hewart's title and his conspiratorial rhetoric is clearly based on concerns about executive aggrandisement. The more complex questions it raised were whether his understanding of the role of Parliament remained relevant and plausible in the late 1920s and early 1930s. While it was generally accepted that Lord Hewart's concerns were overstated, they should be recognised as an important milestone in UK constitutionalism that prompted reflection on the role of administration in parliamentary systems and reforms in relation to the safeguards on regulation-making.

Similar concerns have been expressed by Australian judges, Dixon CJ and Brennan CJ, regarding executive aggrandisement. These concerns are particularly relevant due to these judges' extensive influence in shaping Australian public law. In the *Communist Party* case Dixon J stated:

> History and not only ancient history, shows that in countries where democratic institutions have been unconstitutionally superseded, it has been done not seldom by those holding the executive power. Forms of government may need protection from dangers likely to arise from within the institutions to be protected.[12]

While the *Communist Party* case involved a challenge to an Act that provided numerous regulation-making powers, it is usually recognised as a landmark in Australian constitutional law rather than administrative law. Similar concerns have also been made in administrative law contexts. Justice Brennan in *South Australia v Tanner* stated:

> Parliament is the organ of government in which legislative power is vested and Parliament should not be held to have delegated to another repository more power than is clearly denoted by the words it has used. In my opinion, a delegation of legislative power should be narrowly construed unless the Parliament has, by express provision or necessary intendment, revealed a contrary intention.[13]

[12] *Australian Communist Party v Commonwealth* (1951) 83 CLR 1, 187.
[13] (1989) 166 CLR 161, 174.

Brennan subsequently raised concerns in a published speech about the expansion of executive power and the limited capacity of parliaments to provide a sufficient check on it.[14] The concerns raised by these Australian judges about executive aggrandisement are not as dramatic as Lord Hewart's. They did not prompt substantial debate in legal and academic circles, or inquiries. However, they raise similar concerns to Lord Hewart's.

Accordingly, executive aggrandisement is not only a recent concern prompting academic analysis. It has been identified by judges over the last 100 years. The important point is that executive aggrandisement in relation to regulation-making had its initial debate and primary solutions addressed in the 1930s in both countries. In part one I focused on these debates. While they revealed some problems, and different understandings of the role of parliaments in modern parliamentary democracies, it should also be recognised that not far below the surface of the participants' arguments there was often general agreement about the solutions: the safeguards that provide the democratic legitimacy for delegated powers to make regulations. The safeguards recommended by the Donoughmore Committee and the 1930 Senate Committee were the obvious solution to the concerns raised.

Parliamentary scrutiny of regulations was recognised then, and subsequently through the twentieth century, as the primary safeguard. Unlike the other safeguards, it enables a systemic check by the primary democratic institution in the constitutional system. All Acts and regulations were to be reviewed by parliamentary committees to check for the range of problems included in these committees' scrutiny criteria. As explained in chapter three, this included an escalation function. At times that function was regarded as pushing the boundaries of technical scrutiny and subsequently it became an express part of some of the committees' functions.

These developments are critically important. Regulations, as a form of law in parliamentary democracies, are legitimate when they deal with technicalities that are not suited to analysis by politicians. They may have micro-political significance for a particular set of stakeholders and interest groups, but not macro-political significance. But when governments add macro-politically controversial matters to regulations there needs to be an escalation mechanism. While the line between macro and micro-politics may not always be clear, parliamentary scrutiny committees in both countries have been able to carry out this function.

In both countries the two primary democratic safeguards, parliamentary scrutiny and public consultation should be understood to have inherent complexities. While parliamentary scrutiny is arguably the primary safeguard due to it linking regulation-making to the primary democratic institution in the political system, it is also often regarded as weak. The examination of it in chapters two and three highlight some key points that are not commonly recognised. One such feature of the 1930s reports is that parliamentary scrutiny committees provide systemic

[14] G Brennan, 'Courts, Democracy and the Law' (1991) 65 *Australian Law Journal* 32, 34–36.

scrutiny; all regulations were intended to be checked by parliaments. The high number of regulations made and the technicality of the matters they deal with, creates a difficulty for parliamentary scrutiny providing a deep check. This is one reason why it should not be understood in isolation. It should be regarded as being supplemented by the two other safeguards that have their own contributions to democratic legitimacy.

In chapter four we saw that public consultation has made a very long and important contribution to the safeguards. It also has particularly complex characteristics in both countries. While in the twentieth century it was removed as a generally applicable legislated, mandatory requirement, it still plays a role in the system of safeguards. It is clear enough that public consultation can be regarded as an established norm for regulation-making, even if it is not a generally applicable, enforceable requirement as it is in the US.

Part one also revealed that the implementation of the safeguards, most importantly parliamentary scrutiny committees and consultation, has commonly been controversial. Governments have resisted them at most stages. Governments in both countries were able to remove the mandatory public consultation provisions that were in operation in the early decades of the twentieth century and the attempts to have them reinstated at the turn of the twentieth century were not successful. On the other hand, parliamentary scrutiny committees were added in each country despite opposition by governments. In contrast to the views expressed in Rose-Ackerman's work discussed in chapter one, the historical research for this book reveals that the executive branch should not be understood to have absolute control of parliaments. The executive branch is powerful in these parliamentary democracies but, as we have seen, does not always get its way. This is an important contribution to be taken from part one of the book.

When understood in this way, the safeguards provide the basis for accepting the democratic legitimacy of regulations. Parliamentary scrutiny plays the lead role in this. It is of course conducted by the primary democratic institution in parliamentary democracies and it provides for systemic scrutiny of regulations for which parliaments have veto powers. The regulation-making systems in the UK and Australia with its heavy reliance on safeguards, with parliamentary scrutiny at the fore, provide the normative standard by which to examine changes to regulation-making practices and to identify forms of executive aggrandisement.

C. Executive Aggrandisement in this Century

Drawing on Khaitan's and Cohn's analyses of executive aggrandisement highlights the primary characteristics of its operation in regulation-making. The set of norms for democratic legitimacy provided by the safeguards are well understood. The examples of executive aggrandisement that were examined in part two of the book each involve incremental, yet systemically significant, chipping away at the primary safeguard, parliamentary scrutiny of regulations. As both Khaitan and Cohn recognise, the forms of executive aggrandisement examined in those chapters were facilitated by legislation. Accordingly, Parliament has played a role in enabling it to occur. However, and equally as important, it must be recognised that Parliament is also commonly the institution that raises the concerns about minimising and avoiding parliamentary scrutiny and takes steps to correct it.

In part two I examined four current aspects of regulation-making that work to circumvent or minimise the safeguards on regulation-making. In chapter six I examined the exclusion of tabling regulations in parliaments and the exclusion of parliamentary veto powers. This is an obvious example of avoiding parliamentary scrutiny with risks of executive aggrandisement. When regulations that have general application and affect individuals' and organisations' rights and interests are made according to such processes, an important question arises as to the regulations' democratic legitimacy. On the other hand, the concerns do not arise when the regulation provides for commencement of an Act or regulation or has purely administrative significance. Executive aggrandisement is also not a concern when the regulation that is not subject to parliamentary scrutiny has local significance only; and that is particularly the case if the regulation is subject to local consultation processes. However, the lines between acceptable and unacceptable exclusion of parliamentary scrutiny have not been clearly developed. Excluding parliamentary scrutiny can have important practical consequences as well as raising concerns about executive aggrandisement. The lack of scrutiny by parliamentary committees means that problems such as errors, poor drafting, inclusion of overly broad discretionary powers, will not be raised with the regulation-maker and corrected.

Chapter seven involved an examination of a more recent development in regulation-making; incorporation by reference of guidance and privately made standards. Incorporation by reference in a dynamic manner avoids parliamentary scrutiny. The document that is incorporated by reference is not only the current version but also any subsequent changes to it. Dynamic incorporation means that subsequent changes do not prompt an amendment to the regulation that incorporates the document, and accordingly that there is no parliamentary scrutiny of those changes. The exclusion of parliamentary scrutiny through dynamic incorporation by reference enables a form of executive aggrandisement. It also must be recognised that parliaments can authorise dynamic incorporation by reference, which has most clearly occurred in Australia. Dynamic incorporation by reference of administrative guidance is a straightforward example of executive overreach. It enables administrative control of the content of regulations without parliamentary scrutiny. The same concern arises for incorporation by reference of private standards but this development should be understood as being prompted by a different phenomenon. It relates to trade law and its demand for international harmonised regulatory laws.

Henry VIII powers, examined in chapter eight, have long been recognised as a form of executive aggrandisement. As we saw in that chapter, that is the point of the Henry VIII terminology – it is recognised as the famous form of autocratic executive government in English constitutional history. Henry VIII powers are a form of executive aggrandisement because Parliament's role in relation to Acts is minimised by using regulation-making processes for changes to Acts rather than the parliamentary processes for making and amending Acts. Henry VIII powers featured prominently in the 1930s debates and were directly addressed in the Donoughmore Committee report. A consensus developed that they were appropriate for transitional changes relating to matters of detail. Chapter eight identifies expansions of their use in the UK and Australia beyond the limits that were identified in the 1930s. In the UK the expansion can be seen in statutes with constitutional significance. In Australia, the expansion has occurred in economic legislation. The important point is that, as Khaitan indicates regarding modern executive aggrandisement being incremental and enabled by statutory powers, there have been incremental developments in both countries that have expanded the reliance on Henry VIII powers.

Regulations are particularly important in emergency times, as we saw in chapter nine. On the one hand, they have features that make them well suited to law-making in emergency periods. On the other hand, governments' use of regulations in emergency periods needs to be checked to ensure that the need for exceptional steps and the benefits of regulation-making in emergencies does not turn into ongoing executive aggrandisement. Lord Hewart was unusually tolerant of the expansion of executive action and increased reliance on regulations in emergency periods. However, there was much criticism of governments in both countries during the COVID-19 emergency period for extending executive powers beyond what was necessary in the emergency circumstances. In particular, chapter nine highlights that concerns were raised about the COVID-19 period on a range of grounds, including minimising or removing parliamentary scrutiny without justification by reference to the emergency.

In part two of this book I examined four aspects of modern regulation-making that conflict with the normative standards developed in the 1930s and implemented in different safeguards through the twentieth century. The twentieth-century developments provide a basis to examine whether executive aggrandisement is occurring. As Khaitan highlights, one of its modern characteristics is that it occurs incrementally. This can make it difficult to identify for many aspects of executive action. However, executive aggrandisement in regard to regulation-making is relatively easy to analyse when there is a concern that it is occurring. The conceptual framework for democratic legitimacy of regulations is clear due to the work in the 1930s by judges, academics, legal practitioners and Members of Parliament. It is clear that forms of executive aggrandisement have occurred in recent years and continue in relation to regulation-making. As Khaitan and Cohn make clear in regard to executive aggrandisement more generally, it has involved minimising the restrictions and accountability checks on statutory delegations of powers to administrative officials. Neither scholar focused on regulation-making as a particular area ripe for executive aggrandisement, but recent history of regulation-making powers in each country analysed in chapters six to nine indicates its operation.

D. Ongoing Tensions

The contribution I seek to make to comparative administrative law scholarship is to see through the complexity that there is a system of safeguards on regulation-making in the UK's and Australia's parliamentary democracies that provide for their democratic legitimacy. There are complexities involved, but the three primary safeguards that apply in both the UK and Australia add up to a system that provides for democratic legitimacy. The powerful role of the executive in parliamentary democracies does not necessarily prevent the development of democratic checks on regulations. I have sought to highlight these aspects of regulation-making in the UK and Australia in order to inform comparative administrative law scholars of the primary features of regulation-making in parliamentary democracies in these two countries. I have also examined the history of developments relating to regulation-making safeguards in the UK and Australia in order to provide public lawyers in these countries with the background to regulation-making in each country. My hope is that this history will be an important source of information for current and future public lawyers in their examination, and potential criticisms, of forms of executive aggrandisement that tend to develop in regard to regulation-making. I also aim to draw to the attention of administrative lawyers that for regulation-making the most important institutional relationship is between the executive and parliament, rather than the executive and courts.

Understanding the relationship between the executive and parliament in the UK and Australia's parliamentary democracies as not being a matter of executive control but, as Cohn highlights, a matter of tension and risk of executive aggrandisement, has some practical consequences. Public law scholars, practitioners, and commentators need to be attuned to the tensions and the signs of executive expansion. As regulation-making is commonly below the radar of commentators and media, it is important for public lawyers and others who are exposed to it to escalate their concerns to courts, parliamentary committees, to governments through consultation processes, and potentially to the different forms of media in the current era.

If one were to accept the view that the regulations in parliamentary democracies such as the UK and Australia are democratically illegitimate due to overarching executive control, there would be little reason to look for signs of executive aggrandisement. However, when parliaments are recognised as having powers and techniques for pushing back against executive overreach, as seen historically in part one of this book, there is a need to keep an eye out for it and to identify the best techniques for parliaments, and potentially other institutions, to respond.

As Cohn emphasises, it is a matter of ongoing tension between governmental institutions requiring vigilance of those who are sensitive to the forms and characteristics of executive aggrandisement.

II. Bicameralism

This book also reveals differences between the UK and Australia in relation to regulation-making safeguards. While there are specific differences in respect to developments in regard to public consultation and judicial review of regulations in the two countries, the difference that is most relevant to parliamentary democracy relates to parliamentary scrutiny of regulations examined in chapter three. In that chapter we saw that there are relatively few examples of parliamentary veto of regulations in the UK and minimal time given to debating them in comparison to Australia. This has particular significance for the democratic legitimacy of regulations.

In chapter three I explained that the constitutional arrangements in the two countries are likely to be relevant to the way in which concerns about ineffectiveness of parliamentary scrutiny of regulations arise. In particular, the differences are related to the characteristics of parliamentarism in the UK compared to the semi-parliamentarism that applies in Australia. This analysis is based on parliamentary scrutiny being one of the two main justifications for bicameralism.[15] While scrutiny of regulations is particularly suited to bicameralism in parliamentary democracies, there are important differences in the two countries. The members of the House of Lords are not elected. The House of Lords is made up primarily of appointed peers and some remaining hereditary peers.[16] The members of the Australian Senate are elected according to a proportional representation system.

We saw in chapter three that this difference in bicameralism in the two countries suggests an explanation for the differences in the number of regulations vetoed in the UK and Australia. Concerns about the lack of a democratic basis of the House of Lords and the primacy of the House of Commons in the UK does not translate to Australia. The self-imposed restraint that applies to the House of Lords' veto power regarding regulations, does not feature in parliamentary scrutiny of regulations by the Senate. This difference most likely also affects the scrutiny committees' work in each country. The Senate scrutiny committee's engagement with ministers over regulations occurs in the context of a realistic possibility of disallowance. The rareness of the use of veto powers in the UK must lessen the effectiveness of scrutiny committees' influence on governments' responsiveness to committee criticisms.

[15] M Russell, *The Contemporary House of Lords: Westminster Bicameralism Revived* (Oxford University Press, 2013) 45–46.

[16] UK Parliament, 'Lords membership – by peerage', available at members.parliament.uk/parties/lords/by-peerage.

This difference between the UK and Australia raises a question as to whether either country can be regarded as a special case of parliamentary democracy. My general answer is that both countries have features that enhance or diminish the effectiveness of their scrutiny of regulations. As explained in chapter one, I have avoided referring to the UK and Australia as Westminster-model democracies due to the variations in parliamentary democracies in different countries. While the Westminster Parliament has been a major historical influence on parliamentary democracies, it is worth noting that Lijphart, in his famous comparative work on democracies, recognised the UK Parliament as having differences from his understanding of Westminster-model parliamentary democracy due to its bicameralism.[17] Rather than comparing each country to a particular model of parliamentary democracy, my analysis is limited to a comparative analysis of two parliamentary democracies, the UK and Australia. The relevant difference between the two forms of parliamentary democracy is their different forms of bicameralism and the significance of those differences for parliamentary scrutiny of regulations.

The primacy of the House of Commons has a strong hold on participants' deliberations in the UK. As we saw in chapter three, it affects the way the House of Lords applies its scrutiny powers over regulations, notwithstanding that the Parliament Acts control the relationship between the two houses in relation to primary Acts but not to regulations.[18] The primacy of the House of Commons has also influenced recently expressed proposals for constitutional reform in the UK. The Commission on the UK's Future, 'A New Britain: Renewing our Democracy and Rebuilding our Economy',[19] published in 2022 and led by former Prime Minister Gordon Brown, proposed an elected second chamber that would not have veto powers over Acts and would not affect the House of Commons' primacy.[20] If this proposal were to be adopted the institutional arrangements that currently restrains the House of Lords in its scrutiny of regulations, would most likely continue to operate.

The Australian Senate is recognised as having particularly unusual features for a parliamentary democracy. It has been elected since it was established, and elected according to a proportional representation system since 1948.[21] This has resulted in governments rarely having a majority in the Senate. Section 53 of the Commonwealth Constitution also makes clear that the Senate has equal power to the House of Representatives except for specified exceptions. These aspects of the Senate led one scholar to claim that Australia should not be regarded as a

[17] A Lijphart, *Patterns of Democracy: Government Forms and Performance in Thirty-Six Countries*, 2nd edn (Yale University Press, 2012) 10, 17–18.

[18] D Natzler and M Hutton, *Erskine May's Treatise on The Law, Privileges, Proceedings and Usage of Parliament* (UK Parliament website) pt 4, ch 31, available at erskinemay.parliament.uk/section/5639/practice-of-the-house-of-lords-on-delegated-legislation; Russell (n 15) 84, 140–41.

[19] (December 2022), available at labour.org.uk/page/a-new-britain.

[20] ibid 138, 141, 143.

[21] Commonwealth Electoral Act 1948.

parliamentary democracy.[22] Other scholars have more recently recognised the parliamentary system in Australia as 'semi-parliamentarism'.[23] This is an additional category of democratic system with the primary features being that it has a bicameral parliament in which the first chamber provides confidence in the Government and the second chamber has a general veto power over legislation. The semi-parliamentarism of the Australian Parliament suggests a reason for less restraint on the Senate's exercise of veto powers in comparison to the House of Lords. There is no reason for Senators to consider the House of Representatives to have primacy. Senators are elected, the Government usually does not have a majority, and the Commonwealth Constitution clarifies that it generally has equal powers to the House of Representatives over legislation.

The comparative analysis in this book confirms there are important differences in the forms of bicameralism in the parliaments of each country that are likely to be relevant in decisions to exercise veto powers over regulations. The special position of the Senate in Australia's parliamentary democracy can explain its comparative assertiveness on exercising its veto powers. On the other hand, Hansard Society research into House of Lords' scrutiny of regulations has made suggestions to improve the assertiveness of the House of Lords' scrutiny of regulations in the UK's bicameral parliamentary system.[24] If that is right, the different characteristics of the two parliamentary democracies suggest reasons for differences in parliamentary scrutiny but should not be regarded in a rigid manner.

III. Comparative Research of Regulation-Making

While the comparative research for the book identifies differences between the two countries, it is important to keep those differences in perspective. The similarities in developments regarding parliamentary scrutiny of bills and regulations says a lot about the primary features of regulation-making in the two parliamentary democracies. The differences can be put down to different characteristics of their bicameralism, in particular Australia's semi-parliamentary features, and to judicial developments.

The primary theme of this book has been its focus on the relationship between the executive and parliament. The importance of this relationship for regulation-making in parliamentary democracies suggests that research of it should be

[22] S Bach, *Platypus and Parliament: The Australian Senate in Theory and Practice* (Department of the Senate, 2003) 330–31.

[23] M Taflaga, 'What's in a Name? Semi-Parliamentarism and Australian Commonwealth Executive-Legislative Relations (2018) 53 *Australian Journal of Political Science* 248, 249; S Ganghof, *Beyond Presidentialism and Parliamentarism: Democratic Design and the Separation of Powers* (Oxford University Press, 2022) ch 3.

[24] R Fox and J Blackwell, *The Devil is in the Detail: Parliament and Delegated Legislation* (Hansard Society, 2014) 187–89.

higher on administrative lawyers' agenda than it is currently. I have two particular suggestions for future research.

The first relates to drafting practices in regard to primary legislation. I have sought to highlight in part two of the book that many of the current tensions between the systems of safeguards that developed in the twentieth century and current regulation-making practices are due to legislative drafting practices. The problems arising from exclusion of parliamentary scrutiny, incorporation by reference, Henry VIII clauses and emergency legislation can all be, at least partly, attributed to drafting of primary legislation. While Lord Hewart is often regarded as an idiosyncratic figure in the history of public law in the UK and the commonwealth, his intervention was a historical landmark for public law in parliamentary democracies. He drew attention to the difficulties associated with primary legislation delegating power to administrative officials in a manner that limits and excludes forms of accountability. While privative clauses and other forms of restriction on judicial review have a central place in modern administrative law scholarship, legislative techniques for excluding or minimising parliamentary scrutiny of regulations have been given little attention. More research on this aspect of the accountability of administrative officials would be beneficial.

The second suggestion is for further research regarding parliamentary scrutiny and consultation in practice; research that focuses on weaknesses in practice of these safeguards and proposals to improve them. The systemic focus of this book meant that it has a different methodology than is suited to research of these practices. However, the issues are highly important for understanding the democratic legitimacy of regulation-making. The Hansard Society's sustained research on parliamentary scrutiny has been influential for UK public law scholarship. There is scope for similar research in Australia.

More generally, the research for this book can help to put executive–parliament relations on the research agenda of the current generation of administrative lawyers in each country. I have drawn on research in each country with more of a constitutional focus,[25] but such research is also suited to administrative law scholarship as it focuses on the accountability of government officials for the exercise of powers delegated by statute. There has been work by administrative law scholars in recent years,[26] but the focus of administrative law research tends to be on the relationship between the executive and the courts, then followed by research of

[25] See eg G Appleby, 'Challenging the Orthodoxy: Giving the Court a Role in Scrutiny of Delegated Legislation' (2016) 69 *Parliamentary Affairs* 269; A Tucker, 'Parliamentary Scrutiny of Delegated Legislation' in A Horne and G Drewry (eds), *Parliament and the Law* (Hart Publishing, 2018) 347; J King, 'The Province of Delegated Legislation' in E Fisher, J King and AL Young, *The Foundations and Future of Public Law* (Oxford University Press, 2020).

[26] See eg, A Sinclair and J Tomlinson, 'Plus ça change? Brexit and the Flaws of the Delegated Legislation System' (*Public Law Project*, 13 October 2020), available at publiclawproject.org.uk/resources/plus-ca-change-brexit-and-the-flaws-of-the-delegated-legislation-system; J Boughey, 'Brett Cattle: New Limits on Delegated Law-Making Powers?' (2020) 31 *Public Law Review* 347; J Boughey, 'Executive Power in Emergencies: Where is the Accountability?' (2020) 45 *Alternative Law Journal* 168.

administrative law institutions such as tribunals and ombudsman. It is difficult to see why accountability of the executive to parliament is not researched to the same degree. The benefit of such research by administrative law scholars is that they should be more attuned to characteristics of regulatory systems and the subtleties inherent in accountability relationships. Recent developments in analysis of parliamentary democracies in comparative political science and comparative constitutional law can help administrative law scholars to understand the characteristics and dynamics of that relationship and in particular, to see the role of bicameralism in holding the executive accountable for its regulation-making.

I would like to finish with a call for the kind of research in this book to be conducted for other parliamentary democracies. I have deliberately limited my comparative research to two countries in order to examine them in some depth. However, I also regard regulation-making in parliamentary democracies more widely as being important. While political scientists now usually agree that there are no common characteristics of parliamentary democracies that have evolved from the Westminster Parliament, this book has shown that in relation to regulation-making the similarities between the UK and Australia are striking although there are also important differences. It is unclear whether these similarities and differences apply in other parliamentary democracies.

BIBLIOGRAPHY

Allars, M, 'Standing: The Role and Evolution of the Test' (1991) 20 *Federal Law Review* 83

Allen, CK, *Bureaucracy Triumphant* (Oxford University Press, 1931)

—— *Law and Orders* (Stevens and Sons, 1945)

—— *Law and Orders: An Inquiry into the Nature and Scope of Delegated Legislation and Executive Powers in English Lawn*, 2nd edn (Stevens & Sons, 1965)

Allison, JWF, 'The Westminster Parliament's Formal Sovereignty in Britain and Europe from a Historical Perspective' (2017) 34 *Giornale Di Storma Costituzionale* 57

Apostolova, V, 'Acts and Statutory Instruments: the Volume of UK legislation 1950 to 2016' (Commons Library Briefing Paper CBP 7438, 21 April 2017)

Appleby, G, 'Challenging the Orthodoxy: Giving the Court a Role in Scrutiny of Delegated Legislation' (2016) 69 *Parliamentary Affairs* 269

Argument, S, 'Legislative Scrutiny in Australia: Wisdom to Export?' (2011) 32 *Statute Law Review* 116

Aronson, M, 'Subordinate Legislation: Lively Scrutiny or Politics in Seclusion' (2011) 26 *Australasian Parliamentary Review* 4

—— 'The Great Depression, This Depression, and Administrative Law' (2009) 37 *Federal Law Review* 165

Arvind, TT and Stirton, L, 'The Curious Origins of Judicial Review' (2017) 133 *Law Quarterly Review* 91

Bach, S, *Platypus and Parliament: The Australian Senate in Theory and Practice* (Department of the Senate, 2003)

Baldwin, R, 'Is Better Regulation Smarter Regulation?' [2005] *Public Law* 485

Barber, NW and Young, AL, 'The Rise of Prospective Henry VIII Clauses and their Implications for Sovereignty' [2003] *Public Law* 111

Barber, S, Brown J, and Ferguson, D, *Coronavirus: Lockdown Laws* (House of Commons Library, 14 July 2022)

Beamish, D, 'How the House of Lords has Adapted to the Pandemic' in P Evans, C Salmon Percival, P Silk and H White (eds), *Parliaments and the Pandemic* (Study of Parliaments Group, 2021)

Beatson, J, 'Legislative Control of Administrative Rulemaking: Lessons from the British Experience?' (1979) 12 *Cornell International Law Journal* 199

Blick, A, *The Codes of the Constitution* (Hart Publishing, 2016)

Bond, C, *Law in War: Freedom and Restriction in Australia During the Great War* (New South Wales Press, 2020)

Bottomley, S, 'The Notional Legislator: The Australian Securities and Investments Commission's Role as A Law-Maker' (2011) 39 *Federal Law Review* 1

Boughey, J, 'Brett Cattle: New Limits on Delegated Law-Making Powers?' (2020) 31 *Public Law Review* 347

—— 'Executive Power in Emergencies: Where is the Accountability?' (2020) 45 *Alternative Law Journal* 168

Bremer, ES, 'On the Cost of Private Standards in Public Law' (2015) 63 *University of Kansas Law Review* 279

Brennan, G, 'Courts, Democracy and the Law' (1991) 65 *Australian Law Journal* 32

Brown, J and Kirk-Wade, E, *Coronavirus: A History of English Lockdown Laws* (House of Commons Library, 22 December 2021)

Büthe, T and Mattli, W, *The New Global Rulers: The Privatization of Regulation in the World Economy* (Princeton University Press, 2011)
Cane, C, *Administrative Tribunals and Adjudication* (Hart Publishing, 2009)
Cane, P, 'Administrative Law as Regulation' in C Parker, C Scott, N Lacey and J Braithwaite, *Regulating Law* (Oxford University Press, 2004)
—— *Controlling Administrative Power: An Historical Comparison* (Cambridge University Press, 2016)
—— 'The Constitutional Basis of Judicial Remedies in Public Law' in P Leyland and T Woods (eds), *Administrative Law Facing the Future: Old Constraints and New Horizons* (Blackstone Press Ltd, 1997)
Cane, P, McDonald, L and Rundle, K, *Principles of Administrative Law*, 3rd edn (Oxford University Press, 2018)
Carr, C, *Concerning English Administrative Law* (Columbia University Press, 1941)
—— *Delegated Legislation: Three Lectures* (Cambridge University Press, 1921)
—— 'Parliamentary Supervision in Britain' (1955) 30 *New York University Law Review* 1045
Carroll, P, 'Australia and New Zealand' in C Dunlop and C Radaelli (eds), *Handbook of Regulatory Impact Assessment* (Edward Elgar Publishing, 2016)
Chen B, 'The Principle of Legality: Issues of Rationale and Application' (2015) 41 *Monash University Law Review* 329
Chen, CM, *Parliamentary Opinion of Delegated Legislation* (Columbia University Press, 1933)
Cohn, M, *A Theory of the Executive Branch: Tension and Legality* (Oxford University Press, 2021).
Colombo, C and Eliantonio, M, 'Harmonized Technical Standards as Part of EU Law: Juridification with a Number of Unresolved Legitimacy Concerns?' (2017) 24 *Maastricht Journal of European and Comparative Law* 323
Cormacain, R, 'Keeping Covid-19 Emergency Legislation Socially Distant from Ordinary Legislation: Principles for the Structure of Emergency Legislation' (2020) 8 *The Theory and Practice of Legislation* 245
Corry, JA, 'Administrative Law and the Interpretation of Statutes' (1936) 1 *University of Toronto Law Journal* 286
Craig, PP, *Public Law and Democracy in the United Kingdom and the United States of America* (Clarendon Press, 1990)
Daly, P, *A Theory of Deference in Administrative Law: Basis, Application and Scope* (Cambridge University Press, 2012)
de Smith, SA, 'Delegated Legislation in England' (1949) 2 *Western Political Quarterly* 514
Dicey, AV, *Introduction to the Study of the Law of the Constitution*, 8th edn (Macmillan and Co, 1915)
Dorf, M, 'Dynamic Incorporation of Foreign Law' (2008) 157 *University of Pennsylvania Law Review* 103
Eaves, J, *Emergency Powers and the Parliamentary Watchdog* (Hansard Society for Parliamentary Government, 1957)
Edgar, A, 'Administrative Regulation-Making: Contrasting Parliamentary and Deliberative Legitimacy' (2017) 40 *Melbourne University Law Review* 738
—— 'Deliberative Processes for Administrative Regulations: Unenforceable Public Consultation Provisions and the Courts' (2016) 27 *Public Law Review* 18
—— 'The Westminster Model in Comparative Administrative Law: Incentives for Controls on Regulation-Making' (2019) 38 *University of Tasmania Law Review* 47
Elliott, ED, 'Re-Inventing Rulemaking' (1992) 41 *Duke Law Journal* 1490
Elliott, M and Tierney, S, 'Political Pragmatism and Constitutional Principle: the European Union (Withdrawal) Act 2018' [2019] *Public Law* 37
Else-Mitchell, R, 'Delegated and Sub-delegated Legislation' (1943) 17 *Australian Law Journal* 75
Evans, H, *Odgers Australian Senate Practice*, 14th edn (Department of the Senate, 2016)
Evennett, H, 'Delegated Legislation in the Lords since 1997' (House of Lords Library Note, LLN 2016/001, 5 January 2016)
Ewing, KD, 'Covid-19: Government by Decree' (2020) 31 *King's Law Journal* 1
Fisher, E, *Risk Regulation and Administrative Constitutionalism* (Hart Publishing, 2007)

—— 'The Open Road? Navigating Public Administration and the Failed Promise of Administrative Law' in E Fisher, J King and AL Young (eds) *The Foundations and Future of Public Law* (Oxford University Press, 2020).

Fox, R and Blackwell, J, *The Devil is in the Detail: Parliament and Delegated Legislation* (Hansard Society, 2014)

Fredman, S, 'New Horizons: Incorporating Socio-Economic Rights in a British Bill of Rights' [2010] *Public Law* 297

Ganghof, S, *Beyond Presidentialism and Parliamentarism: Democratic Design and the Separation of Powers* (Oxford University Press, 2022)

Ganz, G, 'Delegated Legislation: A Necessary Evil or a Constitutional Outrage?' in P Leyland and T Woods (eds) *Administrative Law Facing the Future: Old Constraints and New Horizons* (Blackstone Press Ltd, 1997)

Ginsburg, T and Versteeg, M, 'The Bound Executive: Emergency Powers during the Pandemic' (2021) 19 *I•CON* 1498

Grez Hidalgo, P, de Londras F and Lock, D, 'Parliament, the Pandemic, and Constitutional Principle in the United Kingdom: A Study of the Coronavirus Act 2020' (2022) 85 *Modern Law Review* 1463.

Griffith, JAG, 'Delegated Legislation – Some Recent Developments' (1949) 12 *Modern Law Review* 297

Grogan, J, 'States of Emergency: Analysing Global Use of Emergency Powers in Response to COVID-19' (2020) 22 *European Journal of Law Reform* 338

—— '(Un)governing: The COVID-19 Response in the UK' in J Grogan and A Donald (eds), *Routledge Handbook of Law and the Covid-19 Pandemic* (Routledge, 2022)

Harlow, C and Rawlings, R, *Pressure Through Law* (Routledge, 1992)

Harrison, CM, 'Assessing the Impact of Regulatory Impact Assessment' (2009) 16 *Agenda* 41

Hayhurst, JD and Wallington, P, 'The Parliamentary Scrutiny of Delegated Legislation' [1988] *Public Law* 547

Hewart, G, *The New Despotism* (Ernest Benn, 1929)

Hickman, T, 'Abracadabra Law-making and Accountability to Parliament for the Coronavirus Regulation' in P Evans, C Salmon Percival, P Silk and H White (eds) *Parliaments and the Pandemic* (Study of Parliaments Group, 2021)

Hofmann, HCF, Rowe, GC and Türk, AH, *Administrative Law and Policy of the European Union* (Oxford University Press, 2011)

Hooper, HJ, 'The Use of Parliamentary Materials by Courts in Proportionality Judgments' in H Hooper, M Hunt and P Yowell (ed), *Parliament and Human Rights: Redressing the Democratic Deficit* (Oxford University Press, 2015)

Jacobs, C, 'The Evolution and Development of Regulatory Impact Assessment in the UK' in C Kirkpatrick and D Parker (eds), *Regulatory Impact Assessment: Towards Better Regulation?* (Edward Elgar, 2007)

Jensen, CB and McGrath, RJ, 'Making Rules about Rulemaking: A Comparison of Presidential and Parliamentary Systems' (2011) 64 *Political Research Quarterly* 656

Kavanagh, A, 'Proportionality and Parliamentary Debates: Exploring Some Forbidden Territory' (2014) 34 *Oxford Journal of Legal Studies* 443

Kelly, R, *Statutory Instruments* (Commons Briefing Paper, Number 06509, 15 December 2016)

Kersell, JE, *Parliamentary Supervision of Delegated Legislation* (Stevens and Sons Ltd, 1960)

Khaitan, T, 'Balancing Accountability and Effectiveness: A Case for Moderated Parliamentarism' (2021) 7 *Canadian Journal of Comparative and Contemporary Law* 81

—— 'Executive Aggrandizement in Established Democracies: A Crisis of Liberal Democratic Constitutionalism' (2019) 17 *I•CON* 342

King, J, 'The Province of Delegated Legislation' in E Fisher, J King and AL Young, *The Foundations and Future of Public Law* (Oxford University Press, 2020)

Laski, H, 'Judicial Review of Social Policy in England: A Study of Roberts v Hopwood' (1926) 39 *Harvard Law Review* 832, 833, 847–48.

Laski, HA, *A Grammar of Politics* (George Allen & Unwin Ltd, 1941)

Laws, J, 'Judicial Remedies and the Constitution' (1994) 57 *Modern Law Review* 213

Lazarus, L and Simonsen, N, 'Judicial Review and Parliamentary Debate: Enriching the Doctrine of Due Deference' in M Hunt (ed), *Parliament and Human Rights: Redressing the Democratic Deficit* (Oxford University Press, 2015)
Lee, C, Brown, C and Hamlyn, M, 'The Impact in the Commons Chamber' in P Evans, C Salmon Percival, P Silk and H White (eds), *Parliaments and the Pandemic* (Study of Parliaments Group, 2021)
Lijphart, A, *Patterns of Democracy: Government Forms and Performance in Thirty-Six Countries*, 2nd edn (Yale University Press, 2012)
Lim, B, 'The Normativity of the Principle of Legality' (2013) 37 *Melbourne University Law Review* 372
Loughlin, M, *Public Law and Political Theory* (Clarendon Press, 1992)
Maitland, FW, *The Constitutional History of England* (Cambridge University Press, 1913)
Manwaring, R, *The Search for Democratic Renewal: The Politics of Consultation in Britain and Australia* (Manchester University Press, 2014)
Marshall, G, 'Metric Measures and Martyrdom by Henry VIII Clause' (2002) 118 *Law Quarterly Review* 493
Mashaw, JL and Harfst, DL, *The Struggle for Auto Safety* (Harvard University Press, 1990)
Mason, A, 'The Interpretation of a Constitution in a Modern Liberal Democracy' in C Sampford and K Preston (eds), *Interpreting Constitutions: Theories, Principles and Institutions* (Federation Press, 1996)
McGarrity, TO, 'Some Thoughts on 'Deossifying' the Rulemaking Process' (1992) 41 *Duke Law Journal* 1385
McGrogan, D, '"It is Unarguable that what happened under these Regulations Amounted to a Deprivation of Liberty": Dolan v Secretary of State for Health and Social Care' [2021] *Public Law* 671.
Meagher, D, 'The Principle of Legality as Clear Statement Rule: Significance and Problems' (2014) 36 *Sydney Law Review* 413
Meyerson, D, 'Rethinking the Constitutionality of Delegated Legislation' (2003) 11 *Australian Journal of Administrative Law* 45
Mill, JS, *Considerations on Representative Government* (Floating Press, 2009)
Missen, A, 'Senate Committees and the Legislative Process' in JR Nethercote (ed), *Parliament and Bureaucracy: Parliamentary Scrutiny of Administration – Prospects and Problems in the 1980s* (Hale and Iremonger, 1982) 125
Moe, TM and Caldwell, M, 'The Institutional Foundations of Democratic Government: A Comparison of Presidential and Parliamentary Systems' (1994) 150 *Journal of Institutional and Theoretical Economics* 171
Moens, GA and Trone, J, 'The Validity of Henry VIII Clauses in Australian Federal Legislation' (2012) 24 *Giornale Di Storia Costituzionale* 133
Mulgan, R, 'The Australian Senate as a "House of Review"' (1996) 31 *Australian Journal of Political Science* 191
Murphy, CN and Yates, J, *The International Organization for Standardization (ISO): Global Governance through Voluntary Consensus* (Routledge, 2009)
Natzler D, 'How the House of Commons has Adapted to the Pandemic' in P Evans, C Salmon Percival, P Silk and H White (eds), *Parliaments and the Pandemic* (Study of Parliaments Group, 2021)
Natzler, D and Hutton, M (eds), *Erskine May's Treatise on The Law, Privileges, Proceedings and Usage of Parliament*, 25th edn (2019), available at erskinemay.parliament.uk
Page, E, *Governing by Numbers: Delegated Legislation and Everyday Policy-Making* (Hart Publishing, 2001)
Patapan, H, *Judging Democracy* (Cambridge University Press, 2000)
Pearce, D and Argument S, *Delegated Legislation in Australia*, 5th edn (LexisNexis Butterworths 2017)
Port, F, *Administrative Law* (Longmans, Green and Co, 1929)
Priddy, S, *Coronavirus timeline: End of Hybrid Proceedings in the House of Commons* (House of Commons Library, 8 September 2022).
Prosser, T, *The Regulatory Enterprise – Government, Regulation, and Legitimacy* (Oxford University Press, 2010) 214.

Rawlings, R, 'Modelling Judicial Review' (2008) 61 *Current Legal Problems* 95

Reid, GS, 'Parliament and Delegated Legislation' in JR Nethercote (ed), *Parliament and Bureaucracy: Parliamentary Scrutiny of Administration – Prospects and Problems in the 1980s* (Hale and Iremonger, 1982)

Rippon, L, 'Constitutional Anarchy' (1990) 11 *Statute Law Review* 184

—— *Making the Law* (Hansard Society, 1993)

Rippon, R, 'Henry VIII Clauses' (1989) 10 *Statute Law Review* 205

Rizzi, M and Tullich, T, 'All Bets on the Executive(S)! The Australian Response to Covid-19' in J Grogan and A Donald (eds), *Routledge Handbook of Law and the Covid-19 Pandemic* (Routledge, 2022)

Rose-Ackerman, S, *Democracy and Executive Power: Policymaking Accountability in the US, the UK, Germany, and France* (Yale University Press, 2021)

—— 'Policy-Making Accountability: Parliamentary versus Presidential Systems' in D Levi-Faur (ed), *Handbook on the Politics of Regulation* (Edward Elgar, 2011)

Rose-Ackerman, S, Egidy, S and Fowkes, J, *Due Process of Lawmaking: the United States, South Africa, Germany, and the European Union* (Cambridge University Press, 2015)

Russell, M, *The Contemporary House of Lords: Westminster Bicameralism Revived* (Oxford University Press, 2013)

Russell, M and Cowley, P, 'Modes of UK Executive–Legislative Relations Revisited' (2018) 89 *The Political Quarterly* 18

Russell, M and Gover, D, *Legislation at Westminster: Parliamentary Actors and Influence in the Making of British Law* (Oxford University Press, 2017)

Schepel, H, *The Constitution of Private Governance: Product Standards in the Regulation of Integrating Markets* (Hart Publishing 2005)

—— 'The New Approach to the New Approach: The Juridification of Harmonized Standards in EU Law' (2013) 20 *Maastricht Journal of European and Comparative Law* 521

Schwartz, B and Wade, HWR, *Legal Control of Government: Administrative Law in Britain and the United States* (Clarendon Press, 1972)

Scotford, E, *Environmental Principles and the Evolution of Environmental Law* (Hart Publishing, 2017)

Scott, E, *House of Lords: Remote Participation and Hybrid Proceedings* (House of Lords Library, 8 July 2021)

Seaward, P, 'Emergency Powers in Parliament: A Short History' in P Evans, C Salmon Percival, P Silk and H White (eds), *Parliaments and the Pandemic* (Study of Parliaments Group, 2021)

Selinger, W, *Parliamentarism: From Burke to Weber* (Cambridge University Press, 2019)

Shaffer, G, 'How the WTO Shapes the Regulatory State' in F Bignami and D Zaring, *Comparative Law and Regulation: Understanding the Global Regulatory Process* (Edward Elgar, 2016)

Souter, G, *Acts of Parliament: A Narrative History of the Senate and House of Representatives Commonwealth of Australia* (Melbourne University Press, 1988)

Stellios, J, *Zines's the High Court and the Constitution*, 6th edn (Federation Press, 2015)

Stewart, R, 'The Reformation of American Administrative Law' (1975) 88 *Harvard Law Review* 1669

Strauss, PL, *Administrative Justice in the United States*, 3rd edn (Carolina Academic Press, 2016)

Sumption, L, 'COVID-19 and the Courts – Expediency or Law?' (2021) 137 *Law Quarterly Review* 355

Taflaga, M, 'What's in a Name? Semi-Parliamentarism and Australian Commonwealth Executive-Legislative Relations (2018) 53 *Australian Journal of Political Science* 248

Taggart, M, 'From "Parliamentary Powers" To Privatization: The Chequered History of Delegated Legislation in the Twentieth Century' (2005) 55 *University of Toronto Law Journal* 575

Thio, SM, *Locus Standi and Judicial Review* (Singapore University Press, 1971)

Tucker, A, 'Parliamentary Scrutiny of Delegated Legislation' in A Horne and G Drewry (eds) *Parliament and the Law* (Hart Publishing, 2018)

Van Geelen, T, 'Delegated Legislation in Financial Services Law: Implications for Regulatory Complexity and the Rule of Law' (2021) 38 *Company and Securities Law Journal* 296

Vangimalla, D, *Compendium of Legislative Standards for Delegating Powers in Primary Legislation* (Hansard Society, 25 April 2022)

Varuhas, JNE, 'The Principle of Legality' (2020) 79 *Cambridge Law Journal* 578
—— 'The Public Interest Conception of Public Law: Its Procedural Origins and Substantive Implications' in John Bell, Mark Elliott, Jason NE Varuhas and Philip Murray (eds), *Public Law Adjudication in Common Law Systems: Process and Substance* (Hart Publishing, 2016)
Williams, G, Brennan, S and Lynch, A, *Blackshield and Williams, Australian Constitutional Law and Theory*, 7th edn (Federation Press, 2018)
Willis, J, *The Parliamentary Powers of English Government Departments* (Harvard University Press, 1933)
Windholz, EL, 'Governing in a Pandemic: from Parliamentary Sovereignty to Autocratic Technocracy' (2020) 8 *Theory and Practice of Legislation* 93.
Wood, S, 'Exploring the Relationship between Administrative Norms and Competence in Transnational Governance: ISO, ISEAL and Sustainability Standards' (2016) 21 *Tilburg Law Review* 193

INDEX

www.ingramcontent.com/pod-product-compliance
Ingram Content Group UK Ltd.
Pitfield, Milton Keynes, MK11 3LW, UK
UKHW020258051026
15470UKWH00020B/1111

9 781509 972241